Traveling Blind

Traveling Blind
Life Lessons from unlikely Teachers

Laura Fogg

Medusa's Muse Publishing
Ukiah, California

Medusa's Muse Press
410 W. Mill St.
Ukiah, CA 95482
To order this manuscript as a Electronic Book or Audio Book visit us at
www.medusasmuse.com

Front cover photograph by Richard Wismar
Back cover photograph by Laura Fogg
Book design by Richard Wismar
Minion Pro Font was chosen for its high degree of readability.

ISBN 978-0-9797152-0-4
ISBN 0-9797152-0-2

For:

Pete Wurzburger
Mobility Instructor and Mentor extraordinaire

And the late Lou Delsol
Who believed in me when I was so very green

And all of my extraordinary students
and their families

PS: Laura and Medusa's Muse would like to encourage the reader to take a look at the Love Bike as described on page 119. It is now known as the Buddy Bike. Find it at www.buddybike.com. Good Guys with a good idea! Check them out.

THANKS

Without Pete Wurzburger I wouldn't have had a career, and without a career I wouldn't have had a story—or at least I wouldn't have had this story. Pete is the reason I love this work I do. Every time I laugh at the craziness or the wonderfulness or the downright strangeness of my unusual and fascinating students being themselves, I think of Pete and hear his contagious chuckle. So to Pete—a heartfelt thank you!

A thank you also to my students and their families, whose stories I have used in this book. All of the people and events I have represented are real. The descriptions of my students' lives are not embellished, though the names I use are fictitious in order to protect their privacy. I want to honor these children and their families, and the communities that contain them, with truth. I see no shame in the difficult details or the unavoidable failures, and I want to acknowledge and celebrate both the joy and the sorrow of these unforgettable human beings who have touched my life in so many ways.

My apologies to readers from Mendocino County who will be completely perplexed by the geographical descriptions that don't match any map they have ever seen. I changed, mixed and confused names of towns, rivers, roads and other features that could be used to identify where my students live. Believe me, I know better!

Another word of thanks to Robert Madrazo, an adventure-loving boss from years ago. He listened patiently to my accounts of the day's events when I returned to the office at the end of both exhilarating and devastating work days. Bob was the person who first encouraged me to get some of my stories down in writing.

And a final thank-you from the bottom of my heart to the two women who are the entire staff of Medusa's Muse, the small publishing company that launched this book of mine into print. Terena Scott, the mother of Cari in my story, took a risk by asking if she could publish the manuscript I showed her, and she gave me more useful feedback on the crafting of my stories than anybody else who read them. She asked questions, encouraged me to use dialogue and applauded when I turned a decent scene into a good scene. Jane Mackay, the editor from the "East Coast Office," had the insight to ask me to describe the theme of my book in four short sentences. Then she and Terena made me stick to it. Without the two of them this book would still be a manuscript.

Light

elusive, ephemeral

yet an end in itself

not touched

but felt

with senses I never knew

I see it

and am drawn

to discover the source.

No, compelled

for when I stand

still

it goes away.

17 July, 1984

PRELUDE

Shaynna will never go on another adventure with me. After ten years and countless hours of working and playing with this funny little mixed up, badly behaved, headstrong and hilarious blind child, I got what I had always wanted for her. She left home at the age of twelve to begin attending the residential program at the California School for the Blind. I was excited and hopeful for Shaynna, imagining that she would have blind friends for the first time in her life, and be part of a class where most of the academic program would finally make sense to her. I hoped for a better life for Shaynna, where she could learn skills that we couldn't teach her in rural Mendocino County, and where she could have a chance to eventually discover her elusive potential and achieve the degree of independence that was her right. Shaynna left for the place where my career as an Orientation Mobility Instructor for the Blind had started more or less by accident, after a bad dream, a quarter of a century before. I felt that I had come full circle professionally, and that it was time to tell my story.

I began writing. The structure of my book emerged as I thought back to those long-ago days volunteering at the very institution where Shaynna was now a student. I would write about the most interesting and challenging of my blind students, and lead up to the final and best one, Shaynna. However, to my dismay, the success I imagined for Shaynna never happened. Her new life at the School for the Blind turned into a disaster, and I couldn't bring myself to end my book with Shaynna's tragedy compounded by my grief for her, her family and myself. My will to tell my stories abandoned me.

During the lull in my writing, I began to realize that this book was not going to be about what I was teaching my students, but about what they were teaching me. Shaynna's lesson was too hard for me to accept at that time, but I knew that once I could look squarely at the complicated ways this child and her family affected me, I would have a better story to tell. I needed to take some time and live some more, and learn to look at myself from a greater distance. I had to develop an ability to accept what I couldn't change.

I waited, slowly learning to live with my feelings of loss and discouragement over Shaynna, hoping for a renewed sense of excitement about my future in my chosen profession. This finally appeared, seven years after I saw Shaynna for the last time, in the form of Mike. It took a while, but I eventually recognized this quiet, brilliant child as the new focal challenge for my most creative teaching energy. He filled the hole in my professional life and gave me the emotional jump-start I needed to resume writing after the long hiatus.

I've taught other students in those years between Shaynna and Mike who are fascinating, demanding, and all kinds of fun to work with, but up until now nobody besides Shaynna has been able to challenge me to the very depths of my abilities. Mike does that, and more. In helping him find his power, I am finding my own. This amazing boy's story is my favorite, and I am grateful to him for his rock-solid lesson about belief in one's self.

So now, with revitalized confidence in the present and restored hope for the future, my writing continues. Here on these pages I weave the stories of my haphazard existence as an itinerant teacher in a huge rural county. I am hired to work one-on-one with my far-flung students, but over the course of my thirty-five year career I have spent almost as much time driving as I have teaching. The road has become as important a part of my day as the work I do with blind children. I can no longer think about my students without putting them into the context of my journey to get to them.

The road is my teacher too, and my adventures in the county car parallel my experiences with my students and their families. On the road, in all of its changing conditions, as well as with the families I visit, I have learned to observe carefully, plan my strategy, and proceed with a sincere belief that I am capable of making good decisions. I try to remember to look for places to pull off to rest or enjoy the view, both metaphorically and in reality, and I am no longer ashamed to turn around and go home on occasion, when the going gets too tough. The weather and the scenery throughout the county reflect my moods, and I look forward to the gift of time that driving adds to each of my workdays. The road has literally become a character in my life, and in my book, as I follow it to do the work I love. I both drive and teach with curiosity, some trepidation and a great amount of joy, never quite knowing what to expect around the next blind turn.

A NEW DIRECTION

Each step in my nightmare brought me closer to an airless chamber below the museum. Dusty, dark and cramped, the room was invisible to throngs of visitors in the building above, as they wandered the halls admiring works of the ancient masters. No voices down here below ground level—just echoes of the dull thud made when each painting was carted down the steps and dumped on top of the one before it. Piles of forgotten artwork towered around me, brown and unrecognizable with age and layers of crazed yellow varnish. It was my job to scrape each canvas down to the original paint and catalogue it. I stared hopelessly at the stacks and the chamber grew smaller, the walls moving in towards me. I stood paralyzed, sentenced to an eternity in this subterranean purgatory without light or sound.

I woke up from my bad dream sweaty and exhausted, yet charged. Convinced in my very core that the time had come for me to change direction. I had lived in Italy for the previous year, surrounded by cathedrals and palaces filled with masterpieces from the Renaissance, and had fallen easily into an Art History major upon coming home to the University of California at Berkeley. I was about to graduate to an uncertain future, with no job possibilities that were even remotely interesting to me. It was becoming more evident as each day passed that studying the two-dimensional creations of people who had been dead for three hundred years was not my calling. I needed a strong shot of life, in the here and now, with people who were still breathing and talking. I was ready for anything that would put an end to my recurring nightmare, but had no idea where to turn for inspiration.

On one particularly gray Berkeley day, I walked out of an art history class, miserably watching groups of students bustling around, all looking like they knew exactly where they were going. My final quarter as a senior was almost over and desperation about my future was looming dangerously close. I headed towards my apartment to cram for a test, changed my mind, and decided to go buy an ice cream first. Taking an unaccustomed path, I passed a rack of newspapers and saw that the new issue of the Daily CAL had come out. I grabbed a copy with the intention of stuffing it in my backpack to read later, but something moved me to scan the headlines before walking on. An article caught my attention and I stood there reading it, turning the paper over when it continued onto the back page. I never finished the article.

My eye went straight to a smallish advertisement, set within a simple black rectangle. "Volunteers needed at the California School for the Blind," the letters spelled, followed by a contact number. I read the short ad a second time, my mind already gearing up to imagine myself spending a few hours a week tutoring some cute children who would benefit from my help. The idea was appealing—the CSB campus was close to my apartment, and going there would be a fun project for the rest of the quarter. I had never possessed the slightest desire to become a teacher, but this would be something useful to keep me occupied while I came up for air and tried to make some serious decisions about where I could search in the world of the living for an eventual career. It would be a welcome break from the routine of studying for classes I had lost interest in.

Within two days I was signed up at the School for the Blind and walking with a certain amount of trepidation towards my assigned classroom. Moving through the dim corridor that smelled of a hundred years of floor wax, I was stunned to realize how depressingly similar this place was to the chamber under the museum in my nightmare. I considered bolting. Never one to back out on a commitment, though, I missed my chance to flee and found myself in the classroom, face to face with Miss Hertz.

All business in her navy blue skirt and buttoned-to-the-neck white blouse, Miss Hertz immediately ordered me to sit next to Sarah Jane, who was busy banging out spelling words on her Braille writer. Sarah Jane was not cute, or even easy to look at. Her lumpy body stretched the seams of her out-of-style plaid dress, and she sported a whole lot of protruding teeth and greasy hair that looked like she had cut it herself. She smelled unwashed. None of the students in the room looked much like the groomed and orthodontured suburban kids I was used to baby-sitting. The inmates of Mrs. Hertz' classroom all rocked and flapped their hands and rolled their heads around, and some of them had their knuckles inexplicably stuck into their eye sockets. I made myself quit staring, realizing a bit sheepishly that nobody in this sightless environment was aware of my rudeness. I buckled down to the project of trying to be of some use to Sarah Jane and her mysterious page of raised dots.

Our progress was suddenly interrupted by Miss Hertz shouting across the room in exasperated tones, "Sarah Jane, your eyes are backwards again! You get out of here this minute and put them in right!" I took five slow breaths and prayed that my lunch would stay where it belonged. Miss Hertz glared my way and instructed me to accompany Sarah Jane out of the classroom, to see to it that the offending eyes were indeed replaced in their correct sockets. Sensing that there was no graceful way out of this situation, I did as I was told. I was beginning to work up an unpleasant fantasy about exactly what I might be expected to do, but Sarah Jane, bless her heart, had the technique down. Bending over the drinking fountain in the hallway, she popped both artificial eyeballs into the palm of her hand, wetted them down and deftly re-inserted them. No big deal. I couldn't make myself look to see if the eyes were actually relocated where they belonged, and probably wouldn't have known the difference even if I had found the courage to examine them. I toddled into the classroom behind Sarah Jane and forced myself to attend to her spelling list during the remainder of the period.

I came back the next day, though I really wanted nothing more than to find a good reason to back out on my newfound tutoring commitment. I felt trapped in the dull confinement of the classroom, and Miss Hertz reminded me unpleasantly of my childhood piano teacher, the brittle old lady who made me endure my hour-long lesson the one day of my entire California childhood that it snowed. Sarah Jane never appealed to me much either, but having signed up to work with her three times a week, I decided I had better get used to her. I concentrated on her braille and may have even helped her a little.

Sarah Jane wasn't the focus of my attention for long, though. A few weeks into my volunteer job, on the day of my twenty-second birthday, I was walking towards the school celebrating the heady spring weather that contrasted deliciously with the previous months of Berkeley fog. I'm a bit of a dreamer, slightly inclined towards magical thinking, and I was musing that the perfect weather on the first day of my twenty-third year of life might be an omen of good things to come. At that moment I looked up and noticed an elderly, pleasant-looking man out on the sidewalk in front of the main building, following a blind student with a white cane in his hand. The man appeared to be giving the student a lesson of some kind, directing the boy with quiet words and a gentle hand on the shoulder when the boy hit something with his cane or had trouble walking straight. I had never seen anything like that in my life, and puzzled over it a bit, slowing my pace so I could watch. There was no socially acceptable way to continue standing on the sidewalk gawking, and I was getting late for Sarah Jane, but I was compelled to walk over and ask the man, "Could you please tell me what you are doing?"

Leo Bailey, the Orientation and Mobility Instructor at CSB, grinned at me, asked my name, and shook my hand with an enthusiastic grip. He introduced his student, a young teen-ager named Jeff, who needed no prompting to reach towards my voice and shake my hand also. Jeff could hardly contain his delight at the novelty of suddenly having an audience for his lesson. He tried to stand politely still, but his body twitched with excitement and the hand clutching his cane contracted repeatedly with a pent up desire to move. I guessed that Jeff's lessons with Leo were his favorite time of the day.

Something inside Leo immediately shone through to me ... there was a happiness and an energy about him that I hadn't noticed in any of the classroom teachers I had met so far. Leo didn't appear to be crabby or jaded with his job, though he was clearly old enough to have been doing it for a number of years. He was visibly excited by my interest, and the spontaneous enthusiasm in his voice stirred that part of me that was looking for the answer to my nagging and increasingly worrisome question regarding what I wanted to do for my own career. My mind ran fast-forward to a vision of myself in Leo's shoes, out on the sunny sidewalk with a student of my own.

I love to be outside. I need to be outside. I've known that about myself ever since I was a high school student refusing to take a typing class because I didn't want to ever entertain the possibility of falling back on an office job if all else failed. As a tiny child my mother taught me to marvel at flowers, seasons and all kinds of weather. She and I spent hours watching insects or sitting on a rock waiting for birds to land near us. My greatest thrills were helping her garden or going on long walks in the hills with my father. Slow summer days were spent on a swaying perch in a treetop, and I got to sleep under the stars all summer long. My bedroom for the other three seasons was the one with the most windows. I have always gone outside to celebrate the best times and to mourn the worst—it is where I belong.

I have never liked being in school, though I was a good student. It wasn't the learning that bothered me—it was being stuck in a classroom all day. I could hear interesting things going on outside while I was forced to sit at my wooden desk, facing the blackboard for fear that the teacher would chastise me for staring out the window. I had to endure hours of not watching it rain or not looking for the migrating birds I could hear calling, while inhaling that ubiquitous school smell.

Office buildings have the same effect on me as classrooms. My closest experience to working in an office was a part-time job I had in a large shopping mall, the first one built in Northern California, during my junior college years. I would park my car, come in by a side door in the concrete wall and disappear into the climate-controlled recesses of that huge building for eight hours at a time. Without a single window or skylight to offer natural illumination, and no place but the parking lot to go out to eat lunch, I began to feel trapped like a wild animal in a zoo.

Refocusing on Leo and Jeff, I was enjoying the pleasant feelings generated by a vivid mental picture of myself doing Leo's kind of work, when I realized that he was talking to me. "You're really interested in this, aren't you?" he was asking with a smile that hinted he didn't need me to tell him the answer to that question.

Jeff chimed in with enthusiastic approval, "Mr. Bailey is my favorite teacher. You're welcome to come and watch what we're doing any time you like." I immediately started playing hooky from an Art History class at Cal to take my new friends up on their offer.

It didn't take many hours of tagging along behind Leo and Jeff to get the picture about what they were doing. Leo explained that Orientation and Mobility Instructors get hired by schools and institutions that serve blind people to teach them how to travel safely and independently from one place to another. The teaching is done one-on-one, the classroom is the community, and the curriculum is individualized for each student. No dreary tutoring on boring academics and no getting stuck in stifling classrooms on sunny days! I knew by the second outing with Leo and his charge that this was the job I had been waiting through four years of college to find. It had fallen out of the springtime sky as the best birthday present of my life, and I was ready for it. I hurried back to the UC campus to make up for lost time in the Art History class so I could graduate and get on with my newly discovered career. Leo recommended me for the Master's program in Orientation and Mobility at San Francisco State College, and I was enrolled within the month.

LEARNING THE TRADE

Nobody told me-or it didn't sink in-that, as a student in the Orientation and Mobility Program at San Francisco State College, I was going to have to learn to be a proficient cane traveler myself. And I was going to have to do it without vision, just like my future students. The very first day of class, along with the other nine fledgling mobility instructors in the program, I was measured for my own long white cane by Pete Wurzburger. Pete would fill the multiple roles of main instructor, mother hen, group photographer and funny guy for our little group over the ensuing year and a half. Pete was a pro—he was one of the four ex-rehab instructors from the Hines VA Hospital in Chicago who had invented the white cane technique we were about to learn, and there was nobody on the planet who could do a better job teaching us the skill.

Blind people have used all kinds of sticks and canes throughout the history of civilization to randomly probe for obstacles or wave around to warn others to clear the way. Pete and his compatriots in the Veteran's Administration developed a cleaner and more efficient technique that would meet the needs of the thousands of soldiers who came home from World War II blind, but who otherwise were mentally and physically intact. These veterans were eager for a dignified means of regaining the independence that had been theirs before the war. What Pete Wurzburger, Leo Bailey and their co-workers developed was the "touch technique." Moving a long fiberglass cane in a controlled arc in front of him, a blind person lightly taps the ground at the outer edges of the arc and "clears" a path in front of himself that is just wide enough to move through safely. The cane, when used according to this technique, detects obstacles, steps and changes in the surface underfoot, and provides information about the immediate surroundings that is pertinent to orientation. Specific training in the use of hearing, smell and touch augments the learning of white cane skills, and a blind individual can learn to travel confidently and safely just about anywhere he wants to go.

It was pure good luck that landed me at San Francisco State College where Pete had chosen to continue his career, though now he was training teachers instead of soldiers. Pete's love of his job was contagious, and he didn't waste time lecturing his new class about what we would be learning over the ensuing weeks. He issued each of us a light-occluding sleepshade to put on, and sent us off down the hall in our sudden state of simulated blindness … each of us clutching the elbow of a fellow student whom we had not yet learned to trust.

"Sighted guide" was the technique we were supposed to be experiencing and learning through this hands-on approach. You depend totally on your guide to get you where you are going and to look out for your safety. This trained, or possibly untrained, person is supposed to remember you are there as he guides you. He is supposed to leave room for you to fit as the two of you negotiate doorways, hallways, and stairs—and ultimately traffic. You follow half a step behind your guide and read, through the "body English" of your hand firmly gripping his arm just above the elbow and sensing his motion, what is about to happen. You step up when your guide steps up, down when he steps down, and stop when he stops. You hope he remembers you are there, sightlessly attached to him, when you pass a garbage can in the middle of the hallway. Nothing is louder than a metal garbage can getting accidentally kicked in the silent hallway of an institution of higher learning. You pray that when your guide positions you to sit down in a chair, he has turned you exactly the right amount so that the chair is squarely behind you. You learn to check.

After this first week of sighted guide training, I realized, to my complete surprise, that I wasn't hitting as many things as I had been in the beginning. Nor was I getting surprised as often by turns in the hallway, walls in front of me, or the awareness that a person was standing next to me. I realized that I could now "feel" space, or the lack of it. I could detect a sudden sense of openness as I came to the end of the wall next to me and began to walk across an intersecting corridor. An increasing awareness of pressure on my face became palpable as I walked closer to an unseen wall looming in front of me, and I learned to stop a foot before I hit that wall, without ever touching it. Something changed in the air if a person moved past me, like an invisible shadow. While under the sleepshade, I was learning to listen to echoes, just like dolphins and bats—and blind people. Echoes come back faster when things are closer, and take longer when they bounce off objects that are farther away. You can "hear" walls, doorways and the contrast between a roof and the sky overhead. If you get really good at it you can judge the size of the room you are in, and even walk around signposts (and garbage cans) without crashing into them.

If you pay attention you can use the echoes reflecting from the wall next to you or the buildings across the street to walk in a straight line—you just have to keep the return time of the echoes constant. Some highly practiced blind people can even detect a curb in front of them and step down neatly in the right place. That's considered to be the ultimate skill by those who are adept at walking without sight.

Other issues came up for me during the sighted guide training besides the fairly straightforward challenge of learning the proper technique. While blindfolded, I encountered people I had never seen before, and was introduced to some of them, but not to others. I was not allowed to remove my sleepshade to see any of these strangers, so each interaction left me frantically trying to fill in the missing pieces of my mental picture. The first challenge was immediate—who, among all of the unfamiliar voices near me, was I supposed to be engaging in conversation? With vision, I could have figured that out in an instant, and done it without stress. Functionally blind however, I could not tell if the people I was talking to were those I had just met, or if I was inadvertently addressing mystified passers-by. It was also disconcerting never knowing who was listening to my conversation. Was I talking to just those people in my circle of acquaintants, or was everybody in the room listening? If other people were in fact listening, how many of them were there, and who were they? Should I be talking louder or more softly to include or exclude those unknown ears?

Even when fairly certain I was talking to the right person, I could not gather anywhere near enough information about them through my auditory sense alone. All I could tell about a person I had just sightlessly met was whether they were male or female, and that was never with 100% certainty. My usual efficient and stereotypical methods for sizing people up didn't work. There was no quick shortcut, equivalent to vision, for determining anybody's age, social status, probable intelligence, or sex appeal. Stories were told later at school parties about each one of us blindfolded mobility students standing on street corners in San Francisco with our white canes in hand, earnestly engaged in conversations with bums and derelicts. Pete passed around Polaroid photos he had gleefully snapped, from his usual post across the street, for humorous proof of the irony of it all. These were people to whom most of us never would have given the time of day had we been able to see them—but lacking our usual ability to censure on sight, we responded to them without judgment.

I was also somewhat unnerved by the complete absence of visual feedback during conversations with groups of acquaintances. One-on-one, with a single person, a visionless verbal exchange was similar to talking on the telephone, where turn taking was fairly straightforward and easy to work out even if we both started talking at once. However, in a group of friends, I always felt an insecure two steps behind everybody else. Without the eye contact, nods, affirming smiles, and those lovely and encouraging little lifts of the other peoples' eyebrows when we reached a momentary pinnacle of emotional consensus, I never knew where I stood in terms of the relationship we were experiencing. Were my friends still interested in our discussion, or were they slumping in their seats getting bored? Did they believe in what I was saying? Or were they looking at their watches and rolling their eyes at each other? In the absence of the positive it was easy to assume the negative, and I found myself trying harder and being just a little louder to compensate for my imagined deficits. Without the mirror I was used to creating in other people, I couldn't see myself reflected. I couldn't tell whether to match, override or play second fiddle to my friends' conversational gestures. The only clues were in the tone of their voices, the speed of their vocal responses, and the content of their conversation—all impossible for me to size up accurately without being able to read their faces.

Blindfolded, I realized how much humor depends on cues other than the words that are spoken. Some jokes are funny just because of what is said—those are the ones that you read in magazines and laugh at if they are good—but there is a lot of humor in daily human interaction that is far more subtle. A wry face or a naughty gesture completely changes the meaning of what is said, and an exchanged look with no words at all can cause two people to suddenly roll in the aisle with laughter. Without vision you have to take words at literal face value, and though I never knew exactly what I was missing, I was always sure that all of the juiciest nuances were going right by me.

Eating blindfolded was another memorable, and distasteful, experience. All of us students were required to have a sighted guide adventure into the college cafeteria for lunch, and it was akin to being stuck in a clumsy two-year-old body with the exaggerated social conscience of a stage-shy adult. I couldn't see the food that my guide helpfully described and loaded onto my compartmentalized metal tray, and I had no way to predict whether or not I would find any of the dishes appetizing. Were the string beans fresh and green or boiled to a gray pulp? Was the lasagna delightfully striped with fresh layers of cheese and red sauce, or was it squashed and overcooked? How big were the servings, and how much salad dressing had been accidentally slopped over my dessert? The heightened smell sense that automatically turns on with the absence of vision wasn't encouraging either. Without being able to see individual dishes I couldn't smell their distinct aromas—all of the scents combined into the unpleasant stink of the greasy cafeteria.

Trying to keep my tray balanced and level as I swerved to the seat I didn't get to choose was unnerving. I hit the edge of the table with the tray as I tried to set it down and knocked my fork on the floor. The act of eating was harder yet. I was convinced that every person in the room was staring at me as I discreetly tried to find a morsel of food with one finger of my left hand, so I could spear the elusive little bugger with the fork in my right hand without pushing it all the way off the plate. After going through all that, there was no way of knowing whether the fork would turn up empty, or reach my mouth with an unstable load of dressing-drenched salad that would fall all over my front the minute I tried to bite into it. I experienced about an even number of both kinds of humiliation.

Then there was the insurmountable challenge presented by beverages—no matter where a glass full of liquid was placed on the table, it ended up directly in the path of my hand as I was searching for a napkin, the butter dish, or even the glass itself. No movements on my part were slow or careful enough to prevent my knocking over the glass every time I reached for anything. My guide uncomplainingly fetched more napkins and dabbed at my sodden lap, without asking me if I'd prefer to do that chore myself. I quickly decided that if I were blind I would live on peanut butter and jelly sandwiches and milkshakes ordered "to go" with a tight lid and a straw. Less chance for mess, and I would know for certain what I was going to get in my mouth with every bite. I was finding it almost assaultive to be expecting scalloped potatoes the few times I actually managed to get something on my fork—and to come up instead with a sweet mouthful of sliced peaches. My admiration blossomed for my blind classmates who functioned neatly and inconspicuously in the cafeteria.

Before beginning our outdoor training in the next phase of the program, Pete announced that we would be having a guided tour of the SF State campus and surrounding neighborhood. I gathered with my fellow students in the lobby of the Education Building at the appointed time, waiting for our guide to arrive. I heard him before I saw him, tapping down the hallway towards us. A tall, fit man appeared from around the corner, walking erect and confident behind his white cane. He stopped squarely in front of us and oriented himself towards his audience. "My name's Steve," he announced, "and I'll be showing you around this morning. Do you want to see the major walkways between buildings, or shall I show you the shortcuts?"

Steve commenced explaining the layout of the campus that he knew better than any of us who had vision. He ushered us out the door, using his cane unobtrusively to negotiate the stairs and locate the path he wanted—a narrow gravel one that branched off from the main path and headed downhill through the trees. While talking and laughing with Pete, Steve led us along at a speed that left me breathless. We arrived at the parking garage in half the time it had taken me to walk from there to the Education Building using the normal route. Once there, Steve cocked his head a little, located a sidewalk that was about three steps in front of him, and led us at his breakneck pace past all of the other major buildings on the campus. He did not make a single misstep or wrong turn. Even in my newness, I was aware of the message our instructor, Pete, had just communicated through this guided tour. He had silently expressed a masterful statement about our profession that he never could have described in words. Here was living proof, demonstrated by Steve, of the best that a white cane could do for a person.

The day finally arrived for our first outdoor white cane training. We were given the long, red-tipped fiberglass canes that we had been measured for at the beginning of the summer, and were instructed to meet Pete at the corner of Ulloa and 31st Streets. It was a pleasant residential neighborhood near the college, with a minimum of traffic and a maximum of straight sidewalks and predictable four-way intersections. We had been practicing the "touch technique" in the safety of the hallways of the Education Building for a couple of weeks, learning to move the cane from side to side in a perfect arc that was just wide enough to check that the path in front of us was clear of obstacles, yet not so wide as to come into contact with objects or people that were not in our way. By now we were used to reacting fast when we hit a wall or came to a drop-off, and we had learned to "shoreline," which is the skill of following an edge such as the straight line where a sidewalk meets a lawn.

We had already taken our first little blindfolded baby forays outdoors on the campus paths, experiencing for ourselves the terrible openness of the unseen world when it is not limited by the close security of walls. People depend so much on boundaries to keep their perspective of the world human-sized. We relate to the hugeness of space by searching for its edges. We create visual walls for ourselves even when there are no buildings, by unconsciously looking for roads, tree lines or horizons to hem us in. We never realize the desperation of that drive to define space until we can't see our limits. Without vision the outdoor world goes on forever into emptiness. The echoes don't come back, and what we sense is fear.

The challenge now, standing uncertainly on Ulloa Street with sleep-shades in place and anxiety partially under control, was to put our fledgling cane skills to use out in the real world. Here at the intersection there were streets and cars and people and noises, all mixed up in a setting that we had never seen. The assignment was simply to set off one by one, walk clockwise around the block without crossing any streets, and end up safely back at the starting point.

My turn came altogether too soon, and I launched myself, completely forgetting to take an initial swipe of my cane to "clear" so that I wouldn't run into a pole or some other unforgiving object with my first stride. I felt a strong hand over my outstretched cane arm, preventing me from taking the step that would have smacked me face-first into a power pole. Pete, quietly and efficiently doing his job as safety monitor, was hovering on the spot to prevent any injuries worse than a minor scare. He manipulated my cane arm in the correct clearing motion so that I contacted the lurking pole as I should have in the first place. Pete then guided my free hand over to touch the pole and discover how close it was to me. No words were necessary. I knew I would never need to be re-taught that lesson. I took a deep breath, sidestepped, cleared again without Pete's assistance, and bravely set out a second time. I shuffled stiffly down the sidewalk and hugged the curb so I could shoreline along something solid and maintain a straight line of direction. This time, no problems. I was doing every move by the book.

Then came a driveway, something I had always negotiated easily in my sighted life. One does not ordinarily have to think much to walk across a driveway. Without vision, however, I had no warning of the driveway's presence except for my cane dropping down into its slope one step before the sidewalk under my feet tipped downhill. I was suddenly launched from the relative security of my flat sidewalk onto this out-of-level plane of concrete that didn't have any curb-boundary for me to follow between it and the street full of moving cars. The sideways incline felt exaggerated, and I had to put all of my conscious effort into maintaining my balance. I found myself veering down the slope out towards the street and had to keep correcting to maintain what I hoped was a straight line of travel. One step and another and yet another, like time-lapse photography, I forced myself to continue my slow motion odyssey. Panting and loaded with adrenaline as if I had just finished crossing a steep talus mountain-side in the Sierras where a single misstep would send me plunging to a certain and horrible death, I survived the ordeal and once again found myself on level ground. The curb was just where it was supposed to be, square and hard on my left—a welcome indication that I was indeed reunited with the known entity of my sidewalk and not lost out in the middle of the street.

Continuing to the end of the block, I negotiated a few more driveways with decreasing anxiety, and arrived at what I believed was the corner. Again, I was deluged with a terrible overload of doubts. Was this place where I had stopped really the corner, or was this some kind of busy driveway that would lead me into an unknown parking lot or back yard that I would never find my way out of? Making the right turn required an enormous amount of faith, and more guts than I felt I had. However, the alternative of standing there on the corner for hours was unappealing. It was getting chilly, and I wanted to make it home across the bay in time for dinner. Most of all, I did not want to have to be rescued by Pete for a second time on my first mobility lesson. So I took another deep breath and willed myself to turn. The sun that had been shining on my forehead now warmed my left ear, and the breeze blowing off the ocean was no longer in my face. I knew I was traveling north, since it was afternoon and the sun was on its way down. Things were adding up with a solid feeling of rightness—the sidewalk felt smooth under my feet, lawns were on my right and traffic was where it belonged in the street on the left. I knew I was on the second side of the square that made up the block that was neatly mapped in my brain, and that there were three right turns ahead of me. Driveways were coming along regularly and beginning to feel like old friends. As long as I paid attention to those things and didn't break a leg, I should be able to get back to the starting point with flying colors. Piece of cake.

It's a mistake to get smug. I sailed happily into one of those old-friend driveways and plowed full-force into a car that was parked across the sidewalk. No injuries, to me at least, but the noise of my cane whacking the sheet metal of the car door was deafening. I could hear people in the yard making some kind of commotion, like they were feeling awful about causing this accident to a poor blind person. Or maybe they were feeling awful about the scratches I was sure I had just put on their car. I didn't care too much—I just wanted to get away from the scene and put this lesson behind me. I wondered, as I bashed my way around the offending vehicle, why none of these people said anything to me as I was approaching. A word or two of warning would have prevented the whole noisy incident. Maybe my calling card, the scratches on their car, would remind them in the future that blind people respond to simple spoken words just like anybody else.

Turning right at the next corner, I knew I was on Taraval Street because I could hear the familiar streetcar clattering by. No doubts here about whether or not this was the corner. It was a commercial block, full of traffic and stores, not to be confused with a driveway or anything else. The stores were all open, with people passing by me on their way in and out. Some of the doors must have been propped ajar on this pleasant afternoon, because I could identify various shops by their smells as I walked by. The neighborhood grocery store smelled of sawdust on the floor in the butcher department, and the dry cleaners reeked of cleaning fluid and steamed wool. I could identify the unmistakable odor of polished leather emanating from what must have been a shoe store. Some of the smells were old and familiar—I knew they had been a part of my life since childhood, but it took a few minutes to peg them. I was not used to having the odor be the only clue. Smells had always been paired with more important visual information, and served to embellish the picture rather than to paint it.

Almost at the end of my maiden voyage around the block, I came to the end of the stretch of Taraval I was traveling, and tried to make the necessary right turn. There was grass in front of me, grass on my right, and the curb on my left. Nowhere to go. I poked and prodded with my cane and could not find any sign of the sidewalk that I knew was supposed to be there. I backtracked and tried my approach all over again, to no avail. Totally frustrated, I stood on the corner and jabbed around helplessly until Pete took pity on me from his vigilant post across the street, and came over to explain the lay of the land. He used words I understood perfectly well, but nothing he said shed any light whatsoever on my present situation—I literally could not get the picture. Pete finally led me about three feet to the place where the sidewalk started and got me launched on the last leg of my journey, but I had no idea where I was or how I had gotten there or why I was so confused. My frustration was so intense that I went back to that corner when the lesson was finally over, so I could see it. With vision, it was just another ordinary street corner, except that there was a wide planter strip of grass growing between the sidewalk and the street, unlike the other three streets I had just been walking along. This insignificant strip of green had prevented me from finding the curb where I thought it should be, and the confusion had wrought havoc with my mental map. Without an intact mental map I was helpless, and the feeling of helplessness prevented me from trying to find another way.

Street crossings came next on our lesson plan. Simple. You stand on the corner and listen. When it's safe, you go. Taken step by step, the technique isn't as life threatening as it sounds. Traffic patterns are blessedly simple, probably because drivers, whether or not they are very smart, have to understand them too. Everybody more or less stops at stop signs, and you can tell by standing on a corner and listening for a minute or two whether there is a two-way stop or a four-way stop in front of you. Having figured that out, you wait for the sounds you are expecting and go with them. When an idling car beside you accelerates forward into the intersection, you move with it because you are both going the same direction, and if it's the car's turn to go it's your turn too. If you hear a car idling on the cross street in front of you, you wait for it to go, because it could kill you if you don't. Then you make a large sweep with your cane and step off the curb before the next car is ready to accelerate.

With traffic signals you wait for the surge of traffic at the beginning of the green light going in your direction, stick your cane out in a purposeful I-am-really-doing-this manner and cross. It's actually safer and easier to cross streets with moderate traffic than those with very light traffic, because the sound cues from cars are unmistakable, and there is an established rhythm of waiting and going.

The hard part about crossing streets is going straight. I learned that in a hurry out there in the Ulloa neighborhood. Without any edges to follow except the painted lines of the crosswalk, which were no help at all to me with my sleepshade on, I tended to veer. Sometimes to the left and sometimes to the right, and I would never know for sure which way I was going wrong until I began to get nervous about not having reached the opposite curb in what I guessed would be the appropriate amount of time. Then I would begin to rapidly compute all the information that was available to me—the slope of the street, the sound of the traffic, and the direction of the sun on my head or face. Sometimes I could get myself back on course and find the sidewalk within a few feet of the corner, and other times I took long unplanned walks down the middle of a street, never correcting enough to get all the way over to the edge. Occasionally I managed to cross an intersection diagonally and end up kitty corner from my starting position, completely flummoxed and having to ask a passing pedestrian to get me back where I belonged, which is embarrassing but considered to be fair play. Just as getting lost is part of traveling blind, so is getting found. Learning where and how to ask for assistance is a valuable life skill. Old Pete just stood across the street and laughed to himself when these things happened, adding to his arsenal of good stories to tell at parties. He must have directed traffic to go around me at times, and he was always there to get me out of messes that were seriously threatening, but the rest was my job to figure out.

The most lost I ever got was on a straight and easy length of Taraval Street, in a business district. I had just made a close-to-perfect street crossing, and had climbed up the curb onto the sidewalk. Continuing in the same direction, I walked about ten steps and ran up against another curb. Now what? There were cars moving in all directions around me, and a few idling where I didn't think they ought to be. I figured that somehow I must not have finished crossing the street after all, and that all these cars must be milling around trying to dodge me or waiting for me to get out of their way. I stepped onto the curb and tried to go forward. Something was in the way, and there wasn't room to squeeze between it and the curb, but I had no desire to step back into the street with all those cars moving around. Trying the other side of the object that was blocking my path, my cane dropped off another curb. Panic was beginning to crowd in around the edges of my reasoning. There was absolutely nowhere for me to go, and I stood paralyzed. When I calmed down a bit and quit moving, some interesting clues began to filter into my overloaded brain—the sound of car doors opening and closing, the smell of gas. GAS! I reached out to touch the object that was blocking my path, and sure enough, I contacted the hose on a gas pump. There I was, foolishly stranded on an island in a gas station, thrashing around among the pumps and probably entertaining everybody who was there filling up. There was no way to finesse a graceful retreat out to the sidewalk, but I did manage to make it a hasty one.

Midway through our training at San Francisco State, our small group of fledgling Orientation and Mobility instructors was treated to a weeklong trip to the east coast to visit some of the major institutions and organizations that provide services for blind people. Seeing Eye Institute, the famous guide dog school in New Jersey, sponsored the entire trip. Pete accompanied us as our guide and entertainer and, most importantly, driver. He was an old hand at cold climate winter driving.

Hines VA Hospital in Chicago, the very place where Pete and Leo Bailey had pioneered their white cane technique after World War II, was our first stop. I slipped and skidded with Pete and my fellow students across the frozen parking lot on a miserable January morning, toes and hands frozen, shocked to encounter a real winter for the first time in my life. Wind shrieked off the lake and caused the cold to bite right through my pathetically inadequate California outerwear. I had never heard of "chill factor" before, but here it was emblazoned on every outdoor thermometer just below the actual temperature. Today the mercury showed -4 degrees with a chill factor of -40. I pondered loudly to my friends how much worse it could be in hell. Chattering and complaining about our misery in the cold, the group of us crowded through the revolving door of the VA hospital and immediately started shedding layers in the superheated lobby. The real shock of that day, however, wasn't the weather. It was being ushered to the blind ward of the hospital and finding myself confronted by dozens of terribly injured Vietnam veterans. The horrible reality of war-caused blindness was something I had not expected, and it hit me like a blow to the solar plexus. I had to fight to keep breathing. Up until that moment, learning to travel blind had been a fun challenge for me—a clever and unusual skill that required intense concentration and awareness of all of my senses. I danced through my lessons, thoroughly enjoying my developing proficiency. I had not yet been touched on the emotional level beyond my initial discomfort around some of the strange students at the California School for the Blind, having only seen blindness as a painless condition that some people happened to be born with. In my safe world I was insulated from even imagining what could cause sighted adults to lose their vision. The pictures in my textbooks were black and white photographs of various eye conditions, some unsightly, but none showing the human beings that the injured or diseased eyes belonged to. My exposure to adventitious blindness had been sanitized and clinical.

There was nothing sanitized or clinical about the blind soldiers confronting me in the ward at Hines. They were real and destroyed and terrifying with their missing limbs and blown-up faces. Some of them must have been younger that me, and all of them looked like they would have been grateful to have been left to die on the battlefield. I felt horrible staring at men who could not see me as our group was guided past the rows of beds and parked wheelchairs that contained their ruined bodies. What sense, I wondered, did it make for me and my fellow students to walk past these people? There was nothing any of us could do to help any of them, and what were we supposed to learn from observing them in their misery? I felt like we were violating the privacy of each and every veteran on the ward. I felt ashamed of my undamaged body and perfect vision. I fought tears and quit looking at the wounded men.

On the next ward we were introduced to a couple of men who had made it most of the way through their intense rehabilitation programs at Hines. They were up walking around and both were smiling and eager to show off the skills they had learned. One man, with an artificial leg, had a white cane fitted to a specially designed holder strapped over the stump of his remaining arm. Totally blind, he could walk about as well as any of us, and he was excited about heading back to home and work. He had been at Hines over a year and desperately missed his wife and children. The other man, legally blind and also missing both arms below the elbow, joked with the counselor accompanying us and asked if he could show off his newest skill. He adjusted his prostheses and laboriously picked up a matchbook with one hook and tore out a match with the other. After about three tries he lit the match and brought it up to the cigarette hanging from his lips. He took a long satisfying draw, exhaled a luxuriant cloud of smoke, and grinned at us. I tried to imagine these two men lying broken and hopeless in the previous ward, where they must have been when they first arrived at Hines. The rehab counselors at Hines had truly given them back their lives, and I fervently hoped the same would be true for the newer arrivals in the first group we had visited.

The other memorable stop on our east coast trip was our final destination, Seeing Eye Institute in Morristown, New Jersey. Situated near a rural postcard-perfect village, the entire campus was buried under a picturesque yet treacherous foot of packed, frozen snow. It was almost impossible to pick our way along the partially shoveled sidewalks without slipping, and here we were supposed to blindfold ourselves and learn how to use guide dogs. My skepticism increased when we were told that the large breeds used for this work walk between three and four miles per hour. I'm a fast walker and can easily manage that pace sighted on dry pavement, but I had no idea how any of us were going to perform on the Morristown ice without our vision.

Luckily, we started in the safety of the hallways at Seeing Eye, just like we had with our white canes in the Education Building at San Francisco State. After taking a few minutes to make friends with our assigned dogs, we were taught the voice commands and arm motions to signal the dogs to go forward, left, right or stop. Something of a melee ensued as the ten of us sleepshaded mobility students gave confused commands to the bewildered animals. I didn't like the feeling of moving through space attached by my left hand to my dog Baxter's constantly shifting harness. My connection to the dog seemed too loose and I felt out of control. I missed the security of my white cane contacting every obstacle or bump that was in my path—Baxter just steered me past any landmark that might have given me a sense of where I was in space. I wobbled uncertain and lost in my dog's wake, though he seemed to know exactly what he was doing.

The outdoor component of our brief guide dog training began on the second morning. With little of the step-by-step getting-ready-to-go-outside guidance that would have been on the program for regular blind students at Seeing Eye, we were launched onto the sidewalks in record time for a walk of about ten blocks. Happy to be outdoors, Baxter strained to set a pace that he considered decent. I pulled back to slow the dog, losing my balance and slipping repeatedly as I fought to find my center of gravity. There was nothing about this experience that I was enjoying, and I was terrified with every step I took that I would plunge facedown on the ice or stumble and break an ankle.

My vanity saved me. Having gotten this far in the program with flying colors on my white cane skills, I wasn't thrilled at the prospect of failing miserably with the guide dogs. I decided to alter my approach and see if I could find a rhythm that worked for me with this dog on the ice, instead of fighting every step of the way. I figured that I would be well looked after if I had a disastrous fall, and if that turned out to be the case at least my training at Seeing Eye would be memorable. It would make a good story for Pete to tell.

Remembering my years of modern dance training in high school, I did a mental check on my posture. My left hand and shoulder were thrust forward and my weight was pitched off balance as I tried to follow Baxter's lead. Every muscle in my body was tense. I threw caution to the icy wind and started walking fast enough to catch up with the hand that clutched the dog's harness. That returned my shoulders to their proper alignment. As I allowed my stride to lengthen my center of gravity found its natural place of rest over my hips, and I began to walk more freely. I quit slipping. Baxter no longer pulled, and I had the first inkling that we were beginning to work as a team. I could sense my dog right where he needed to be, just to my left side. All I needed to do was trust him, stay conscious of my body's well-trained sense of balance, and keep walking.

Baxter and I went a successful block, and then another. I realized that I could still use all of the auditory and tactile skills I had learned with my white cane, with the added advantage that I wasn't hitting anything. Everything began to fit into place and work as it was supposed to. As Baxter steered me in a clean, straight line, my confidence grew and I picked up my pace. Now I was able to walk with a limber swing in my hips, at the pace I usually walked without the blindfold. I was myself again, happy and confident in my body, thoroughly enjoying the unbelievable experience of walking blindfolded on ice in New Jersey.

I laughed out loud and reached down to scratch Baxter's ears at the next corner. He turned and licked my hand. "Forward, Baxter," I told him as soon as the traffic quieted. "Let's beat the others." I knew in that moment that my greatest hope as a mobility instructor would be to eventually get to work with a student who used a guide dog. I didn't care how long it would take for that day to come—I knew I would be ready for it. I mentally thanked Seeing Eye for this incomparable opportunity to experience the unique sensation of walking freely and fearlessly with a dog.

The grand finale of my Orientation and Mobility training at San Francisco State was a blindfolded adventure on public transportation from the campus to downtown San Francisco and back, during the height of the Christmas shopping season. Each of us ten mobility students had to independently board a streetcar in front of the university, transfer to a bus at a specific stop along the way, and then walk about ten blocks along downtown Market Street to check in at the Lighthouse for the Blind. By then I was a good enough cane traveler that this wasn't too daunting a proposition. The Muni was easy—the only car that came by the campus was the J car, and I had practiced the route to the stop many times. I could hear the train coming over the racket of the traffic, and there were little dots on the pavement right where the car doors would open, so I could climb aboard without assistance. All I had to do was find a pole to hang onto, stand by the door, and wait for the third stop to climb back down the steps and hop off.

The bus experience was a little more daunting. I could hear the bus rumbling towards me and squealing to a stop, but I had to ask people standing near me what number it was to make sure I boarded the correct one. There was no way to tell, like I could with the streetcar, exactly how far away from me the bus was stopping or where the door was. I had to poke and bash around with my cane to get in, and then find a seat since it was going to be a long trip. With my eyes closed behind my sleepshade, I prayed that I wouldn't plop down in some stranger's lap on a seat that I assumed was vacant.

It was scary riding the unfamiliar bus through streets I couldn't see, trusting that the harried driver of the overloaded vehicle would remember to tell me when to get off. Without vision I had no sense at all of how much distance we were covering as the bus lurched and wove past what might have been intersections, slowed traffic or official stops. Though I knew the basic layout of San Francisco, I was utterly lost within a few minutes. I decided, on second thought, not to trust the driver to tell me when we were at the Lighthouse, and ended up asking some passengers near me for help. They immediately tapped into their Christmas spirit and formed a leaderless committee, amusing themselves for the rest of the trip arguing over which stop would be the best one for me. That "help" was more unnerving than trusting the driver would have been, though consensus was eventually reached and I was deposited at the unanimously decided correct stop.

Once off the bus, I set out for my destination with confidence. I had been smart enough to ask one of my bus mates to tell me the name of the cross street where I was getting off, and it fit neatly into my mental map. I was sure of my technique and clear in my orientation, happily looking forward to the successful conclusion of this adventure. After marching along for a block or two, I became aware of a soft male voice behind me every time I came to a curb. "Step up" or "Step down," it said. Nothing more. I would walk another block, and there would be the voice again at the appropriate moment, "Step down." On the other side of the street, "Step up." Never too close to me, but always vigilant, my self-appointed guardian angel followed me all the way to the Lighthouse. There he disappeared silently into the darkening afternoon. Maybe he sensed too that my training had reached its culmination.

LOST

MaryBeth caught my attention as she walked backwards down the hallway between classes. She was in her junior year at a public high school in the well-to-do suburbs of Contra Costa County, where I was assigned for my first two months of student teaching in 1970. My master teacher, Sheldon, had mentioned that he had a student with some bizarre habits, but I was completely unprepared for the scene I found myself gawking at. Why, I wondered, was this girl being so weird in front of all the students swarming through the hall, and why wasn't anybody doing anything about it? Why didn't she seem embarrassed? I would have been able to accept the strangeness if the girl had looked like Sarah Jane, who had obvious disabilities, but this girl appeared so perfect.

Slim, blonde and model-beautiful except for her sunken eyes, Mary-Beth was dressed expensively and impeccably. Not a hair strayed out of place, and her lipstick was applied more evenly than my own. Sheldon told me that she was an exemplary student, earning A's in most of her college prep classes. She was able to take care of her own personal needs, and she could eat without spilling a thing. I could see that she used her white cane in the hallways with almost flawless technique—as long as she made a conscious effort to walk facing the right way.

Nobody in my college program had spent any time addressing the issue of exactly how one was supposed to teach a real student with real problems. Sheldon, not as supportive in his master teacher capacity as I would have liked, wasn't forthcoming with useful suggestions either. He hailed MaryBeth as she cruised past us, oriented forward by now, and went through the formality of introducing the two of us. He suggested that I take this strange girl—right now—to practice street crossings. He didn't offer any pointers about where he and MaryBeth had been practicing this drill, or any information pertaining to her skill level. Sheldon's one helpful hint was that MaryBeth got confused whenever she turned a corner. Then the bell rang and he hurried away with the last students scrambling to get to their classes before the dreaded tardy bell. MaryBeth, waiting for a direction from me, stood passively, leaning on her cane in the empty hallway.

Feeling dumbfounded and annoyed at Sheldon for his failure to support me on this initial lesson with my first real student, and terrified that I would make a total mess of it, I frantically scanned my memory bank for essential, teachable elements of street crossing skills. I couldn't imagine how any of my remembered lessons might apply to this girl standing next to me if she didn't even know which way to face when she walked. How do you teach somebody to orient to traffic if she stands there with her back to the moving cars? What did MaryBeth already know about crossing streets—or, more precisely, what *didn't* she know? What other huge holes were lurking under that exquisite surface of hers? How was I even going to engage her to come along with me on this lesson we were supposed to be having? Would she trust me, a completely new person who had just dropped from nowhere into her blind life, to guide her off the relative safety of her high school campus?

I made a hasty decision to ignore Sheldon's direction to practice street crossings, and decided instead to aim for something I hoped would be more achievable in the thirty minutes MaryBeth and I had left for this already dubious lesson. I told her as much of my plan as I had created in the preceding fifteen seconds, gave her my arm and guided her on foot across the busy street in front of the high school to a residential neighborhood that looked predictable. I could see square blocks, straight sidewalks and regularly spaced houses—a comfortable place, I hoped, with no big challenges. All I wanted to do was get to know MaryBeth a bit while she walked in a straight line. I needed to establish at least the beginnings of a comfortable rapport with her, so I could leave her with the impression that she and I could have some fun and hopefully some success in our time together. "Here we go," I told MaryBeth. "I'm going to let go of you now and follow you while you walk on to the next corner. Just go straight."

"What?" she turned to ask me, losing her orientation before she had taken a single step. "Sheldon never makes me walk out here by myself."

"Don't worry," I tried to reassure her, "I'll be right behind you and I won't let you get hurt. Come on, let's get going and let's see how far you can go. That's right, use your cane and tell me if you think that's grass or gravel over on your right. Where do you think this driveway goes?"

"What?" MaryBeth asked me again.

It didn't take me long to realize that MaryBeth couldn't talk and walk at the same time. My friendly attempts at conversation distracted her from what was, for her, the tremendously difficult task of walking without veering where there were no walls to trail. She kept waiting for me to give her directions that would solve her immediate problems, but I needed to find out what she could do without my support. I quit yakking and tagged along nervously behind her, hoping to at least ascertain her strengths related to orientation and mobility. I watched as the poor girl got lost in almost every driveway. When she found the sidewalk again she frequently stepped out in the wrong direction. She wandered down driveways into the street and walked along in the gutter, unable to differentiate it from the sidewalk. By the time we arrived at the corner we had been aiming for she was hopelessly disoriented. She thought she should be back at the school by now when, in fact, we had been walking away from it for the last ten minutes. I gave up on the hopeless lesson and offered MaryBeth my arm to guide her back to her next class, feeling more perplexed than when I had met her an hour earlier.

I learned a few more things about MaryBeth as my weeks with her progressed. She had grown up in a caring and educated upper middle class family. She belonged to what was known as the "RLF" generation. Her story was the same as that of every other blind child raised in the 1950s—born prematurely, saved from death by high amounts of oxygen administered to her in her incubator, and inadvertently sentenced to a life of total blindness caused by the very oxygen that had kept her alive. The retinas in MaryBeth's eyes had been destroyed by scarring caused when she was taken off the oxygen. Faced with a school system that wasn't prepared to educate a blind child, MaryBeth's mother had learned braille and doggedly fought to have her daughter included in regular education classrooms from kindergarten on up through the grades. What I was looking at was the result of that long, partially successful struggle.

What MaryBeth couldn't do was create a reliable mental "map" of where she existed in space. She couldn't tell up from down, literally having no inkling what "up" or "down" meant. She was as likely to walk backwards down the hall as forward, and she could get lost if she stood in one place and turned around. This lovely girl, who at first impression seemed so "normal," was in reality an empty shell of groomed appearances. The emphasis of her training had been on teaching her to superficially act like all the little sighted kids in the neighborhood, rather than on getting down and dirty and learning how her body and the world were really put together. She was totally unaware of how her limbs moved and bent and related to each other, and equally helpless with spatial concepts such as "in front of you," "across the street," or "around the corner." MaryBeth was totally and perpetually lost in a world full of disassociated bits of half-understood information.

One of the roadblocks that MaryBeth faced in terms of functioning in her sighted world was her vocabulary full of a huge percentage of "hollow" words—words she could use fairly appropriately because she was smart and had heard them all her life in the stories her mother had dutifully read to her as a tiny child, but which were meaningless to her because of her limited "real" experiences. What is a cloud to somebody who has never seen one? Or a lion? A fluffy cotton ball or a stuffed lion toy have only visual qualities in common with their real counterparts, and though these objects are frequently used in an effort to convey the meaning of cloud or lion to a blind child, they are ineffective, confusing, or both. Even objects that can be touched, like trees and trucks and horses, have limited meaning if the child doesn't have access to the entire object with all of its moving parts and multitude of functions. The words "hallway" and "street" and "corner" have to be specifically taught by moving through them, on hands and knees if necessary, to feel and investigate every feature. These new concepts have to be experienced over and over again from every possible angle, with somebody there to guide the child's exploring hands and attach relevant vocabulary to each sensation.

And then there are the verbs—the even less tangible action words. I knew about skiing and square dancing for years before I ever set foot on a snowy mountainside or swung through my first do-si-do, because I had constant access to a world of pictures. Hundreds of fascinating actions and events were depicted in my childhood storybooks, shown at the movies, and even printed on my pajama fabric. MaryBeth missed all of that. I tried to make a wisecrack one day as we walked past an overgrown parking strip where the tall weeds kept getting tangled with her cane—that somebody really needed to mow the grass. MaryBeth didn't get it. "Mow" to her meant a certain loud noise in the distance, but for her the racket of the lawnmower was unassociated with making grass shorter. There is no incidental learning of words if you don't see, and trying to build concepts using words you don't understand is impossible.

MaryBeth moved around in her confusing world by the "cookbook" method. She could follow a series of memorized directions and get from the resource room at school to her math class. "Go out the door, trail along the lockers with your left hand, and go in the first door you come to." She got from her math class to social studies the next period using a similar "recipe." But she had no idea how to walk directly from the resource room to social studies—there was no mental map that linked them without stopping at the math class in between, even though the math class was not located between the other two familiar points. MaryBeth could not imagine the classrooms on a grid in relation to each other, let alone understand that it was considerably shorter to go to social studies by turning right instead of left when she came out of the resource room, to go around the short side of the rectangular route. The long way was the only way for MaryBeth.

Feeling a little braver after knowing MaryBeth for a couple of weeks, I tried to teach her how to walk home from her school bus stop—ignoring, with all of my fresh student teacher zealousness, the fact that her regular Orientation and Mobility instructor, Sheldon, had already failed miserably at that same goal. It was a short three-block route with a couple of straight street crossings and one turn. Nothing tricky. I could have done it on the first try with my eyes closed. The process, however, was almost identical to the sequence of directions and confused responses of our first attempt to walk a block.

"MaryBeth," I began, "this is where you would be if you had just stepped off the bus into the street. You've done that before. There—find the sidewalk with your cane and climb up. Good, you're on the sidewalk where you belong. Now all you have to do is start walking towards your house."

"Where do I go?" she asked me with a face that was already set in an expression of blank incomprehension.

"Try to figure it out. Which way does your mom take you when she meets you?"

"What?" my student asked me.

MaryBeth and I struggled at this project for several frustrating weeks, but made little headway. MaryBeth did eventually learn which way to turn when she got off the bus, but she couldn't get over her confusion over the concept of turning and crossing the street she was walking along. She was totally flummoxed by the fact that the traffic ended up on the other side of her after she made the crossing. I tried all of the teaching strategies that were fresh in my mind from my own training. I had her cross and re-cross the street, and then stand in one place and make 180 degree turns, hoping that she would comprehend how she could make the direction of the traffic change relative to her own orientation. Pete Wurzburger had done that with me and I understood the concept almost instantly, but MaryBeth looked ready to cry. I tried walking down one side of the street talking to her while she walked down the other side, to give her the idea that space continued to exist on the other side of the street even if she could not touch it with her cane. She could never figure out where my voice was coming from. I made a simple tactile map that represented the street and the sidewalk, and had MaryBeth trace her way down the miniature cardboard "street" with her fingers to explore the location and direction of the turn. That, too, had been a useful tool for me when I was disoriented, but with MaryBeth my efforts were all to no avail. The more I talked and explained, the blanker MaryBeth looked; and the blanker she looked, the more exasperated I became. I heard myself beginning to shout at her in the utterly futile and thoughtless hope that louder would somehow get through better and increase her comprehension. When I realized what I was doing it finally became clear to me that there just were not enough functional words in MaryBeth's vocabulary for her to grasp the concept that there were two sides to the street. I couldn't recall ever *not* knowing that.

At seventeen MaryBeth was too old to start all over again on concept training. She was too big for me to lift into treetops and over fences, or to carry while I ran madly down a hill and jumped over a creek. Having spent her entire life learning to stay clean, she was not open to the dirty work of up-close exploration of sidewalks, curbs and gutters. MaryBeth's family would not support my efforts to get her down on her hands and knees to learn to differentiate gravel from blacktop from dirt by touching them. They had worked too hard all those years ago to coax their blind daughter up off the floor so she could walk like everybody else. For MaryBeth, the natural and childish delight in exploration was past.

MaryBeth and I didn't get very far with our mobility lessons. They kind of petered out, and then I was sent on to my next student teaching assignment in another town. My failure with MaryBeth actually opened a door for me—it showed me the direction I wanted to take as a teacher. Through my frustration at my inability to help MaryBeth learn a simple route, I developed a fervent conviction that Orientation and Mobility had to be opened up to preschoolers, and even infants, to teach them the body awareness and spatial concepts they would need to become confident and independent travelers as adults. I wanted my future students to walk backwards because they felt like it—not because it wasn't any different to them than walking forward. I wanted them to learn that they have two sides to their body, and to extrapolate from that to understand that there are two sides to a street. I wanted them to climb and run and fly and dance, and to know the meaning of those words from the first-hand thrill of doing it. I vowed to give my future students the chance to fit into a fun, meaningful and ever-expanding world.

THE PERMANENT REALITY OF BLINDNESS

I had completed half of my student teaching stint at the Albany Orientation Center for the Blind when I was assigned the job of getting Doug through the next few lessons on his program. He had been at OCB for a while, learning a whole new way of life after his car accident. Handsome and athletic in his mid-forties, and graying slightly, Doug exuded confidence with his white cane and strode along at a good clip, handling every obstacle with well-rehearsed technique.

Doug's scars didn't show much. His face was pretty well healed from his headlong flight through the windshield, and it was only after weeks of my working with him that he told me his wife had left him because she couldn't handle the idea of being married to a blind man. Doug didn't complain—this was just a fact that related to who he was now. He couldn't find it in his heart to blame his wife, and had not fought the divorce. The only real regret he had, Doug told me, was that he had also lost his sense of smell as a result of the head injuries he sustained in the accident, and he couldn't enjoy the fragrance of flowers or the taste of food the way he used to. He was getting weary of the blandness of everything.

At OCB every student goes through the same sequence of daily mobility lessons, beginning with indoor cane technique and progressing to streets and crossings and public transportation, just as we students did at San Francisco State College. Every lesson is numbered in order and written out in detail, right down to the cross-streets where it is to begin and end, including exactly what the student is supposed to purchase in what store. Lesson plan in hand, I set off with Doug one day to accomplish the prescribed goal—he was to walk to a certain coffee shop on the main drag and enter it alone, find the counter, sit down, and order a cup of coffee.

As we neared the coffee shop I noticed that Doug was sweating. He was also making uncharacteristic mistakes—veering on a street crossing, stumbling on a curb and smashing harder than usual into obstacles. He finally stopped in the middle of the sidewalk and told me quietly, with his head bowed, "I can't go into the coffee shop."

"Sure you can," I responded as brightly as I could. "What's the problem?"

"I'm afraid I'll do something dumb like knock over a glass of water and make a fool of myself," Doug confessed to me. "Then the waitress will be all mad at me."

"I don't think so," I responded, "and I'll bet you never knock your water over in the dining room at OCB. Why don't you just give it a whirl?"

"I can't. I'm sorry."

"Listen, I'll be right here outside the door waiting for you. How about if you just go in, turn around and come back out again? Then you can do the rest of the lesson tomorrow."

"No, I can't do this. I don't want to hurt your feelings, but I really can't go in there."

I couldn't think of anything else to say to Doug to encourage him, fearing that more pushing on my part would just make him feel worse. I felt uncomfortable trying to support this man in his emotional crisis, never having learned much in my years of growing up that gave me any idea what to do in a situation like this. In my small family, extreme feelings were ignored, counteracted or punished. A few giggles or tears were acceptable, but I remember being sent to my room if anything escalated to a higher pitch. We, and my mother included herself in this "we", were all expected to put on a happy face and cope, no matter what. If something was really bad, the only solution was to close the door on it, walk away and never look back. I didn't even have the appropriate words in my vocabulary to express support or caring to a person in pain, and I completely lacked the self-confidence to reach out to Doug, who in my eyes belonged to the unapproachable "adult" generation, even though I was the teacher and he was my student. All I could do was tell Doug, "OK, we'll try again tomorrow." We turned around and silently returned to OCB without finishing the lesson.

We tried the same lesson again the next day, and the next, and every day after that for two entire weeks. We walked and talked and repeated previous lessons for lack of anything else to do, but nothing I could say from my earnest 21-year-old perspective could convince Doug to take the plunge and put himself through what was, for him, the dreaded public test of his new identity as a blind man. Everything he had accomplished up until now in his cane training had been a matter of skill and concentration, both of which he possessed in abundance. Doug could take that cane and go anywhere, providing he didn't have to interact on a personal level with anybody besides instructors. He was a machine out there, safe and strong as long as he kept walking away from the truth that was stalking him.

Maybe Doug got tired of listening to me. Or it's possible that he actually heard what I was trying to tell him. Maybe he just figured it out for himself. One day, for the dozenth time, I asked him, "What do you think will happen if you knock over your glass of water in the café?" Doug stopped and considered for a moment while I looked at his blind eyes through his sunglasses. Then he turned abruptly and headed in the direction of the coffee shop without saying a word to me. I followed him to the door, expecting to see him to stop there as he had so many times before, and I tried to think of what to say that would be supportive in light of another failed attempt to purchase this over-rated cup of coffee. This time, though, Doug kept going and charged in, head down, moving like a robot towards the showdown with his demons.

I stood out on the curb, alone and worried, watching the traffic signal at the corner go through its cycles and trying to live Doug's pain for him. Having prevailed on him after so much agonizing and negotiating, I wasn't sure either one of us was experiencing anything even close to triumph. I wanted to rush into the restaurant and pull Doug outside to the safety of the busy sidewalk. I didn't want him to be without support in this place where he was scared, and I wasn't happy with the responsibility of having pushed him so far.

After what seemed like enough time for him to have consumed an entire greasy meal in that awful place, Doug strode out and waited, like a blind person must, for me to come and find him. He stood on the sidewalk with his shoulders square and proud, and the confidence was back in the way he held his head. I could see that he was trying to control an ear-to-ear grin. I couldn't wait to hear his story.

"Yep," Doug told me, "I did it all. I knocked over my water right off the bat, and the waitress was a real sweetheart about it. She just came over and mopped up without complaining, and she even poured me another glass of water. Nobody around me even seemed to notice. They just kept on with their meals and conversations. It wasn't that bad."

"Did you get your cup of coffee after all that?" I wanted to know.

"I sure did. And you know what? The waitress kept coming back to chat with me while I was drinking it. She was real nice."

I suggested to Doug that it was about time to start heading back to OCB to celebrate his triumph with the other mobility instructors. He took a couple of steps, stopped, and turned towards me.

"You know," Doug blurted out, "I'd really like to go back to that cafe tomorrow."

I didn't have any more lessons with Doug, as I was assigned a new student at OCB for the remainder of my stint there. However, on my last day, I was summoned to the office. There I found Doug holding a large box of chocolates for me. He had brailled a beautiful note of thanks for my patience and perseverance with him. The head mobility instructor later informed me that gifts from students to teachers were strictly forbidden at OCB, but they had made an exception for Doug. It was only then that I realized that I had made a huge impact on Doug's life, just by hanging in there with him during his struggle to fully accept his blindness. My shyness and clumsiness about finding the right words to support this man in his pain had been inconsequential. What Doug had needed from me was simply my willingness to be present.

LEAPING INTO THE UNKNOWN

There weren't any jobs for an Orientation and Mobility Instructor in Mendocino County in 1971, but there were plenty of positions in the San Francisco Bay Area, where I remained after finishing school. The logical choice would have been to stay there and apply for one of those perfect openings at the School for the Blind or at one of the many excellent rehabilitation facilities for blind adults in the area. However, being newly and blissfully married, I didn't even think to question my husband's desire to leave the financial security of the overcrowded city and return to the home where he grew up—to his parents' property in rural Mendocino County.

I was all for the idea of a move. The unrelenting pace and constant noise of the Bay Area were becoming overwhelming, and I was weary of the growing number of scary people accosting me every time I walked out the door of our apartment. One year post-People's Park and Cambodian Invasion, Berkeley continued to exist in a state of remembered siege. The tanks and riot gear were gone, but the police still felt threatening as they marched through the streets in a show of force that undermined any sense of peace. Too many of the street people were in-your-face aggressive with their panhandling. I had been physically assaulted twice, and was tired of feeling nervously compelled to look over my shoulder, ready to bolt, every time I heard footsteps behind me on the sidewalk. There was no respite unless I hid indoors, which wasn't an alternative I was willing to consider. Even indoors nothing was safe. One morning my husband and I found the wheels had been stolen off our locked bicycles in the basement of our apartment building. The last straw was realizing that I had to lock the apartment door behind me just to run down the back stairs to take the garbage out. This place wasn't feeling much like the peaceful rural home I yearned for.

The decision to leave Berkeley was made quickly. We packed our belongings, including what was left of our bicycles, and divided the awkward heaps between the cavernous interior of our '59 Ford sedan and the bed of our even more ancient Chevy pick-up. Looking something like Mom and Pop Judd from *Grapes of Wrath*, we caravanned north, colorfully and rather slowly, on account of the decrepitude of our vehicles and the lack of visibility caused by our piled furniture and great lengths of an over-grown split-leaf philodendron coiled up against windows of the car. We weren't in much of a hurry. In spite of the fact that Mendocino County feels like it's located in another country, it's only a three-hour drive from the city—four hours if you stop for a leisurely lunch along the way *and* drive what we were driving on a hot day.

I felt a delightful sense of absolute certainty as we crossed the Rich-mond Bridge, heading *out* of the foggy Bay Area summer towards our new home to the north. Layers of weight peeled away from my civiliza-tion-stressed psyche with each of the succession of cities we left forever behind us. Highway 101 narrowed from its teeming five lanes to three lanes each way, and finally down to a reasonable two—before it quit being a divided freeway altogether. Finally, past the congestion of Santa Rosa, the highway quietly reverted to the two-lane road it had been in my childhood. It dawdled through the tired agricultural towns of Gey-serville, Cloverdale and Hopland. We drove past ramshackle open faces of feed stores, grungy diners, IOOF halls and used car lots casually lit-tered along the downtown drags in these fading centers of bygone com-merce, all reminding me of the way of life I had missed so much in the overpopulated Bay Area.

A few hot miles later, we crossed the Russian River for the last time on this trip and descended into the orchard-patched expanse of the Ukiah Valley. Here Highway 101 enjoyed one last shot at importance. A full twelve miles of it stretched out in front of us in a relatively straight line to be-come a bona fide freeway, the only section of freeway in all of Mendocino County. Starting here, the four divided lanes continued in a large sweep through the pear ranches surrounding the county seat of Ukiah, passed an ugly commercial strip along the old highway, and ended abruptly at the north end of the valley. That was it. And that was the end of the line for us. Taking the last off-ramp, we gladly left the freeway behind. My husband's parents, grandparents and younger siblings were waiting to help us move into the family home a mile away in Redwood Valley.

Redwood Valley isn't really a town. It's an intersection with its own ZIP code, located in the middle of a pretty valley with almost no redwood trees left in it. There isn't much else in Redwood Valley either. Houses, small farms, mobile homes, decaying barns and old head-pruned Italian vineyards are scattered haphazardly across the landscape, separated by fences in various states of disrepair—all jumbled up in each other's way, but used to it, and consequently co-existing rather peacefully. Similarly, the population of old farming families, new back-to-the-land hippies and well-to-do ranchette owners seem to accept and tolerate, if not love each other.

I turned a full circle, like Dorothy when she landed back in Kansas, surveying my new home on its surrounding acres of vineyards and woods. I glowed with a self-conscious feeling of righteousness. My husband, at least, was returning to the home where he grew up—and I, through association, now belonged here too. I was no longer a "country wannabe" from Berkeley—I was now a legitimate farm girl, and a legitimate farm family had just accepted me with open arms. I inhaled and filled my lungs with the warm afternoon air that smelled of plowed dirt and growing things, knowing in my soul that this place would nurture me. I immediately settled into an energetic routine of organic gardening, canning and cooking with my mother-in-law, happily occupying every hot summer minute. The weeks flew by until September was one calendar page away.

It was time to set out and see to the daunting chore of getting employed. The prospects of my landing a job in this chosen rural oasis of ours seemed depressingly unlikely. Mendocino County only had a population of 50,000, which had been slowly declining for years, and of all the scattered little towns, only four were incorporated. Ukiah was by far the largest town, with about 10,000 people in and around it, followed by Fort Bragg, Willits and Point Arena, in descending order of size. These "bigger" towns (Point Arena boasted a population of approximately 400) had high schools, most of the smaller towns had elementary schools, and some of them had a visually handicapped student or two on their rosters. No resource rooms anywhere, though, and no concept of what Orientation and Mobility was all about, let alone any defined need for a teacher with my specialized credential.

My father-in-law suggested that I drive into Ukiah and announce myself to the Mendocino County Office of Education, even though they weren't advertising any teaching positions at all. I ignored his advice and drove all the way to neighboring Lake County, where they were actively searching for a Teacher of the Visually Handicapped. Once there, I discovered that Lake County wanted to hire a person for an hour or two a day to assist some kid with low vision through reading assignments that were hard for him. I heard myself say to the administrator who was interviewing me, "You really don't need to pay for a credentialed VH teacher to do that." I lessened my chances of getting the job by continuing, "I think you can save your money and use a classroom aide or a volunteer, or even another student, since it is just run-of-the-mill, unspecialized tutoring you need." I walked out of that interview with many thanks for my advice—and obviously no job.

So, back to the drawing board—I still needed a job. I finally decided to follow my father-in-law's earlier suggestion and see if somebody at the Mendocino County Office of Education would talk to me. I marched into the office unannounced, sweating and uncertain. I told the receptionist my name, and before I had a chance to formulate an intelligent opening sentence, I was ushered in to meet the Superintendent himself. Lou Delsol greeted me cordially with a big handshake, waved me to a chair, and immediately put me on the spot. "What do you think you can do for MCOE?" he asked me bluntly, skipping the pleasantries that might have put me at ease, such as asking what *he* could do for *me.*

I swallowed a few times in an effort to will my voice to function. "I teach visually impaired children," I stammered, painfully aware of my almost complete lack of experience. "I can do the regular classroom things like supporting students who need braille or large print, but I'm really more interested in finding a place where I can teach more basic skills."

"What do you mean?" Lou prompted me.

Grateful that my words finally started flowing unimpaired, I launched into all of my ideas about working with very young visually impaired children to try to teach them more about their world than my first student MaryBeth had managed to learn. "I want to try to help these kids before they get too confused or frustrated to make sense of their world," I explained to Lou. "I want to teach them while they still love to play, and I want to show their parents and siblings fun and effective ways to interact with them. I want to make a difference before it's too late."

Lou was surprisingly interested and started asking me questions. "How do you think you can do that?" he wanted to know.

"I'm convinced that it's absolutely critical to begin teaching blind children while they are babies, in their homes. If you wait for them to begin kindergarten you miss the first five years of their lives, and then you are playing the futile game of catch-up before you even start. And you never really get to know the families, which is critical if you are going to learn to trust each other. That doesn't make any sense to me."

"How do you feel about working with children who are multi-handicapped?" Lou asked, looking intently at me.

"Then it's even more important to start while they are young," I replied, recalling a fascinating hands-on class I had taken at a development center at San Francisco State. In that center I had been able to work directly with a number of severely impaired preschoolers, under the tutelage of a highly skilled master teacher, and I was excited at the possibility of putting to use some of the good ideas I had gained there.

A huge grin spread across Lou's face. "You," he told me, "have arrived here at exactly the right time for both of us. You are the answer to our prayers. We have four visually impaired preschoolers in the county right now. Two of them are multi-handicapped. And there is another older girl who is totally blind with so many other disabilities that she is not in school. Until this minute I had no idea how in the world I was going to provide a program for them, and I've been worrying about it for months."

By the time my unofficial interview ended, Lou had created a position for me. He asked me to start the following Monday with an itinerant program, where I would be required to drive to each of my students' homes for an hour every day to provide them with some kind of direct, one-on-one instruction. I was given free rein to design my curriculum however I saw fit, and Lou told me he would see to it that I had a generous budget for materials and travel expenses. My office would be my car, and a telephone on somebody else's desk would be available to me if that person didn't happen to be using it at the moment. That was all I needed to know. The rest would be worked out on the job.

"You are truly the answer to our prayers," Lou repeated to me as I danced out of his office. I was pretty sure that the reverse was true. Lou's open-hearted reception of me and my ideas was exactly what I had experienced when I moved in with my husband's family a few months earlier, and for the first time in my life I knew that I truly belonged in a place. In the people of Mendocino County I found the trust, the support and the appreciation that had always been missing in my life. I felt whole, and I knew I would never leave.

Three days later I loaded up the trunk of my huge pink Ford with materials I pillaged from a storeroom in the basement at MCOE, borrowed a map of the county so I could find my scattered students, and set out to become a real teacher.

MY FIRST LESSON ON LOSS

Darleen came first. Four years old on the Fourth of July and scrappy as all get-out, she peered at me through her blue-framed Coke bottle glasses and staked out her claim to independence. She was going to have nothing to do with this unfamiliar teacher invading her territory, no matter how much fun her twin brother and I were having playing games at her family's dining room table across the room. This was her house and I didn't belong there. Period.

Darleen held out for the entire first week of my daily lessons at her home. Always in the room, always watching, she steadfastly refused to respond to my earnest new- teacher invitations or to her mother's pleas to come over and join her brother and me with our tactile puzzles, darkly outlined drawings and colorful large print books. Then one day when I showed up, Darleen just walked over and climbed into my lap as if she had been doing it all along, snuggling her raggedy strawberry blonde head under my chin. Gracious and sweet as you please, but the message was clear—the ball was in *her* court.

The ball stayed in Darleen's court for the entire year that I knew her and worked with her in her home. She liked it that way and so did I. What she gave she gave from her heart, with no calculations, manipulations or ulterior motives. She possessed a pure and innocent self-centeredness that was completely uncomplicated and unequivocally expressed. Bad days with Darleen were indescribably bad. When she needed to take a stand over some issue that I couldn't allow her to win, she graced everybody in her immediate environment with a tantrum that wouldn't quit. Darleen's good days were like sun shining through rain—full of freshness and ex-citement and wonder that were heightened by their very transience. I loved Darleen like I had never loved the children I had babysat in my teenage years, learning from her that there is endless magic in simply watching an unspoiled person being herself.

Darleen had a will to learn and a tremendous drive to function with confidence in a world that she could barely see. Born with cataracts, as was her twin brother, she had had surgery early in her life to remove them. She consequently needed to wear thick glasses that gave her clear central vision at only one distance, about twelve inches from her face. Everything else was like looking through a windshield sheeted with rain—full of blurry colors and movement, but devoid of clear shapes or spatial definition. For some reason Darleen's vision was considerably worse than her brother's, but that just caused this exceptionally intelligent child to fight harder to make some sense out of the inadequate visual information she was able to take in.

Darleen possessed a strong inner drive to confront her poorly seen world with all of its challenges, and was actually better prepared for kindergarten than her brother by the end of my year of working with the two of them. Responding to my one-on-one instruction and using adapted materials that she could understand for the first time in her life, Darleen absorbed information with an appetite that astonished me. She learned to count, identify pictures, read dozens of large-lettered words and illustrate fantasy stories that she and I dreamed up. She learned to walk safely on the route to school and handle herself with confidence on the playground equipment. She couldn't wait for school to start in September.

Darleen never made it to kindergarten. One summer day, a few weeks before the beginning of school, she begged her mother to be allowed to go in the Jeep with her high school sister to pick berries at a neighbor's place. A quarter of a mile from home, Darleen inexplicably stood up in the doorless Jeep and bounced out, landing on her head on a concrete bridge abutment. She lay where she had fallen, unmoving. She was rushed to the local hospital by ambulance and subsequently transported to the intensive care unit at a major regional hospital. I saw her there, lying in a coma, hooked up to enormous life-sustaining machines pulsing and blipping in a vain attempt to sustain her life. I looked at the shell of her body in the oversized steel-railed hospital bed, but I couldn't find Darleen. Her glasses removed, her head shaved and bandaged, and her eager little face a still mask of bloodless white, she died.

Three decades later I drive to Anderson Valley for a meeting concerning another student. It's the same unspoiled valley that it was when I first ventured out there on a daily basis to visit Darleen and her brother, full of cattle pastures and hayfields by the river and patches of corn rustling in the autumn breeze that smells of rain. I drive in one road and out the other like I always did, for the same reason I always did—the valley is so beautiful I want to see all of it, on both sides of the river.

I go by Darleen's old house and pass the graveyard where she was buried so many years ago in a new party dress that she never got to choose, with white gloves and a neatly styled wig. I didn't attend her funeral because I couldn't bear the thought of seeing the little child I loved imprisoned and quiet in her tiny casket, with her messy pigtails gone. I didn't know at the time what to say to her grieving family, and I was afraid to let them see me cry. I didn't realize that my presence might have been the best comfort I could have offered, and I sadly wish that I could go back in time to do it over.

I park and get out of the car to wander for the first time in the overgrown cemetery. Tears come to my eyes again as I realize that I don't even know for sure which of the small fenced gravesites is Darleen's. Winter is approaching and it's hard for me to think of Darleen's little body lying alone in the cold and rain for so long. She would be thirty-nine years old now.

THE "PERFECT" BLIND CHILD

Every teacher of the visually impaired fervently hopes to have at least one "perfect" blind child on their caseload at some point in their career. More than one would be better yet, but "perfect" blind children are rare. To be "perfect," a child has to be functionally blind, smart, minus other extreme physical impairments, and blessed with one or two parents who can eventually embrace this completely unexpected world of braille and white canes. We teachers brag to our colleagues about our "perfect" blind children and thrill at every opportunity to work with them—these are the children who allow us to use the finest and best skills of our highly specialized trade.

In the early '50s, a virtual epidemic of totally blind children was inadvertently created when doctors discovered that premature babies could be saved by administering high doses of oxygen while the tiny babies were struggling to hang onto life in their incubators. The oxygen unexpectedly ruined their retinas, but tens of thousands of infants who would have perished without it lived to grow up without additional impairments. By the end of the decade doctors learned exactly how much oxygen they could safely use, and today the condition, now known as Retinopathy of Prematurity (ROP), is extremely rare. Now most of the visually impaired children in the school system have low vision and multiple handicaps caused by an assortment of untreatable genetic conditions, diseases such as meningitis, or drug and alcohol exposure in utero. These children are interesting and challenging to work with, but most are unable to benefit from the high-intensity Braille and white cane skills we all love so much to teach.

Ironically, fifty years ago, when there were so many high-functioning totally blind children needing an education, there were few teachers of the visually impaired. Blind children up until that time were almost never educated in the public school system. They were either sent to state schools for the blind or kept at home. Resource rooms for blind students in their neighborhood public schools were unheard of, and many parents in the '50s found themselves needing to learn braille as the only viable means of giving their blind child the necessary support to get through the years of public schooling. The universities finally caught up with the demand, but then had to modify their teacher-training curriculum to address the needs of the next generations of less academic blind children.

I have had three "perfect" blind children in my thirty-five-year career. To my heartfelt dismay, they have all moved away to more populated places where their parents could find better jobs or new spouses. I hear through the grapevine that all three of my lost students have continued to thrive and learn new skills without me, but it kills me that some other lucky teacher had all the fun of nurturing and fostering that growth. Jerico, Jewel and Nicole probably don't even remember me any more, but I hang onto and treasure my memories of them.

Jerico was exhausting. He was so smart he glowed. He walked early (almost unheard of for a blind child) and learned to hear walls before I had a chance to even think of teaching him that skill. He talked precociously and incessantly. He filled his space wherever he went, asking new questions before his beleaguered parents and teachers had finished answering his previous ones. When he ran out of queries about how and why things in his environment worked, he broke the silence by yelling at least once a minute, "Where is everybody?" or "What are you doing now?" And he hollered louder if he didn't get an immediate answer.

I didn't work with Jerico long enough to teach him braille or get him very far along in his living skills. I watched him eat a few meals, though, and I thoroughly admired and supported his parents for their approach of letting Jerico's every encounter with food be a "sensory experience." That's an educational euphemism for a tremendous mess caused by the child doing it himself. It's great for the development of body awareness and cause-effect relationships, but an awful lot of cleanup.

Jerico's mother, Gina, had their day-to-day life, with all of its new challenges and demands, comfortably and efficiently under control when I first met her with her beautiful blind infant in her arms. She smiled at me and looked confidently into my eyes as she offered to let me hold her baby. I knew instantly that Gina would find the inner strength to tackle all the extra things she would have to teach Jerico, and that she would do it all with a fearless and loving competence. She was physically and intellectually up for the challenge.

Gina hadn't heard of, but was already living, a parable that I read years later in an education journal. It was written by Emily Perl Kingsley, the mother of a child with Cerebral Palsy. The parable applied perfectly to Gina. It went like this:

"I am often asked to describe the experience of raising a child with a disability—to try to help people who have not shared that unique experience to understand it, to imagine how it would feel. It's like this... When you're going to have a baby, it's like planning a fabulous vacation trip—to Italy. You buy a bunch of guide books and make your wonderful plans. The Coliseum. The Michelangelo David. The gondolas in Venice. You may learn some handy phrases in Italian. It's all very exciting. After months of eager anticipation, the day finally arrives. You pack your bags and off you go. Several hours later, the plane lands. The stewardess comes in and says, 'Welcome to Holland.' 'Holland?!?' you say. 'What do you mean Holland?? I signed up for Italy! I'm supposed to be in Italy. All my life I've dreamed of going to Italy.'

But there's been a change in the flight plan. They've landed in Holland and there you must stay.

The important thing is that they haven't taken you to a horrible, disgusting, filthy place, full of pestilence, famine and disease. It's just a different place.

So you must go out and buy new guide books. And you must learn a whole new language. And you will meet a whole new group of people you would never have met. It's just a different place. It's slower-paced than Italy, less flashy than Italy. But after you've been there for a while and you catch your breath, you look around ... and you begin to notice that Holland has windmills ... and Holland has tulips. Holland even has Rembrandts. But everyone you know is busy coming and going from Italy... and they're all bragging about what a wonderful time they had there. And for the rest of your life, you will say, 'Yes, that's where I was supposed to go. That's what I had planned. And the pain of that will never, ever, ever, ever, go away... because the loss of that dream is a very, very significant loss. But ... if you spend your life mourning the fact that you didn't get to Italy, you may never be free to enjoy the very special, the very lovely things ... about Holland."

Gina was clearly getting used to Holland, and was adjusting beautifully to her daily nurturing of Jerico—but I began to sense a little too much brightness in her tone as we talked about her baby's development. I felt self-conscious about the fact that two of my own children and several of my nieces were crawling and toddling around in the home of a mutual friend where Gina and I were having our first encounter. I was afraid that all of these active, sighted children were practically screaming at Gina, "Look at us—we can see and we've got all of our developmental milestones checked off right on schedule!"

My sweating armpits reminded me uncomfortably of my lifelong fear of anything that might even possibly escalate into an emotional issue. I wanted this visit with Gina to be over so I wouldn't have to go through the intense discomfort I knew I would have to face if she started to cry. I was good at interacting with parents at happy times, and even good at problem-solving challenging situations, but tears were still something that froze me in my emotional tracks. My only way of coping was to leave, and if I couldn't do that physically I had to put up an invisible wall between myself and the feelings I had lacked the skills to embrace.

My instincts about Gina were right. Her infant's blindness was still, on a deep and unexplored emotional level, a tremendous sadness for her. Gina's real worry, her overwhelming concern that she had never dared voice, came bursting to the surface within half an hour of our introduction. "Do you think he'll ever get any Valentines?" she blurted out through a torrent of tears.

There was nowhere I could go. Picking up my own children and loading them into the car to flee was out of the question. Sitting there like a lump while this lovely woman wept seemed inhuman. Gina solved my problem by instinctively moving closer to me to reach for Jerico, who was still cuddled in my arms. The two of us sat side-by-side, silent, both stroking the baby—waiting out the storm.

I had no idea on that day that the new parent I was supposed to be helping would offer me far more than I was able to offer her. I saw for the first time in my life the effect of sharing tears instead of running from them. Gina did the work for me that day, but I have been able to do it for others, and myself, since then. Gina helped me remember how to cry.

Years later I think back to Gina's heart-wrenching question, and see it on another level. I know that what she asked me is the simplest, most direct measure of my effectiveness as a teacher. If the answer to "Will my child ever get any Valentines?" isn't "Of course he will," I am doing something terribly wrong. All the braille and white cane skills in the world cannot begin to compensate for the unnecessary tragedy of social isolation, which occurs in epidemic proportions in the blind population. I learned at a conference that the majority of otherwise healthy blind teenagers spend over fourteen hours a day in bed. That is because it is always so hard for them to get out and do things with other kids, and they become depressed. Sighted buddies run too fast, throw balls that the blind kids can't see, go to movies and play video games. Summers and weekends are worst, without the structured hours of school, when everybody else is at camp in the mountains or skateboarding across town or signed up for Little League. Blind kids spend a lot of time sitting at home, frequently alone or interacting with their parents.

It takes a strong commitment and hours of extra work to make everyday fun activities accessible for a blind child, or to design alternate activities that are appealing to their sighted friends. It can be done—and it needs to be done—over and over and over again. Every activity, with every new group of friends, needs to be adapted to fit the current situation, and kids are rarely able to do that by themselves. It requires an adult to be there and care and take the initiative to do the right thing at the right time—an adult who knows when to intervene and when to become scarce. An adult who will start working with sighted peers from the first day of school and teach them how to be a friend to a blind child. Teaching academic skills is tremendously important, but it is only part of the whole complicated picture of helping a blind child grow into a life that is happy, full of options, and socially fulfilling.

Jerico's family moved out of Mendocino County shortly after I started working with him, so I missed the opportunity to do all the things I would have liked to plan with him and his little friends. I know that Jerico experienced some hard times as he grew to adulthood, but that he was rarely, if ever, among the depressed number who sat at home. His blindness was not a tragedy for himself or anyone else, and it did not hold him back from accomplishing everything he wanted to do. As he went through four years of being on the honor role in high school, he played in a garage band, went to a wonderful summer camp for children with visual impairments, traveled to Europe, excelled in martial arts and made friends all over the state. He graduated from college with a major in documentary film-making and now has a full-time job as a sales representative for a winery. And, to his mother's delight, Jerico has always gotten his fair share of Valentines.

Jewel must be in second or third grade by now. I haven't seen her since she was three years old, just beginning to strut her stuff with the tiny white cane I had just given her. Another talker, Jewel knew exactly what she wanted, and she wasn't inclined to grant anybody one iota of slack when they didn't meet her needs fast enough. She was just beginning to exhilarate in the power of a good tantrum, and I was trying assiduously to teach her the alternate and more desirable behavior of "Use your words." On the previous lesson she had thrown her cane on the ground in a fit of frustration at my correcting her technique. The last day we worked together, I tried again to correct her on something I thought she could do better, and she stopped in her tracks. This time, instead of throwing her cane and howling, she took on an imperious expression, paused for maximum effect, and declared in measured tones, "Laura, I would rather do it independently!"

Jewel is the only child I ever turned loose with a white cane after just a single session of showing her parents how it is supposed to be used. I usually see too much I don't like in the child's beginning technique, or I doubt the family's ability to support the lessons, and I prefer not to have to un-teach bad habits that get learned by accident away from my supervision. But I just couldn't imagine Jewel's parents doing anything "wrong" with her, as they had always accepted their daughter's blindness so completely and compensated with such innate intuition. Jewel's parents were also delighted with the independence their tiny daughter enjoyed with her cane the first time she picked it up, projecting delight instead of fear as she toddled down the driveway away from them. My only regret was that this wonderful family moved too far away, too soon for me to watch Jewel grow.

Then there was Nicole, who also came and went altogether too fast. A tiny little imp of a newborn with a pointed chin and a Kewpie doll curl on top of her head, she looked like she would be at home among the butterflies and flowers in the garden, in a delicate cradle spun of spider silk. I met Nicole sleeping in the arms of her great grandfather, with her grandmother and teenaged mother, Marie, anxiously focused on questions about her future. They wanted to know everything in the first hour of my first home visit with them. Could Nicole have a career? How would she manage reading and writing in school? What does braille look like?

What are all of the organizations nationwide that offer support to families of visually impaired children? How does a blind person get a guide dog?

For the first year of Nicole's life, I focused most of my energy on her very supportive extended family's needs and questions. I tried to help them comprehend as well as possible what Nicole's completely visionless world was like, and made dozens of suggestions for ways they could interact with her that would be fun for them and productive for Nicole. I had little direct time with Nicole, though, as she was usually sleeping, eating or fussing when I visited, no matter how her mother and I tried to juggle my schedule to dovetail with Nicole's "good" times of the day. That goes with the territory of home visits with an infant—no matter what brilliant activity I had promised Marie we'd do together, it all came to a grinding halt if Nicole's little baby body was needing something else at that moment.

As Nicole progressed into her second year, despite everybody's best efforts to interact with her, she did what many blind babies do—she turned inward instead of outward for stimulation and entertainment. She twiddled her own hands and feet, rubbed the rug repetitiously with her fingers, and repeated quiet little sounds to herself. Though she could be highly responsive to her mother and other known adults when they initiated a familiar interactive routine, she preferred to lie undisturbed for hours. Her needs for bottles, dry diapers and cuddling were met at her first whimper, and that was all she wanted. She reacted to most other kinds of stimulation as unwanted intrusions, and would frequently respond to intervention by howling and arching her back in a frenzy until she was put back down in a quiet place by herself.

The more Nicole got used to being left to her own resources on the floor, the more she resisted being taken to new places or introduced to new activities. That's the classic blind baby "Catch 22." They can start reacting negatively to interaction and stimulation, mostly because they get scared or overloaded with too many things coming at them that they can't see approaching, and because they have no way to predict what the outcome of any interaction will be. Unlike a sighted child who can tell what is about to happen to them from across the room and prepare themselves for the kind of interaction they are about to experience, blind children can't predict what part of their body will be touched, if they will be touched by something hard or soft, if they will be picked up, or if something will be pushed into their mouth. Even the gentlest interactions can become aversive, and result in fussing or crying. Faced with a baby who obviously dislikes being held, played with and talked to, parents naturally end up doing less and less with them, resulting in greater fear and resistance on the part of the baby the next time a new activity is introduced. After a while the family members, no matter how loving or caring they are, get frustrated and end up leaving the child alone. This pattern was beginning to develop with Nicole, and it worried me.

In Nicole's case there wasn't too much I could do with her directly in the first two years of my home visits, given her negative reactions to unfamiliar stimulation and her young mother's anxiety about her baby's crankiness. All of us who have offspring want to see them shine in public, and we glow when our child will show off something she has just learned. Nowhere is our fear of scrutiny and judgment exacerbated more than when some special education teacher is walking into our home, telling us what to do with our child, and getting treated to a display of rotten behavior in the bargain. Marie was always polite and gracious to me, but I know it was hard on her to accept my constant intervention and witnessing of her daughter's difficult behavior.

I tried to downplay everything that wasn't working and concentrate on slowly building trust not only with Nicole, but with her mother. I knew I'd never get Nicole out of the apartment for a real mobility lesson if Marie couldn't enjoy the sight of her little daughter having a good time at home in my company. I got down on the floor next to Nicole, telling her that I was coming near her. I tried talking in a low voice and making a small amount of noise with a rattle within easy reach of her hands. I waited silently until she moved a tiny bit, and then repeated my action as quietly and non-intrusively as I could. When Nicole indicated her interest by becoming totally still so she could hear every sound I made, I picked up the toy, rattled it quietly again, and touched her fingers very gently with it. Then I waited, without moving or talking, to see what Nicole would do. The goal was to let this be Nicole's game—not mine. I had to allow her to call the shots on every move, and respond only to what she did, without adding new and confusing elements, so the control would remain in her hands. When Nicole finally responded by patting the rattle with her fingers so she could hear the beads shake inside it, I reacted by doing the same thing and whispering "shake, shake." That was as far as I got that day, and I was sure Marie was wondering why I bothered to come if that's all I was going to do with her child.

It was incredibly difficult for me to avoid the pitfall of overdoing it with Nicole. I tried to savor my small successes, though my nervous "teacher" tendency was always to try to get Nicole to do just a little bit more or perform just a little bit better—in order to make myself look better. The important thing, I had to keep reminding myself, was to demonstrate to Marie that little steps were good steps, and that my expectations for Nicole were being met. On days when I tried once too often to help Nicole get up on her hands and knees to crawl or to manipulate an object in a certain way, she would have a meltdown and I would lose the ground I had gained with both her and her mother. On days when I left Nicole giggling and cooing I knew Marie would be happier to see me show up next time.

Nobody ever knows when the really hard stuff is going to explode in their face. For Marie, it was at Nicole's second birthday, when her daughter had piles of lovely presents purchased and wrapped elaborately for her by her mother, grandparents, aunts, and family friends. Marie started describing the large party before I even had a chance to sit down after showing up for a home visit the following day. Marie talked fast and breathlessly, without looking at me. "Nicole was the center of attention," she started, "all dressed up like a fairy princess. This is the dress she wore—my mother bought it for her—don't you love the pink rosebuds?" Marie showed me an exquisite little pink baby dress that I'm sure cost more than dresses I buy for myself to wear to parties and which probably would never be worn again. She continued, "I set Nicole down in the middle of her gifts, with everybody gathered around watching, and everything was going fine. Then I reached for Nicole's hands to show her how to tear the wrapping off the first box. Nicole came unglued the instant she heard the paper ripping, and she just started howling." I could see tears welling in Marie's eyes, but she rushed on with her sad story. "I picked Nicole up and tried everything to calm her, but the harder I tried the more she screamed. Even her blanket didn't work—she was inconsolable." By now tears were streaming down Marie's face. "All I could do was put her down in a back bedroom for the whole rest of her party, and she never came out until it was time to go home. We had to have her party without her—even her cake."

Marie continued telling me how the projected evening of fun and celebration had turned into a heartbreaking, not to mention embarrassing, expose of everything Nicole couldn't do. The other children present had all acted perfectly, according to Marie. Nicole was the only one who hadn't been able to handle the excitement. I could tell that Nicole's meltdown was interpreted by her mother as her own failure at parenting, because Marie kept comparing Nicole to her little peers and asking me why I thought Nicole couldn't act more like them. "What else should I be doing?" she asked me over and over. We had a long talk about the peculiar reactions of blind children to new and different experiences. I tried to point out how much time it can take to help a blind baby learn to like an auditory or tactile experience that they are not used to. Marie was determined, telling me that she wanted all the help she could get to try to bring Nicole out of her shell. She asked me as I packed up to leave, "Could you try to teach Nicole to like wrapping paper before Christmas gets here so she can enjoy opening her presents then?"

By the time Nicole was two and a half, we had the groundwork laid for a truly satisfying program. She would be in a toddler class three mornings a week, with me serving her there, at her home and in the community. Nicole was beginning to enjoy some little walks around town with me to explore surfaces, textures and sounds, with her mother's wrapping paper goal foremost in my mind. I snuggled Nicole in the security of a slightly too small, forward-facing frontpack buckled to my chest, and kept my arms hugged around her as I walked. At Marie's suggestion, we hauled one of Nicole's favorite blankets with us for added security. Nicole slowly learned to let me take her hands and guide them to touch whatever we were passing—walls, windows, trees, fences, and eventually things on the grocery store shelves. The triumph was the day Nicole reached out to touch a crunchy cellophane-wrapped bag of dried fruit that I was scrunching near her. She reached for it over and over as we walked around the store, crinkling it with her hands with no encouragement from me. The next day I bought her a roll of wrapping paper to experiment with at preschool.

Christmas vacation came and went and I didn't see Nicole for several weeks. When I showed up at her house early in the new year, Marie opened the door before I knocked and greeted me, uncharacteristically bubbling with excitement. "Nicole is reformed," she announced.

"What do you mean?" I asked. "She's what?" I wondered what was going on in Marie's occasionally volatile mind.

"You'll see," she told me in a voice filled with confidence. "Just come in and watch what she's doing."

Marie was right. Things that had sent Nicole into a panic just weeks before suddenly interested her. She reached out to me the minute I let her know I was in the room and happily interacted with me while I moved her arms up and down to a nursery rhyme, something she had never let me do in the past. She was beginning to say some words in a soft little voice—another major milestone. Marie told me her little daughter was staying awake longer and suddenly liking to go places. I asked Marie if she had any idea how all of this wonderful progress had come about, and she responded that she was clueless. The two of us decided that we'd just take what we were getting and run with it.

Now that Nicole was suddenly willing to work with me, I couldn't wait to expose her to the entire process of honest-to-goodness orientation and mobility lessons—learning the names and functions of objects, buying things, differentiating stores, and walking routes. The lawyers, sheriffs and store clerks around the downtown courthouse had already gotten used to the sight of us exploring and doing errands, and they were totally in love with Nicole. I was all ready with my planned crusade—to teach the abundance of fascinated adults in our community how to enjoy Nicole and help her when necessary, without smothering her in the process.

Well-meaning adults seem to have a hard-wired tendency to over-help children with obvious disabilities. Especially cute blind children. Without thinking, they seem to say to themselves, "Oh, what a precious little blind child!" as they literally run to open a door, bestow a kiss, or hand out a piece of free candy—all things they would never dream of doing to any other child they didn't know. I love peoples' desire to interact with my students, but I abhor the boxing of a blind child into the outdated stereotype of helplessness and dependence, or the tendency to single them out simply because they are blind. In a small town, the overwhelming adult attention can completely sidetrack a normal experience if the child is accosted by people on every block who want a "feel-good" moment for themselves. It's the same kind of attention that is innocently lavished on twins, and even though the intent is caring, it gets tiresome when overdone.

I wanted Nicole to learn to delight in her ability to do things independently as she grew older, while at the same time learning to interact appropriately with the people in her town to get help when necessary. As with other students, it would be a long haul of meeting people one at a time. Nicole and I would work together to slowly let folks know how to approach the novel situation of dealing with a blind child in their store or watching her wait on the street corner for a safe time to cross. Nicole would have to learn to speak up for herself and explain to people what kind of help she needed. She would have to learn to remove herself from invasions of her personal space. She would have to learn to thank people for their assistance. Just like anybody else. I glowed, laying plans for my time with Nicole and looking forward to years of fulfilling adventures with her.

I was preparing to do some planning with Marie about goals for Nicole's next year with me, when everything stopped. Marie gave me two week's notice that she and Nicole were moving to southern California for Marie to begin a new marriage. I was hopeful and excited for Marie, but devastated about losing Nicole. My official good-bye didn't even happen—my last planned lesson with Nicole was missed over a confusion regarding when I was supposed to show up. By the time I called to rearrange my visit, the phone had been disconnected. Nicole was gone.

I always assume I'll have my students forever, especially the "perfect" little ones like Jerico and Jewel and Nicole. I make long-term plans for them like I made with my own children, and I enjoy fantasies of my participation and glowing pride in their progress. It seems logical, to me at least, that I'll be there for their high school graduations and first jobs and apartment-warmings, and maybe even marriages. I don't get used to the reality that they can leave before I have had enough time with them.

WHY?

Forrest was the most perfect child—utterly blameless and innocent with his cloud of flaxen hair and baby-soft ivory skin blushing to rose petals on his cheeks. So pure he was almost transparent. A fallen angel, dashed to the ground by a terrible vagary of fate.

Born healthy and full of promise, Forrest contracted meningitis at the age of three weeks. The raging fever destroyed most of his brain. Then gangrene set in, necessitating the partial amputation of most of his fingers. He lived for six and a half difficult years, blind and unable to move or talk, waiting patiently to die.

I worked—or tried to work—with Forrest for three long years of his life. Even my college practicum on working with multi-handicapped children hadn't taught me anything about what to do for a child like this, so I experimented with every idea that came into my head. Forrest occasionally showed some response to light, so I attempted to create light shows for him in a darkened room. I propped Forrest up in his wheelchair or on pillows on the floor and flashed colored lights on and off in front of him. I moved flashlights from side to side for him to try to track with what vision he had, and I illuminated colorful and interesting toys with the flashlight beams. Over and over again, I tried variations on those themes, aware that I wasn't getting anywhere. Once in a while Forrest seemed to show a glimmer of reaction with a momentary focused gaze or a wan smile at my efforts, but there was never any consistency in his response. I felt myself growing desperate for validation that there was some reason to continue. My normally productive well of ideas was utterly and painfully dry, and I didn't know what to do.

Every time I came to work with Forrest my mind turned involuntarily to the fortunate and disability-free lives of my own three children. When I first heard about Forrest and what the meningitis had done to him, I was terrified that I could somehow carry germs from him home to my family. I had to make a special appointment with the pediatrician to hear directly from him, in person, that my fear was ungrounded. Only then did I dare to touch Forrest and breathe the same air.

I have no idea why some people live blessed, healthy lives and some people don't, but I wonder about it frequently. There is certainly no cause-and-effect relationship between how good the parents are and how their kids turn out. The most wonderful parents occasionally have the most tragic things happen to their children, and the most incompetent and neglectful adults sometimes manage to bear and raise highly functional offspring. I wish good people could be rewarded with immunity to tragedy, but nothing about life is ever as easy as I would like it to be.

Knowing children like Forrest made me inclined, in the beginning, to be hyper-vigilant of my own children. The practical side of me prevailed, however, before any of them got very old. For starters, I knew that nothing I could do could prevent all illnesses or accidents. My three caught all of the bugs and maladies that made their unpleasant way through their grade school classes, and they all survived, probably with immunities they needed to fight off worse diseases. Occasional accidents happened in spite of my efforts to ensure that everybody was taught the basic concepts of safety. Fortunately, none of the falls and scrapes were too severe, and everybody lived through them with nothing worse than a few scars.

It always makes me uncomfortable to realize that the difference between a normal illness or accident and a life-threatening disability causing emergency is impossible to quantify or control. Why did Forrest end up having all the bad luck? Why have my own children managed to avoid catastrophic events so far? Will my kids continue to have good luck as they move into their fully adult lives? What about the children none of them has borne yet? I fervently hope for the best, and I work consciously with myself to calm my nagging fear for all of the people I love. This job makes me far too aware of all the things that can go wrong.

I don't think I made much of a difference in Forrest's life. I have made my peace with that reality. When I heard the news that he had died in the night, I was grateful to imagine him free at last from his ruined little body. I had a vision of him dancing through the sky with angels, gleefully flapping and swinging his arms and legs that hadn't worked when he was alive. For me, Forrest's tragedy was his life, not his death.

WHO AM I TO JUDGE?

Jed was not at all interested in mobility lessons the first time I met him. He hadn't finished going blind, and didn't see any sense in working hard to learn a skill that he didn't want to need. He would rather shoot baskets with his cousins, even though he could no longer see the hoop. He would even prefer staying home in his room if that would keep me and my blind services away from the sighted life that he was doggedly hanging onto. Seventh grade boys are like that, and this was clearly not a time for me to push. I left him alone.

A year later, in the middle of eighth grade, Jed went totally and painlessly blind. He woke up one morning with his retinas completely detached, destroyed overnight by the hemorrhaging blood vessels in his eyes. Juvenile diabetes can do that, along with a lot of other awful things. Jed had already had a colostomy as a result of the poor blood supply to his intestines, and his physical strength was severely compromised. What he had to look forward to was many years of getting worse and trying, for as long as possible, to maintain the fine line of marginal good health between the extremes of insulin shock and diabetic coma. Jed had the additional disability of being moderately hearing impaired as a result of too many childhood ear infections, unrelated to his diabetes. He wore hearing aids in both ears.

Total blindness, once it came, didn't seem to have much of an effect on Jed. He kept attending school and applied himself with a matter-of-fact concentration to learning braille. No sense of urgency, no emotional outpourings, and no demonstrations of frustration at the difficult chore of having to learn to read all over again with his fingertips instead of his eyes. He got pretty good at deciphering those mysterious rows of colorless little dots, and was soon reading his thick braille volumes of history and literature with a slow and determined independence. Jed accepted the assistance of an aide at school to help him manage the material that wasn't available in braille, and continued to receive the same kind of mediocre grades he had been earning as a sighted student. He hadn't been participating in physical education for years, on account of his colostomy and lack of strength, so losing sports wasn't the kind of crisis it would have been for a more athletic student.

The members of Jed's large and extended family accepted him blind and included him in everything they did, just like they always had when his vision was intact. Nobody seemed all that worried about him, and he consequently didn't worry much about himself. Life just went on with a few adaptations. I was inclined to grieve for Jed and his loss of sight, but realized how silly I would have appeared making more of a fuss than he or his family did—so I simmered down and tried to match their emotional level.

Sighted or blind, Jed was always big on puns, the most sophomoric of which he repeated ad nauseam. Jed never minded being the brunt of his own humor, and he made up countless blind jokes to dovetail with his new sightless situation. The one I heard most frequently was, "What were blinded German soldiers called during World War II?" Allowing only seconds for his listener to fail to come up with an answer, Jed would break into an exuberant grin and shout in his booming voice, "Not sees!" followed by gales of mirth. Jed's standard greeting to me at the beginning of a lesson was, "Let's go raise cane," and his favorite and oft-repeated farewell was "Keep in touch."

Jed was fascinated with trucks and loved to draw them before he lost his vision. He would spend hours at it. He seamlessly transferred that skill from a pencil to his braille writer, and continued spending endless solitary hours pounding out detailed raised-dot images of every imaginable kind of truck. He embossed a row of dots, checked them painstakingly with his fingers, and went on to the next row, planning where every detail would be as he progressed from the top of his thick manila paper to the bottom. Dot by dot he fashioned tactile images of the cab, windshield, fenders, bumpers and trailer of each individual truck. He even figured out how to make the wheels and hubs round—an exacting task since Braille dots have to be made on a rectangular grid. To a sighted person these braille trucks all resembled somewhat bland white-on-white cross-stitching—not much to look at from across the room. However, when viewed up close, this intricate art form possessed an exquisite beauty. Every adult who worked with Jed was presented with at least four truck "drawings" a week.

Once it was an indisputable fact that he needed mobility lessons, Jed accepted them gracefully. He actually liked our lessons, and practiced hard on our daily outings to downtown Ukiah during what would otherwise have been his PE period at the high school. Getting off campus in the middle of the school day was a big draw—to Jed it felt like cutting class. Using his newly learned skills to go buy treats at the stores he remembered from his childhood but could no longer patronize independently added to the attraction.

Jed never complained about working outside in the extremes of inland Mendocino county weather—neither rain nor cold bothered him in any way that I ever observed. He kept dogging along one horribly hot day, paying attention and doing his best, taking one step after another on pavement that was melting in the sun. I, on the other hand, was gasping and mopping sweat out of my eyes with the hem of my shirt, about to pass out. I caught a glimpse of the thermometer on the bank down the block—117 degrees! Heat is the only weather phenomenon that really causes me to wish we had a huge, roofed-over, climate-controlled shopping mall somewhere in this county. I can always put on more clothes or zip up my Polarfleece a little higher to ward off the biting cold during the winter, but there is no cure for having to work outside during a summer heat wave. I told Jed we were done for the day. He was surprised, completely clueless about my discomfort that was rapidly escalating to desperation in the blistering sun. We headed to the car for a sweltering drive home. Jed plodded in and I beat a hasty retreat.

Mentally and emotionally Jed wanted to get out and do things like everybody else, but he lacked the physical capacity to realize his desires. I struggled to set up challenges that would be difficult enough to give Jed a sense of pride that he had accomplished something by the end of each lesson, yet not so physically taxing as to discourage him. The line between the two was always a fine one, since Jed was deteriorating medically. His balance, coordination and stamina varied from day to day, and even from hour to hour. All three depended on his blood sugar level, which was related in turn to the amount of exercise he had or had not been getting throughout the day. Jed's condition was also directly affected by what he had or had not eaten during the past day, week and month.

While I was able to do the mechanics of assessing Jed's abilities in the moment and adapting lessons to suit his energy and ability level on any given day, I never got used to watching what I considered to be serious mismanagement of his diabetes. Jed lived on what I dismissed as "junk" food. He had grown up on it, he was used to it, and he liked it. Even though his mother learned to cook nutritious, diabetic-friendly meals for him, he kept on eating the junk he preferred. I knew that lots of people everywhere in the country consume a diet of highly processed meals loaded with fat, sugar, preservatives and empty calories, and that bothered me intellectually in my organic gardening, back-to-the-land mindset. But that junk-eating populace consisted of other people—strangers to me. I didn't have to come face-to-face with the quality of their lives.

With Jed, the lousy eating habits of our fast food culture hit me on a far more personal level. I was involved with him on a daily basis, and I truly cared about his well-being. I made it my job to see that he got plenty of tips on what the brochures I'd read touted as a healthy, balanced, low-sugar diet. I believed in those brochures and always helped Jed look for diabetic-friendly snacks and meals that he could manage himself, even on days when nobody at home was available to help him shop and cook. Jed and I worked together to dream up nutritious menus that included enough of the foods he liked to be appealing to him, and I wrote up the ideas in braille for him to keep at home. We planned ahead of time how he would handle the inevitable situations when his cousins invited him to go out drinking, to little or no avail. Jed was fully aware of the risks. Even on insulin, diabetics have to be extremely careful to eat and exercise well, and avoid alcohol. Jed knew that as well as I did. He didn't care about the consequences as much as I did, though. Jed couldn't see his future clearly enough to want to change the lifelong habits that I was sure were pounding nails into his premature coffin.

In hindsight, I wish I had not questioned how much Jed and his family cared about his well-being. I realize now that he was probably more loved by more people than any other student I have ever had on my caseload. Jed lived surrounded by dozens of relatives who would drop whatever they were doing to come and help him with anything he needed at any hour of the day or night. They neither complained nor looked for praise for their services—they just showed up even if it meant getting in the car for a long drive at an inconvenient hour. What they did for Jed was simply different than what I would have done for my own offspring if one of them had been in Jed's medical predicament. Thinking about it now, I recognize that my philosophical leaning in the field of education is decidedly towards the school of thought that supports achievement of the maximum amount of independence. I passionately promote the teaching and maintenance of self-help skills. I also am an advocate of working closely with both the mainstream and alternative medical systems to attempt to assertively manage a disease, with the goal of holding off the development or worsening of symptoms for as long as possible. Jed's family naturally gravitated more towards the provision of custodial care as his symptoms worsened, doing things for him as daily routines became more difficult for him to manage alone. They chose to accept Jed's disease and its outcome, instead of altering their lifestyle to try to change its course. They did everything for him that they could, and they held him close until the end.

Throughout my years with Jed I struggled to decide which way was better. Now I wonder if "better" is even a concept that can be pondered under these circumstances. Who grants me permission to try to do it my way with somebody else's child, or to try to convince a family that their approach to their own child's care isn't right? Thinking back to Jed, I wonder if there are times when I should forget about my college degree and all of the things I have learned from books and celebrate, instead, the fact that this young man was loved during his life exactly for who he was. His family did what was best for them, in their situation, at that particular time, and they did it wholeheartedly. Could anything be more right than that?

I enjoyed Jed and all of his exasperating habits. My goofy student loved to plague me with tricks and jokes. His favorite prank, once he became good enough at cane travel to be sent alone into stores, was to hide from me. The first time this happened I had instructed Jed to go into a neighborhood grocery store to buy himself a package of salted nuts. I checked with him to assure myself that he knew to walk out and meet me on the sidewalk when he was done. I dropped him off as planned, parked the car, and came back to wait for him in front of the store. Too many minutes ticked by while I waited with increasing nervousness at the appointed rendezvous spot, and there was no sign of the little urchin. After shifting my weight from one foot to the other for as long as I could stand my mounting anxiety, I slunk into the store to look for him, hoping that nothing awful had happened—sure that nothing awful had happened, but not absolutely certain. I searched up one aisle and down the next, and there he was, his body pressed into an empty area between two shelves. He knew he could not be seen from one end of the aisle or the other, but he completely forgot that I had a full view of him as I walked past his not-so-good hiding place. When I busted him he doubled over in his characteristic and unrestrained belly laugh.

Jed got me again and again—I would invariably see his black head or his cane tip poking out from where he thought he was crouching out of sight behind the greeting cards or the baking ingredients in some store. When I confronted him he would break into an ecstatic ear-to-ear grin, knowing that he had caused me to come near panic at the thought of losing him. A few times Jed even managed to sneak completely out of the store before I found him. He would duck around the corner or into a doorway and flatten himself against the wall, forgotten cane sticking out like a beacon, and wait. Then would come that laugh of his when I discovered him. Weary as I was of this exceedingly worn-out joke, I always had to laugh too. I've never seen anybody enjoy a game as thoroughly as Jed could, nor have I ever met anybody who could enjoy the same game as often.

Every once in a while I got my chance to laugh back at Jed. One day he was crossing a downtown street at a fairly busy four-way intersection, while I was keeping a vigilant eye on him from across the street. I did that frequently, rather than following him like a shadow, so people would have to interact directly with Jed and whatever he was doing instead of looking to me to take charge of the situation. Jed was about half way across the street and doing just fine, when a lady screeched her car to a stop right in the middle of the intersection, threw open the door and leapt out. She ran, breathless with hair flying behind her, over to Jed and threw her arms around him. "Okay, now what?" I thought to myself. "This is really worth watching." I had never seen this lady before, and wasn't sure Jed had. There the strange lady stood with him, stroking his arms and shoulders in the middle of the street, yakking right in his face and beginning to tie up traffic. Just as my amusement was beginning to change to alarm, the lady abruptly left Jed right where she had accosted him and bolted back to her car. She slammed her door shut and disappeared in a cloud of exhaust. I crossed the street to rescue my bewildered student who, it turned out, hadn't been able to make head or tail of what had just happened to him.

Safely on the sidewalk, Jed and I decided that he must have been either blessed or healed by this crazy lady—or maybe both. I was partly amused, but aware at the same time of a growing sense of violation. I had enjoyed my visceral satisfaction in witnessing this prankster of mine having the tables turned on him so unexpectedly, but what had just happened was too close to an assault. There are always people who feel, just because a person is blind and can't see them coming, that they have license to ignore the personal space that people in our culture feel entitled to maintain. Being blind somehow robs a person of some of that essential ownership of one's own body that causes the rest of us to respect each other. That woman who accosted Jed never would have marched up and put her hands on a sighted person without so much as an introduction, because a sighted person would have met her eye-to-eye to witness her inappropriate actions. Whatever the woman's motives, she made assumptions she had no right to make, and I wished I had been quick enough to figure out what was happening and hurry over to confront her before she flew back to her car.

Jed was patient, but rarely philosophical about his disabilities. He surprised me, though, with his introspection one pleasant morning when we were taking a break. The two of us were resting on a sunny bench in front of the courthouse, watching the world go by. Or rather, I was watching the world go by and describing the action to Jed as he drank the diet soda he had just purchased at the little grocery store around the corner. He always liked those moments here and there when he got a chance to be an observer of others, having lost that ability with the loss of his sight.

"There's a young woman standing across the street from us, trying to cross the street," I told him.

"How come she's having trouble?" Jed asked me. "Is she blind?"

"No, she looks like she has Down Syndrome. She can see fine, but she is mentally retarded, and she's probably worried about having to make so many decisions in such a busy place."

"What's she doing?"

"Well ..." I said, "she's trying to cross now, but she just stopped because a car is coming, and she went back to the curb. Now she's trying again, but there she goes back to the curb. I'm not sure she's going to be able to figure out when to cross. Oh good, there she goes following some other pedestrians. She made it safely across the street."

A fairly detailed discussion ensued between Jed and myself about the difficulties and challenges that young woman must have had to face in every aspect of her daily life.

"What do you think it would be like to be retarded?" Jed asked.

"The hardest part, I think, would be to find the courage to get up and go out independently into a world that moves too fast to understand. If you're retarded it takes a long time to figure out what's happening. Nothing would ever feel safe."

Jed grew silent. After a minute he said slowly, "You know, I'm blind, and I don't hear so good, and I have a colostomy, but I'm sure glad I'm not mentally retarded."

I put Jed through more challenges than most high school students were ever meant to face, but finally found a way for him to even the score with me and re-establish a fair balance. Jed loved the fun of it, and so did I. Every semester when it was time for finals, Jed was stuck with me for the entire two-hour PE period. It seemed pointless to try to design, administer and grade some irrelevant mobility exam, since I already knew exactly how well Jed was doing, and nobody else in the school system really cared about the specifics. I decided instead that the final exam challenge would be for Jed to design a lesson for *me* to accomplish with a blindfold and my old white cane from my training days at San Francisco State.

I became the blind student for the duration of the final exam period, and Jed got to be the instructor. With the assistance of a sighted guide pressed into service for the occasion, he followed me down the street, as I usually followed him on lessons. The guide described to Jed every mistake and blunder I made in my rusty attempt to walk straight along the sidewalk. Jed was ruthless—he planned a route that sent me through the trickiest and busiest intersections, and over three parallel sets of railroad tracks where the pavement was uneven and there was no edge to follow. Jed's special grand finale was requiring me go into a restaurant where he specified that I order a blind person's most dreaded meal—salad. Jed and his sighted guide, of course, accompanied me in for lunch, and my delighted student got a blow-by-blow accounting of every faux pas I made. My student relished hearing about each garbanzo bean that I dropped on the floor, every drop of salad dressing that ended up smeared on my clothing, and all of the vain attempts I made to spear a bite of lettuce only to come up with an empty fork. Jed spent the whole next semester looking forward to repeating this performance when finals week rolled around again.

Jed graduated from high school into a more limited world than I wanted for him. He had already moved with his mother and some siblings from a neighborhood within walking distance of downtown to the Pomo reservation about ten miles out of town. The tribe gave him a new house of his own. He lived there alone, with meals carried to him by his mother, who also provided daily health monitoring. With his increasingly poor physical stamina Jed could not make the mile-long walk down the winding hill to the public bus stop, and other means of transportation to the local junior college were unreliable. He started college a few times and dropped out as often. Thanks to being Native American, there was always a job for him on the land at the Pomo tribe's thriving casino, but it meant that he hardly ever left the reservation.

The last time I saw Jed he was in the hospital, where he lay with his legs partially paralyzed as a result of being in a diabetic coma too long. He and I both knew he wouldn't do much walking any more. The end was coming and he was giving up. As patient and accepting as ever, with his prankster spirit intact in spite of his irreversible deterioration, Jed hollered after me as I left him, "Keep in touch!"

A CLOSE LOOK AT DYING

In the first week of spring I set out at dawn on a cold, rainy morning to drive to Point Arena to take Michelle on a mobility lesson. There was snow in the March rain—enough to make me know it was going to be an exciting trip over the coastal mountains. Since I'd missed seeing this totally blind student of mine the week before on account of the county car breaking down midway to the coast, I decided to see how far I could get, instead of doing the sensible thing and staying in town for a comfortable day of work in the office.

I left the Ukiah valley behind me and headed into the first range of low mountains to the west. The minute the road rose from the valley floor to begin its coastward climb, I was surrounded by the unexpected magic of a snowy Christmas card winter, completely out of season now. White-blanketed hills squatted silently on both sides of the empty road. Trees, which only yesterday had shown the promising green of swelling spring buds, slept again in frozen silence. I slowed to a crawl, wondering if I'd have to cancel Michelle for the second week in a row.

Twenty wintry minutes later, rounding a tight turn on the coastal side of the summit, I was catapulted back into March. Just a couple of feet lower in elevation than I had been a moment ago, I watched the cold black and white world of the winter mountain give way to a heady Anderson Valley spring. Rolling fields of energetic new green sprawled downward to meet the valley floor, highlighted by rays of sunlight bursting through the breaking storm clouds. In every field I passed, yellow daffodils showed off in busy profusion, escaping under fence lines like unruly school children refusing to come in from recess. Bushes of early blooming quince blazed red and wild in gardens and farmyards. New lambs, clean and white in the first week of their lives, nursed frantically, butting their mothers' udders in a frenzy of flopping ears and waggling tails. Steam spiraled upward from the backs of the soaked ewes.

Spring again became a tantalizing memory as I left the valley behind and wended through the redwoods along the rain-swollen Navarro River. Branches whipped above me in the winds of another rapidly developing storm, and by the time I drove the last mile from the river canyon up to the coastal bluffs, I was once again enveloped in the throes of winter.

Rain poured down and up and horizontally in sheets that came close to defeating the windshield wipers. I slowed again, hoping this wouldn't be my day to drive off the road. A hundred feet straight down, huge wind-driven waves collided with the edge of the continent. Tons of ocean water slammed against the beachless coastline, claiming a little more of it with each barrage and madly flinging up spray to douse the road and everything on it as if the deluge pouring from the sky weren't enough.

I continued towards my destination, hoping that enough of the road would remain for me to manage the drive home at the end of my day. Point Arena, twenty miles down the coast, turned out to be peacefully awaiting the beginning of an ordinary morning with no snow, no wind, and a moderate amount of thin sunshine working its way through a break in the clouds. I parked the car and went to find Michelle.

Michelle and her squirrely third grade classmates had been forced to stay indoors for a full week on account of the storms, and I wanted to get her outside while we had the chance, since I was still charged form the magical energy of my drive to the coast.

This break in the weather was all the invitation I needed to abruptly cancel our braille lesson. "Come on," I said to my surprised student, shoving her raincoat into her hand, "We're going out."

"I can't go out in the rain," Michelle protested. "My mom says I'm not supposed to get wet."

"Don't worry. Neither one of us is sweet enough to melt if we get some water on us. This isn't Oz; we aren't like the wicked witch that Dorothy killed."

Ignoring Michelle's continuing complaints, I grabbed her hand and hustled her from the classroom out to the street. Michelle had lost most of her vision; she didn't know much about what happens in the rain to the world that the rest of us can observe, and I was determined to take advantage of this opportunity to teach her something new through a firsthand experience.

We breathed deeply of the cool, moist air to clear our lungs of the stifling heat of the classroom we had just escaped. Sensible people were still holed up indoors busy with rainy day projects, so there wasn't a soul to be seen. In the absence of the usual human activity and noise, the sprites and spirits of another domain emerged quietly from their hiding places to be felt, if not seen, by Michelle and me as we came out to play in this familiar, yet strangely altered landscape. I knew that today I would not be the teacher. Some other source of energy was in charge, and I was only along to offer the most minimal guidance to my student.

"What happened to all the birds?" Michelle asked before we had walked half a block. "It's usually noisy outside." I knew something felt different, but wasn't as quick to put my finger on the absence of the usual clattering of blackbirds high up on the power lines and the raucous cawing of our crow friends in the treetops. Even the seagulls had been driven to shelter somewhere. Without the familiar background racket of the ever-present birds doing their daily bird chores, there was a thick sense of waiting in the air, every molecule poised for something to happen. Something new and special that the rain fairies would arrange just for Michelle and me in honor of our presence in their watery landscape.

What we heard in the silence was the earth drinking. From every direction, high and low, drops of rainwater trickled and dripped from trees, roofs, fence posts and daffodils, moving inevitably downward to the drenched ground in a lighthearted symphony of millions of tiny instruments. No two droplets of water colliding on the surface of a leaf did so silently. No thin rivulet cascading down the rough-barked trunk of a tree merged with the earth without a tinkle of clear bells or a tiny drum roll. No swallow of water was accepted by the earth without a song.

Michelle and I contributed to the symphony as we walked along. We squished. We splashed. We lobbed pebbles of various sizes into puddles, causing a different sounding plunk with every stone we tossed. We created entire songs by gathering fistfuls of stones and tossing them into the water one by one. We conducted a whole symphony, for a moment at least, by walking up to a drenched tree with a low-hanging branch that could be grabbed and tugged. A light tug caused a few dozen drops of water to fall to the ground in an airy staccato, while a harder jerk resulted in a percussive crescendo, soaking us both in the process.

In a beautiful neighborhood of fine old houses and glorious gardens that Michelle couldn't see, we stopped to examine a cluster of wet Calla lilies sticking out from under a neat picket fence by the sidewalk. "Here, Michelle," I directed her, "put your hand on this flower. Reach inside it." In the throat of the sodden bloom she discovered a tiny pool of water.

She poked around a bit with a large smile on her face.

"Yikes!" she yelped suddenly, jerking her finger out of the miniature fairy pond she had discovered "There's something moving in there. It's slimy. What is it?" A tiny green frog had hopped out onto her hand, much to its own and our astonishment. In an instant the frog jumped wetly across Michelle's open palm, plopped down onto the lawn below and disappeared. Michelle, for once in her life, was speechless. She stood motionless, with the fingers of one hand resting lightly on the palm of the other, remembering the touch of the little frog's damp feet on her skin.

We both knew it was time to return to the world of ordinary events. We walked back slowly with Michelle's arm looped through mine for guidance. She chattered on, giddily re-living her brief interaction with her frog, while I pondered the impact of this astonishing hour. Sharing this wet and wondrous morning with Michelle brought back the enchanted child world that I had forgotten when my own offspring outgrew it one by one. Michelle's gift was showing me the path back to that magical land.

Today, twelve years later, I'm forgetting how it felt to play with Michelle. It was easy once, so long ago. Now, while I struggle to plan lessons for her, I search for memories to keep alive as I lose the girl I can no longer reach. Michelle was one of the best readers in her first grade class when school started on a September day fifteen years ago. Her first complaints midway through the year that she couldn't see the board were met with disbelief on the part of her teacher, since Michelle had recently been reported by a local optometrist to have perfect vision in both eyes. Her escalating behavior problems at school were attributed to disruptions at home. Michelle, however, remained adamant that she couldn't see, and I was asked by the somewhat bemused school nurse to do a functional visual assessment on her.

I met a pretty and energetic girl, tall for her age and extremely talkative. She was loud, impulsive and easily frustrated, though she was quick to laugh at the silly things I said to break the ice. I liked that, and I like bratty kids in general, so Michelle and I hit it off immediately. I had to use every trick I knew to keep Michelle on task and happy during my evaluation of her vision, and luckily she responded eagerly to the thinly disguised "games" I pulled out of my box for her. She could read black, inch-high letters at a distance of one foot, but no farther. She chose the wrong color almost every time I asked her to pick a specific crayon to fill in a petal of the large flower I had outlined in black for her. She could not stack blocks one-handed without over- or under-reaching the stack. She needed to use the other hand to determine exactly where in space her pile was located. I knew I was looking at a child who was trying her darndest to please me, and it was apparent to me that behavior had nothing at all to do with her dismal visual performance.

My findings prompted another visit to the optometrist, who found, only seven months after his previous examination of Michelle, that her visual acuity was within the scope of legal blindness. There was, however, no evidence of any ocular defects or disease. Michelle's eyes were perfect in all respects.

Michelle was given an uncertain diagnosis of Hysteria Conversion Syndrome, a bizarre yet real condition where the inability to see is attributed to an emotional trauma resulting from a child witnessing some horrible event that they simply do not have the resources to deal with. No such trauma was ever suspected or documented in Michelle's case, but lacking any better explanation and faced with increasing behavior problems on Michelle's part, school officials recommended that she be placed in a self-contained classroom for severely emotionally disturbed children. She stayed there for two years. I began teaching her braille since even the largest print and the fanciest enlarging machines were, by now, completely useless to her. While the doctors and psychologists continued to ponder Michelle's diagnosis, I drove to Point Arena three days a week to work with her and watch her go totally blind.

College did not prepare me for Michelle. I had a carefully constructed illusion that my caseload would be full of cute little kids, some blind and some with useable vision, all of whom would be waiting for a creative and well-trained teacher like me to come along and make them better. I had learned all kinds of magic tricks to help visually impaired students read, write, tie their shoes, prepare meals, get to the store and even put on make-up. I was also well aware that some children had multiple handicaps and would never be able to learn very much very fast, and that was okay. I wasn't afraid of those kids, and knew that I just had to assess them as accurately as possible and begin teaching them on a level that would meet their needs. But everybody I had run into up until now was already as bad off as they were going to get, and no matter how unhappy or tragic that was, I could usually do something to help them make at least some progress. Not so with Michelle. No sooner did she learn a new way to cope with her present state of vision loss than she deteriorated some more and needed a completely different approach. All of our movement was in the wrong direction. Little pieces of me died with every skill that Michelle lost.

Michelle, astonishingly, never seemed to worry very much about losing ground. She barely appeared to notice when something she had once been able to do became impossible. She would launch her headstrong self eagerly into whatever new compensatory skill I presented to help her cope with increasingly difficult schoolwork. She liked games, she liked rewards, and she liked adult attention. Every lesson was fun for her in the moment, and it was hard for me not to laugh with her as she continued to discover the world with her wide-open child senses.

Not only did I like working with Michelle, but I found driving to the coast two or three times a week to be a pleasant experience, especially in the summer months. The hotter it gets inland, the more likely there is to be a layer of cool, damp fog hugging the very edge of our continent. I can tell if the fog is in when I crest the top of Seven Mile Hill out of Willits. It shows thirty miles away as a formless gray stripe on the horizon, and I happily imagine the coolness that awaits me. The air stays shimmery hot as I travel west, until I emerge from the redwood forest a quarter of a mile from the ocean. Then, before I am even treated to a view of the surf, the county car is suddenly and completely enveloped in nebulous silver. I roll up the windows, turn off the air conditioning, and glance into the back seat to make sure I remembered to bring my Polarfleece.

I learned the hard way about the necessity of throwing a jacket in the car in the middle of July. I tend to forget that I even own a jacket after a week of inland days over 100 degrees, but on the coast it can easily be forty or fifty degrees cooler. Besides freezing in my shorts and tank top while I take my students out on their lessons, I find it embarrassing to look like a tourist. The locals laugh at the swarms of unprepared out-of-towners who disembark from their motor homes and SUVs, expecting hot southern California beach weather. Sporting sunburns they got somewhere else, these unfortunates scurry around to the souvenir shops, restaurants and beaches—trying to enjoy this place they drove so far to see, while hugging their arms together for warmth and sprouting gooseflesh on their naked legs. The cute little shops in the coastal towns do a brisk business in locally designed sweatshirts. I followed Michelle on our lessons, warm in my comfortable jacket, pretending to be one of the coastal natives.

Nowhere did I enjoy Michelle more than on mobility lessons. By third grade she had started running into things both in the classroom and out of doors, so I introduced her to a child-sized white cane and taught her how to use it. I improvised ridiculous songs to help her keep her footsteps in rhythm with her cane's arc, and she learned the technique quickly. With her cane Michelle marched noisily down the sidewalk ahead of me, giddily avoiding imagined dangers that lurked everywhere. She found her way safely around unfriendly poles, stopped neatly without stumbling off the curbs with their invisible toe-grabbing hands, and avoided falling into the drains where the trolls lived. The car dragons and truck ogres were outwitted by Michelle's keen attention to her hearing. She never let them sneak up on her. A special triumph for Michelle was learning to use her white cane to locate every doorway on a downtown block, stick her head in and determine by listening and smelling what kind of business was located inside. She memorized the names and order of all the downtown streets, and soon could lead me triumphantly to the ice cream parlor from any intersection within eight blocks of this favorite destination of ours.

While Michelle and I explored her new world of sound and touch and smell, she continued to undergo medical evaluations to determine the cause of her blindness, which by now was clearly real as opposed to hysterical. A visit to a local neurologist resulted in the recommendation that she go to UC Medical Center in San Francisco for extensive testing to determine exactly what was happening to her eyes and to rule out a number of serious degenerative diseases which have blindness among their symptoms. Noisy, impatient Michelle was going to have to lie awake and still for hours, with electrodes pasted all over her head and chest to measure her brain activity in response to a complex barrage of light flashes in her eyes. Lack of cooperation on Michelle's part would compromise the validity of the tests, as would sedation. I impulsively volunteered to go to the hospital with Michelle and her mother, Cindy, and do everything I could to help my student behave well enough for the doctors to get accurate results. I also knew on some gut level that this trip was going to be a terrible ordeal for us all.

The doctors who examined Michelle were grateful for my presence. Michelle was accustomed to enjoying her time with me and cooperating more or less with the program I set up for her, so I had much better luck than her mother in prevailing on her to lie calmly on her back and submit to having the cold electrodes pasted on for the first test. I leaned over Michelle's railed bed in the darkened room for two hours, held her hands, and talked to her quietly about what was going on, and about anything else I thought she might be remotely interested in, real or imaginary. I had never seen Michelle helpless and afraid before. I had to fight a mother's desire to grab her tense body and tear her away from the alien electrodes. I wanted her to be free and in control of her body again, but I knew she had to finish what she had come to the hospital for.

The dreaded blood test was worse. Michelle had already been pushed far beyond her limits, and was close to hysteria before the nurse even came in with the needle. The maximum dose of sedation was not working, and Michelle couldn't be put out completely because she had to be awake for the next test. I worried about whether I was doing the right thing, decided that somebody else could decide that, and without asking kicked off my shoes and crawled onto Michelle's bed with her. I held her in my arms, talked non-stop, and helped her role play the whole event with a well-loved stuffed teddy bear that Cindy had had the foresight to bring. My efforts eventually paid off well enough so the blood was drawn without a fight from a girl who lay still, if not calmly.

I came back to the hospital the next day with Cindy and her husband to hear the diagnosis. Juvenile Ceroid Lipofuscinosis, we were told. The doctors spelled it for us and explained that it was an extremely rare, inherited metabolic storage disease, where by-products of an incomplete metabolism get stored in the skin, the brain and the retinas. Dry skin and loud, blurting speech patterns are early symptoms. So is blindness. Later comes progressive mental deterioration, increasing behavior disorders and uncontrollable grand mal seizures, followed by contractures of the large muscles and loss of ability to walk or talk.

The neurologist finished speaking, picked up Michelle's file and headed for the door. I bid a hasty good-bye to Michelle and her family and chased the doctor out into the hall as he was leaving. There was one more question I had not dared to voice in the hospital room. I asked the neurologist if the disease was fatal. I had to know.

The doctor clearly didn't want to answer my question. I held my ground, blocking his path, and asked it again. This time he looked straight at me and said bluntly, "The answer is yes." He continued to explain, "People who have this condition in childhood usually die by their early 20's. They slowly lose all of their functions and end up contracted into a ball with no vision, no speech and no cognitive awareness. The seizures become constant. All the doctors can do is watch. There is no cure, and once the seizure medications become ineffective, there is no treatment." The neurologist dodged around me, turned back, and added two more words, "I'm sorry." Then he disappeared down the corridor.

I couldn't find the courage to return to Michelle's room. I had forced this last critical detail of my student's diagnosis from the doctor before Cindy had been told that her daughter was going to die, and the mother in me knew that wasn't the natural order of things. I had no right to know the terrible truth first. The neurologist had told me he would go back to have another talk with Michelle's family to "clarify" the situation, and I couldn't imagine myself intruding any more than I already had into the upheaval of their lives. Knowing that Cindy had her husband sitting by her for support, I took a deep breath in an attempt to check my own tears and walked away.

I was astonished to find Michelle back at school the day after her diagnosis. It took a while for me to realize that there was really no reason for her to stay home. She wasn't sick, and nothing at all had really changed for her during those two days at the hospital. I just knew something I hadn't known at the beginning of the week, and I worried about how I could face Michelle. I would have to look at this eight-year-old child knowing that her life had already gotten as good as it was going to get. Any changes in her life from now on would be for the worse instead of for the better, and none of my skills and no amount of my love could alter the brutal process for a second. Fate didn't care that Michelle had been robbed of her future. Days were going to keep following each other with the same number of minutes and hours, and the same number of mundane tasks would continue to make demands on me. I still had to get up in the morning and take a shower and go to work and cook meals for my own children, even though Michelle was dying. It seemed so unfair—so lacking in drama. Cindy hadn't even called her daughter's teacher or sent a note to school, so nobody there had any idea what was going on. I wanted Michelle's fate to somehow change our little Point Arena world, at least for a couple of days. I needed proof that her life had some real significance, and I wasn't finding it.

Nothing at all changed in my daily dealings with Michelle and her mother. Michelle had not been told either that she was getting worse or that she would die, and even though I saw Cindy every time I delivered Michelle home after a mobility lesson, neither of us ever brought up that awful trip to the hospital. We talked about Michelle's need for a longer cane, decided whether or not Michelle could participate in a beach picnic I was planning, and warily discussed Michelle's behavior issues. The proverbial elephant loomed large between us, but neither Cindy nor I ever took the initiative to breach the gap and start the conversation that, for me at least, felt so necessary.

What Michelle got in honor of her fatal diagnosis was a trip to Disneyland with her family, sponsored by the Make-A-Wish Foundation. She was thrilled, and prattled on about it for weeks afterwards. From her clueless and totally in-the-moment child's point of view, she was having the time of her life. The fact that the price was her impending early death never sank in to her naïve consciousness. That load was for the adults to carry—we are the ones who know how to mourn our losses long before we experience them.

I signed up for a weekend workshop in San Francisco, given by Stephen Levine, on Death and Dying. I knew I needed some help coming to terms with this tragedy that I was experiencing. The room where the workshop was held was packed with adults, some apparently healthy like myself, but many bald from chemotherapy or emaciated with AIDS. People too wasted to sit up in chairs were lying on cots in the front row, close to the speaker. I realized that this weekend was going to be far more intense than I had anticipated.

Midway through the first morning Steven asked the workshop participants if they would like to share their own near-death experiences. Quite a number of people in the audience, it turned out, had been saved from death at some time in their lives, and all recounted their own version of what was essentially the same story—a peaceful unification with a source of white light, free from the pain experienced in their earthbound bodies and minds. Many had been extremely reluctant or disappointed to be rescued and brought back to life, because the near-death experience was so compelling. The members of the audience who were on their way to a certain premature death found that they had developed a heightened awareness of the exquisite beauty of life. Each painted a verbal picture of themselves celebrating the days they had left as a series of precious moments that were happening in the immediate present—the way a child, especially a child like Michelle, experiences life. The past and the future were unimportant. All saw their death as a force which, when embraced without panic or fear, added to the quality of their vibrant living experience.

It had been years since I thought about my own close call with death at the age of nineteen, the result of an accidental and stupid overdose of recreational drugs that prevented my lungs from absorbing enough oxygen for me to stay conscious. Those repressed memories all came flooding back during Stephen Levine's workshop. What struck me most was my recollection of the clarity that enveloped me then, during my semi-conscious hours alone in the hospital room after the doctors had said there was nothing they could do for me. I remembered experiencing myself as a white shape hovering on the ceiling above my still body in the hospital bed. I knew then that the choice to live or die was mine, and through an enormous mental effort I willed myself down off the ceiling and re-entered my body. It was totally clear to me, as I thought about it during the workshop, that fear of death was not a factor in that decision of mine to live. Rather, it was the suddenly compelling conviction that I had more of this life to look forward to, and that I didn't want to be cheated out of a second of it. I was reminded that each moment holds its own special magic, if I can just notice it, and that the magic exists regardless of what is happening or not happening to my mind and body. I thought back to Michelle again and realized that, being a child, she still knew that.

Another surprise in Stephen Levine's workshop was his honesty about death. I had been taught that death is too brutal and awful to mention directly, especially in the presence of a terminally ill person or their loved ones. I had learned to avoid the truth of death and to likewise avoid dying people if at all possible. Stephen presented a different approach. When the topic of the workshop evolved to the actual experience of dying, he turned towards a shadow of a man lying on a cot in the front row and said, "Well David, you're about as close to death as anybody in this room. Would you like to tell us about your experience?" David was silent for a minute or two, and then quietly proceeded to open his heart to the hushed group of a hundred people he had never seen before, sharing his hopes and fears, his dislike of his uncontrollable trembling and his great desire to have a "good" death. He was free of pretense. There was no denial in his hesitating speech. Any awkwardness was the result of his attempt to speak his truth more precisely, rather than to hide it.

I was stunned, not in horror of David's astonishing frankness, but by the beauty of his honesty. He said the un-sayable, and it was poetry. He accepted his reality, and brought the hushed people in the room together into his heart. He helped me more by openly embracing his fear and uncertainty about his impending death than he ever could have by skirting around it behind a brave front of avoidance. I knew that I would never again deny what was happening to Michelle or try to change the subject if her mother needed to talk. David, yesterday a stranger, taught me in that beautiful half hour that the way to honor Michelle's death was to be there for it, with all my heart.

These last twelve years have not been easy with Michelle. She spent the third grade fully and somewhat inappropriately included in a regular education class, with the help of an open-minded classroom teacher and a wonderful aide, Casey. Casey was able to learn braille practically overnight and she was always willing to use her bountiful art skills to adapt materials on the spot, ensuring that Michelle had instant access to the curriculum. Still, much of what went by was completely beyond Michelle's ability to grasp, and that frustration combined with her already legendary behavior problems contributed to a stunningly difficult year for all concerned.

Our main reason for including Michelle in the third grade, our idea that she would benefit from social contact with her non-handicapped peers, backfired rather significantly. Kids quickly grew tired of Michelle's short temper and totally self-centered four-year-old attitude, and either ignored her or taunted her. Michelle preferred the taunting to no interaction at all, and spent many recess periods out behind the baseball backstop on the playground, listening for children sneaking up on her and then lashing out at them with her cane. The baseball diamond was eventually declared off-limits, the cane was taken away at recesses, group counseling with peers was initiated, and nothing changed. Michelle's only friend was the classroom guinea pig, Squeaky, whom she cuddled and mauled with desperate intensity at every opportunity.

The fourth and fifth grades were spent in a self-contained class for students with learning handicaps. Here Michelle experienced less academic frustration and found peers who were willing to play hours of adapted games with her, like braille "Uno" and a version of "Connect Four" with large holes drilled in the centers of all the red checkers so she could tell them apart from the black ones by touching them. We also adapted the rules for the games as we went along, since it was less chaotic doing that than putting up with Michelle's arguing and whining when the games got too difficult or fast-paced for her. Friends wore out fast, however, despite our conscientious interventions. Michelle turned more and more inward and began losing the clear distinction between fantasy and reality. When she turned to imaginary friends she could control the speed and content of the interactions between them and herself, and they never ran off leaving her standing alone. She played the same fantasy games over and over again, loudly and insistently. She invented different voices for all her characters and incorporated advertising jingles she had heard on TV into their conversations, all sung in her startlingly lusty contralto voice.

Michelle's best and favorite fantasy was a "Queen of the Castle" scenario that she immersed herself in every time I took her to the playground at a small park in town. Approaching adolescence and tall to begin with, she dwarfed the younger children playing on the climbing structure and commanded their complete attention. The minute we arrived at the park, Michelle would tear her shoes off and make a blind dash for the suspension bridge at the near end of the structure. I had shown her one time how to climb up onto it, over the horizontal boards that formed the roof of what she immediately named the "dungeon," and under the metal bar that functioned as a railing on the high platform that supported one end of the bridge. Once Michelle knew where to put her hands and feet, she wouldn't tolerate any help, though a misstep could easily have sent her headfirst onto the wood chips six feet below. I reluctantly learned to let her go once she had her bearings, because this was the only place in the world where she could move freely, even for a little while. She tore around the structure, from level to level, over the clanking bridge and down the fireman's pole, back up a ladder, under another bar and down the slide. She always remembered to duck under a low platform when she came around from the bottom of the slide to search for the dungeon, and then she was on her perilous way back up to the bridge to do it all over again.

I watched from my seat on the wooden bench around the play area as Michelle commanded the entire climbing structure from the bridge. She quieted to listen for any children playing on some part of it, and the minute she heard evidence of an audience she imperiously proclaimed in a voice that carried to the next block, "I'm the Queen of this castle! I'm really, really wicked and everybody here is my servant!" Awestruck four-year-olds stopped what they were doing, silenced by this brazen declaration of power. Michelle's loud fantasy began to unfold in a delicious cackle reminiscent of the evil characters in her favorite Disney cartoons, "I have magical powers and I am going to catch all of you in my web. Nobody is going to get away!" The little ones crept closer, sucked in by this adult-sized child who spoke their language. Witches and princesses and black widow spiders were assigned roles and positions on the play structure, and amid much shrieking and laughing, chases were staged and captives held.

A special education administrator witnessed this playground scene while evaluating my teaching skills one day. He questioned me about my motives for letting Michelle engage in this activity that was clearly way beyond the bounds of normal. He told me that he had first been shocked and embarrassed for Michelle to see her so obviously out of place with children half her age. I started to defend my reasons for bringing Michelle to the playground and allowing her to carry on without trying to control anything but her safety, but my administrator interrupted me. "I get it now," he said, "Michelle is truly having fun, and who are any of us to judge whether or not it's appropriate? Why should children like Michelle quit having the right to enjoy themselves because some educator determines that what they like to do isn't socially acceptable any more?"

That question was thrown in my face soon afterwards when Michelle was allowed to participate in the school choir as part of her "mainstream" integration program. Michelle had an astonishing voice—a deep, rich contralto with a tremolo that wouldn't quit, and she walked around much of the day singing bits and pieces of TV advertising jingles and Disney movie theme songs. All of the adults on her case, including me, jumped at the chance to get her in the choir, where she would have the chance to sing with a group of peers and learn some technique from the highly talented music director. Wrong! What we ended up with was a girl who rebelled at every attempt to teach her the words to songs she didn't already know, and who physically fought off any person who dared to put a hand on her to keep her from falling off the risers. We moved her to the floor next to the risers, and still she neither could nor would stand still and pay attention to any of the teaching. What was enjoyable to Michelle on her own terms became an atrocity when she had to submit to the rules and structure of others, and she rebelled in her characteristic way: loudly and actively. Nobody found a way to make the choir work for Michelle, and she had to be pulled from the class because every session turned into a battle. She probably would have liked to spin freely around the room at will, listening and chiming in off-key whenever she felt like it, but that would have been too disruptive to the teacher and the other students, and the possibility was never explored. Thus ended Michelle's short music career.

Middle school came before we were ready. Michelle spent the summer growing physically and deteriorating mentally. By the beginning of school in September she outweighed me by at least thirty pounds and I had to look up to meet the vacant stare of her blind green eyes. Her menstrual cycle started. Adolescent hormones surging through her system compounded her combative behavior, while a sharp progression in her medical condition further lessened her impulse control. Michelle was placed in a class for severely handicapped students, farther removed from the mainstream than before and more protected from the demands of the "regular" world. Here she would participate in an individualized academic program, have plenty of time to practice social skills with "reverse mainstream" peers who came regularly into the classroom to interact with the handicapped students, and she could integrate into electives as appropriate.

Our first middle school fiasco came while trying to teach Michelle to negotiate the hallways with her white cane. At the elementary school the students generally stayed in their classrooms except for lunch and recesses, and then they were all moving the same direction, either to or from, monitored by large, vigilant teachers to ensure that there was more walking than running. Not so at the middle school. I had forgotten what a melee several hundred allegedly normal human beings can create when they are all released into the hallways at the sound of the bell after sitting in an enforced state of semi-inactivity for the length of a class period. They stop paying attention to all input from the teacher exactly five minutes before the bell sounds, focusing every aspect of their awareness on their imminent escape. Poised for flight like cornered animals, they are all on their feet simultaneously the instant the bell begins to ring, and they charge towards the door as a single brainless unit. Experienced teachers have already opened the door by this time to prevent its being torn off its hinges, and they know to stand outside, safe in the eddy created by the force of this sea of hyperactive humanity spewing through the narrow opening.

This was not a good setting for Michelle to be practicing her white cane technique. I had hoped that this new school with its long stretches of interior hallways would prove conducive to her getting around semi-independently, but it was a disaster for her from the first day. It probably would have worked if Michelle had had enough self-control to avoid reacting to the craziness around her and concentrate instead on where she was going. However, every bump, every shout and every minor confrontation elicited a magnified response from her. She rudely yelled back at people shouting around her, even if their noisy interactions had nothing at all to do with her, and she reacted to the frenzied level of activity by swinging her cane around wildly in what looked like real attempts to hit people. The staffing situation was such that no aides were available to monitor Michelle getting around in the hallways before or after the bell, since they were all occupied with other students' academic needs in various classrooms, and there was no way that Michelle could go anywhere alone. Therefore, sighted guide became the mobility technique of necessity, and the white cane was officially discontinued at school.

The white cane was also abandoned at home around this time. It was obvious to me and to Michelle's mother that she could no longer pay consistent enough attention to the information she was getting from the cane for it to be of any real use to her. In fact, we agreed that the cane was probably making Michelle less safe. When she was holding it, we expected her to notice obstacles and drop-offs in front of her, and we would allow her more independence than she would have if she were using a sighted guide. She would do fine for a minute or two and then suddenly slam into a pole that she should have detected with the cane, or just as unexpectedly walk off a curb that her cane should have informed her was there. Michelle was getting hurt far too often, and the small bit of independence she gained by using her cane didn't seem like a very good trade-off for the increasing risk to her safety.

Taking Michelle's cane back probably hurt me more than it did her. She accepted my explanation that it was too hard for her to pay attention all of the time, and that I wanted her to be safer with a sighted guide. That was true, but what I really wanted was for Michelle to be the child I had worked with three years ago, who loved her cane and who took so much pride in her nutty little independent forays and adventures. I knew she had already lost that part of herself, but for me taking her cane was like killing a part of her. I accept now that my sorrow was for my own spirit—unless I really watched myself I depended too much on the hope that I was contributing to a learning and growing personality, which would reflect my competence and wonderfulness as a teacher. I was too attached to nurturing my garden and wanting to watch it grow the way I tried to train it, without honoring the true nature of what I was trying to nurture.

Some of Michelle's happiest times in middle school were in art and woodshop classes. Both tolerated her noise and encouraged her far-from-conformist approach to assignments. What she couldn't do, she and her crazily artistic aide Casey happily ignored, and what she could do, they both relished. When the rest of the students were painting cartoons, Michelle created free-form outlines with an embossing tool on special (and fabulously expensive) aluminum foil "paper." On other days she scrubbed paint into the raised outlines Casey created for her with special "Stikki Wikkis" that I ordered out of my catalogues for the blind. Michelle always remembered what color she had used where, and took great pride in explaining every detail of her energetic creations to anybody who would listen. She and Casey got into "Fimo" bead making for an extended period of time while the rest of the class was working on drawings in perspective, and everybody Michelle knew was blessed with at least one interesting necklace. That was followed by a happy period of weaving squares out of garish shades of hideously bright pink, green and orange loops of polyester material, no use for which was ever discovered.

Passing rapidly on to another medium, Casey and I worked together to help Michelle create "found object" collages. I took Michelle to search for materials during mobility lesson time, wandering off with her in any direction she chose, stopping every few feet to pick up seedpods, dried leaves and flowers, rocks and snail shells. Sometimes we went to the beach and collected tumbled pebbles or bits of broken crockery and glass polished to smoothness by the tides. Michelle always insisted on choosing things and picking them up herself; it wasn't any fun if I did that part. Then she hauled her treasures back to school and emptied out her pockets for Casey to sort and describe again before getting to work on assembling them in a collage. We learned early that things worked best if the glue stayed in Casey's control and the selection of what to put where stayed in Michelle's control. This was Casey's lesson in letting go.

When it was time for Michelle's art class to rotate on to Woodshop, we bit our nails a bit and decided to give it a try. Casey handled the stress with uncharacteristic calm and saw Michelle through an initial footstool-making project with the rest of the class. The two of them used every machine in the shop, mostly with Michelle standing behind Casey and feeling where Casey moved her hands as she sawed and sanded. Surviving that with a wobbly stool to take home and all of their fingers intact, Michelle and Casey moved on to a much safer dollhouse construction which lasted for months and involved a huge amount of hand-sanding and gluing, but very little sawing. While other students turned things on the lathe and drilled holes and pounded nails all around the room, Michelle sat safely at her workbench applying paint, wallpaper and rug samples to her creation, enjoying loudly verbalized fantasies about the doll family that would soon inhabit it. We stretched the finishing touches out to the end of the semester, and were vastly relieved when the class ended. Casey and I agreed that one semester of woodshop was entirely enough for us, never mind how Michelle felt about it.

Eighth grade ended and Michelle made the big move to high school. She stayed there for seven years, in a self-contained class for students with severe handicaps that was about as mellow as they come. Every student had a truly individualized program, and neither the teacher nor the aides seemed particularly overwhelmed by Michelle, her unusual needs, or her increasingly outrageous behavior. Casey, bless her heart, lasted fourteen years as a paraprofessional in our program for visually impaired students, and continued to stick it out with Michelle, though she was functioning more as a baby sitter than an aide. I saw less and less of Michelle, since she had lost her ability to use braille for more than a pointless game of pretending to read her now-shredded books out loud, and she vehemently resisted my efforts to teach her routes around the classroom. All she wanted to do was sit in a small room by herself and play what I characterized as the videos inside her head. She sang and babbled to herself with words I could no longer understand, and fought frantically when anybody tried to intercede. There was nothing left for me to teach Michelle. I dropped direct services and wished sadly that I could come up with more creative suggestions during my consultation time with Casey and Michelle's teacher, but I was totally out of ideas.

More years have passed and Michelle's life continues to get worse, which is not easy for those of us who remember the bright little eight year old who learned her braille so eagerly. Our challenge is to support each other as we watch Michelle decline, and to try to remember what we are learning as this difficult journey progresses. We never know while we are working with Michelle that this will be the last time she will ever do a particular task or use a certain skill, but then a day comes when somebody notices the absence of something that Michelle could do a while ago. She is slipping away, not quietly, but bit by tiny bit, and we mourn these little losses when we can't ignore them any more. And then we go on, because the only alternative is not to go on.

Michelle is out of high school now, in an adult day care program. I haven't talked with her mother in ages. While in my office cleaning out old files to clear space for records of new students, I ran across a self portrait that Michelle had drawn for me the first time we met, when she was seven years old. She was just beginning to lose her vision then. The drawing is all done in red and green crayon. Under green clouds and a blazing red sun, a red and centered stick figure version of Michelle dances exuberantly on her toes across a hilltop, with an ear-to-ear smile and her arms stretched heavenward. I have matted and framed the drawing and will take it to Michelle's mother on my next trip to Point Arena. It needs to be hers.

THE REALITY OF DRIVING IN THIS COUNTY

I have learned to trust. All that separates me in my little Japanese car from the oncoming logging trucks on Highway 20 is a couple of parallel lines of thick yellow paint in the middle of the road. If something big lumbers around one of the countless blind turns taking its half of the road out of the middle, all the leeway I have is three or four inches of pavement on the other side of the fog line, and then a long drop. I don't even like to think about it.

The risk is real—cars and trucks are constantly getting towed up out of the canyon bottoms as a result of one drunken, inattentive or unlucky moment on the part of the driver. I always keep something good to read in the trunk, in the event that I end up with an unwanted ringside seat at a rescue that closes the road for hours. Sometimes I just turn around and go back to the office with a case of the jitters that precludes productivity for the rest of the day. The thought is always there—it could have been me.

In spite of my queasiness at the thought of accidents, there are the rare few that have some entertainment value. I still smile, remembering a hot summer day years ago when a refrigerator truck full of fish lost its load taking a turn too fast coming down the Ridgewood Grade. The shining bodies of hundreds of dead fish spewed across the pavement, creating a sudden and unexpected "Slip-N-Slide" for whatever vehicle came next. The first unlucky victim turned out to be a loaded lumber truck, which didn't have a chance to stop before it started skidding on the fish. The out of control truck jack-knifed and turned over, its load of bundled two-by-fours crashing to the pavement and bursting apart across all four lanes of traffic. Into this tangle of pick-up-sticks and mashed fish plowed the next half dozen vehicles that couldn't react fast enough to avoid the mess. Nobody was hurt, but the smell lasted through the next rainy season.

My own closest scrape was almost getting eaten by a Toscana bread truck. I had been impatiently following some guy in a large rusty car for about seven miles, and we finally got to a paved turnout, where he could easily have pulled over to let me pass and get me off his tail forever. For some reason, just as I was about to accelerate and pass him, the driver decided to stomp on his brakes in the middle of the road, instead of pull-ing off like any normal person would have. I reacted luckily and instantly and slammed on my brakes, missing him by inches. I suddenly felt, more than saw, a tremendous square truck-front looming in my rear view mir-ror as I sat helplessly in the traffic lane. Highway 20 is so packed with tight turns that you can follow close behind somebody for miles without ever seeing them, and I'm sure this truck driver was as surprised to see us parked in the road in front of him as we were to see him about to kill us. He did the only thing he possibly could in the remaining second to avoid crashing into me—he swerved across that double yellow line and came screeching to a halt abreast of me, on the wrong side of the road, halfway around a completely blind turn. The old codger in the offending car finally moved out of the way, allowing the rest of us to sort ourselves out seconds before we got mixed up with a wave of oncoming traffic. I stayed hyper-vigilant for weeks.

Large trucks used to be my personal enemies. I'd be happily zooming along in my sleek little Honda, accelerating into every turn on the perfect racecar line that I learned from my brother as a teenager, and counting the curves I could take without using my brakes. Then, inevitably and to my intense dismay, I'd notice the mud flaps of something huge with too many wheels—a chip truck or a massive beer truck or a propane tank-er—disappearing around the bend in front of me. By the time I arrived at the next tight curve I would be right on the truck's tail, close enough to be annoyed at the polished chrome silhouette of a naked woman swing-ing back and forth at me on each mud flap—and working up a case of elevated blood pressure in a modern-age frenzy of impatience about hav-ing to slow down behind the oversized thing. It always seemed so unjust that I should have to creep along behind those smelly, gear-grinding be-hemoths, and it wasn't fair that I should have to wait until the truck driver was good and ready to finally get around to pulling over, if he was ever going to. I dreaded the possibility that this guy might turn out to be one of the jerks of the world, who would block me from my speedy progress for the entire remainder of my trip to the coast.

It was in this kind of situation that I was unhappily fuming one morning on the way to Fort Bragg, when a realization struck me that was so obvious it almost hurt me. These big trucks have a right to be on the road too, and the drivers are really doing the best they can, given all the hills and turns. I'm sure they don't have anything personal against me, and some of the trucks are really kind of pretty if you think about it. Look at all the work the driver does on his time off to install those extra rows of running lights and keep that vast expanse of chrome all polished up. And think how many times a day they have to deal with impatient people like me stacking up behind them. I tentatively backed off to give the truck some space and allow myself to mellow out a bit. The driver politely signaled and moved over at the next wide place in the road. So did the next truck I came upon. They all did.

Big trucks can be a downright godsend on a winding road. Especially when there is a gawking tourist in a battleship-sized Lincoln poking along in front of me at twenty-five miles per hour, ignoring all the pullouts despite some gentle reminders from my horn. I've learned that I just have to plan things right. The best, time-tested approach is to back off and follow the tourist at a respectful distance until a large truck, hopefully an empty logging truck with its trailers piggy-backed so it can take the turns faster, shows up behind me. I let it pass me at the first opportunity to pull over, and then zip out to follow close behind as it bears down upon the offending tourist. I grin as I hear the truck's jake brake making deafening, suggestive and threatening noises behind the slow car, knowing what is about to happen. If the tourist values the rear bumper on his Lincoln, he is off the road in seconds whether or not there is a turnout, and the logging truck and I go sailing by.

Some days don't work out so well. The absolute worst was the result of a do-good notion I had to offer to drive a little girl to the eye doctor in Ukiah. Her family didn't have a car, so they had no way to transport their daughter from their remote town of Dos Rios for the appointment. I elected myself to do the honors, thinking with some degree of logic that my services as chauffeur could make a difference in this situation where the child had a suspected visual handicap.

Simply getting to Dos Rios on an ordinary day is a project. It's not just off the beaten track—it's thirty some-odd miles of winding river canyon road, parts of which are constantly sliding into the river, to the east of a long and lonely stretch of Highway 101. It takes over an hour just to drive from Ukiah to the Dos Rios turnoff, and then you're not quite halfway there. Once in Dos Rios you still haven't exactly arrived at any kind of memorable destination. The town is a dot in the middle of a perfectly round, incredibly beautiful, almost deserted valley. There is little traffic in town because it is not on the way to anywhere—the road going in is the sole road, and the only other place to go on it is back out.

It was raining heavily the day I had to pick up Nonny and her mother, Cola. It had been raining almost every day for two months, and the flooding rivers and supersaturated soil were wreaking havoc with the county's road system. There had been enough road closures during the preceding week that I phoned the California Highway Patrol's emergency road conditions number before setting out, hoping that something between Ukiah and Dos Rios would be washed out and give me a good reason to abandon this trip. No such luck—all the roads were still open. I loaded a child car seat into the aging county car, congratulating myself on my togetherness for having remembered it, and set off into the deluge.

I headed north at about half my usual speed, with the windshield wipers ineffectively churning back and forth at fast flap. Water immediately began dripping onto my left shoulder through some invisible, but worsening, leak in the door gasket—adding annoyance to my escalating trepidation. Trucks, the big ones that usually come roaring down the grade like stampeding elephants, crept towards me in the slow lane, engines winding high in their lowest gears and water sheeting out from under their multiple wheels like the wake of an ocean liner. The slide that had already taken out two lanes of the highway halfway to Willits had claimed another lane during the night, causing a lengthy delay as foul-weather-geared road crews and sodden highway patrolmen worked amid half a mile of flares and flashing lights to get traffic slowed down even more and safely re-routed. I passed the mess and kept driving north.

The bridge over the river at the Dos Rios turnoff was still high enough above the surging brown floodwater to be open, sabotaging my last possible excuse to abandon this mission. I clutched the steering wheel a little tighter, sat up straighter in a futile attempt to see the road better, and inched my way around the first blind turn on the steep mountainside, hoping not to encounter anything big coming on my side of the road. Nothing approached me, not on that turn or any of the others. It seemed that everybody in Dos Rios had enough sense just to stay there for the day. The only excitement was a section of road in a big cut right by the river where mud and rocks were oozing across my lane.

Finally arriving at the last turn where there was usually a heart-stopping view over the Dos Rios valley, I discovered why there had been no opposing traffic on the road. All I could see before me were huge flakes of falling snow. The white stuff was beginning to stick on the road as I made the final descent to the level of the valley floor. I thought ruefully about my smugness at having remembered the car seat—it wasn't going to do me much good now, when what I really should have brought was snow chains.

Forging ahead, I followed my scribbled directions to Nonny's house (not too difficult in a community of about four streets) and slid to a snowy stop in front of their unhinged gate. Picking my way around toys that would soon be buried in white, I took an extra large step past a missing stair on the front porch and knocked on the door. I waited, then knocked louder. A six or seven year old girl opened the door a couple of inches and stared silently at me. I asked her if her mother was home and she didn't seem to know. She closed the door. I hoped the child might be going to fetch her mother, but nothing happened. The door stayed closed, the minutes ticked by, and the snow continued to pile up in the yard. I knocked again with considerably more energy than before. This time a young man appeared, with the same silent stare as the little girl. He was similarly unhelpful concerning the presence or absence of Cola, Nonny's mother. Once again the door was closed in my face. Having made it this far on such an awful day, I wasn't about to give up without a struggle, and I felt more than ready to stand in front of the woodstove that I had seen glowing warmly in the front room each time the door had been cracked opened. I pounded on the door a third time. Cola herself appeared before me, wet-headed and barefoot, with an open jar of baby food in her hand, apologetic about her disorganization. She did not make any clear sign that she was expecting me, and she did not invite me in.

A little too weary of this day to stand on ceremony, I invited myself in. Nothing I saw gave any indication that anybody was prepared to leave town for the better part of the day with a toddler. I tentatively asked Cola how long it would take her to get ready. She guessed about an hour. I mentally calculated that there would be at least three inches of snow on the roads by then, and asked her if there was anything I could do to help speed things up. My mind raced ahead to the possibility of having to ask for hospitality for the night—maybe I could walk to a hotel if it got too snowy to drive—would there even be a hotel in this town? Cola pondered a minute, trying to towel-dry her hair with her free hand. She suggested that I could help by finishing giving Nonny her lunch. She handed me the baby food jar that was still in her other hand and led me into an adjacent room. There I was confronted with the biggest baby I had ever seen. Nonny was all peaches and cream with a tousled mop of curly golden hair, but her prettiness was completely overwhelmed by her size. At eighteen months of age she must have weighed as much as an average five year old, and I again thought of my well-planned car seat with dismay. There was no way this child was going to fit in it. Oh well, one challenge at a time. I set to work making friends with Nonny and helping her empty the baby food jar, while the little girl I had glimpsed briefly at the door ran around the house helping her mother collect necessary items for the trip. Extra diapers, a blanket, a couple of toys, more food and a change of clothes were piled up in the diaper bag while Cola got her own clothes and make-up together. We actually made it out the door in good time.

Faced with the prospect of having no car seat for Nonny or one that was too small, I opted to wedge her into the seat I had brought for the purpose. We had to take her jacket off and ignore the straps altogether, but we were just able to squeeze the molded harness over her head and across her belly. She was asleep and snoring vigorously before we began the snowy climb out of the valley. That pleased me greatly, since Cola had warned me that Nonny was prone to carsickness.

I didn't breathe normally until we were out of the snow, dreading the possibility that we would run into a place where it was too deep to drive through and I'd have to go back. All I wanted was to return safely to Highway 101. I was just beginning to think we were home free, when we came around the bend by the little slide I'd passed on the way into the valley. The slide wasn't little anymore. The whole mountainside had liquefied and was oozing darkly downward across the road. Half a dozen bulldozers and front-end loaders were churning around in the mess, trying to load as much of the mire as they could scoop up into waiting dump trucks. The muddy machines looked pitifully insignificant in relation to the enormous task at hand. Yellow rain-geared men, looking even more insignificant, waved me to a stop beside a work truck with flashing lights. One mud-covered fellow sloshed over to talk to me. "It'll be at least two hours before they get enough of the hillside carted away to open the road," he announced wearily. I opened my mouth to complain, but closed it before any words even formed in my head. What good would it do to whine at this one powerless human? The man gave me another slow look and said, "I'm not telling you this, but if you wait for that loader to get out of the way, you can probably make it if you go real fast. Make darn sure there aren't any trees coming down, and step on it." I looked up just as a full-sized fir tree toppled off the high edge of the slide and barreled down toward the road, coming to a crashing rest too close to the nearest bulldozer. A few thoughts about the things I still wanted to do with my life flashed through my mind, but were instantly supplanted with my overwhelming desire to get through to a place where returning to Dos Rios would be out of the question. I didn't even ask Cola for her opinion. I looked up, made sure that all of the potentially killer trees were staying put for the moment, stepped on the gas, and cleared the slide in about thirty slippery, adrenaline-charged seconds.

With nerves raw and Nonny still sleeping noisily in the back seat, we arrived safely at the 101 intersection. It was still pouring, but that seemed perfectly fine compared to everything else I had dealt with that day. I looked left and right a couple more times than usual, accelerated onto the highway with extra attention to avoid skidding, and figured we'd hit Ukiah in about an hour, still more or less on time for the ophthalmologist appointment.

Half a mile down the relatively straight highway Nonny stirred in her tight car seat, retched mightily and commenced vomiting up the substantial lunch I had helped spoon into her not so long ago. She covered her front, the seat beside her and much of the floor. As the odor of stomach acid filled the car sickeningly, I looked desperately through the rain for a place wide enough to pull over without risking our lives the minute we opened the car door, as this was clearly going to be a get-out-of-the-car-and-wipe-down-everything kind of operation. I hoped Cola would be able to perform the clean-up unaided, because getting out of the car was the last thing I wanted to do at that moment. She came through heroically despite the fact that she got thoroughly soaked in the process. I sat unmoving and dry in the driver's seat while Cola made good use of the extra clothes her older daughter had helped her pack. The befouled clothes were left where Cola dropped them, in a puddle.

Wondering what could possibly happen next, I set off yet again to see if we could make the doctor appointment within half an hour of the scheduled time. By then I was beginning to fantasize that we would arrive at the office only to find that the doctor had been unable to get to Ukiah on account of the weather. I started planning what to do to ensure that I wouldn't have to make the return trip to Dos Rios. I would even be willing to put Cola and Nonny up in a hotel at my own expense to avoid a re-run of this day.

As it turned out, the ophthalmologist was waiting for us, completely undismayed by our lateness, quite impressed that we had set out at all on such a day. Nonny's eyes were thoroughly checked, and we got the verdict that nothing much was wrong—just a mildly wandering eye that could be corrected with a minimal amount of patching. Susan, the Toddler Program teacher who had signed up to drive Nonny and her mother back to Dos Rios, showed up right on schedule. I beat a hasty retreat, figuring that Susan would be better off knowing nothing about my day.

A CELEBRATION OF PATIENCE

Red's name is really Andrew, but for some reason nobody ever calls him that. Nor does anybody ever ask why he's called Red, even though he has dark brown hair. That's just the way it is, and people accept it. That's exactly how Red's whole life seems to work. He's noticeably different, but perfectly okay the way he is.

Red was born without disabilities, the youngest of three active, strapping boys. He grew and developed the way he was supposed to, began talking at the appropriate age, and had learned to run all over the house when he came down with a fever that kept getting higher. One week after his second birthday he had developed what seemed like a garden-variety cold, and his mother Scarlett thought nothing of watching her husband drive off for a long-planned four-day hunting trip into the uninhabited wilderness of northeastern Mendocino County. That night Red's fever reached 106 degrees, and Scarlett called the hospital twice. She followed the doctor's directions to get the fever down and brought Red into the rural clinic in the morning for a check-up and antibiotics for what was diagnosed as a strep infection. She returned home with Red, who continued to get worse.

By the end of the second day Red didn't recognize anybody in his family, and the nightmare began. Back to the clinic, back home again on the doctor's advice, then hallucinations, which precipitated a fast trip down the road to the nearest hospital in Willits. There Red was diagnosed with meningitis. He was rushed by ambulance another half hour down the road to a bigger hospital in Ukiah, where he was immediately placed in the Intensive Care Unit. Early on the third morning he went into cardiac arrest while alone with his mother. His father still couldn't be located. A team was flown in from San Francisco, Red was put on life support, and he was immediately flown by helicopter to UC Medical Center in San Francisco, where he had his second cardiac arrest.

Red stayed at UC for two months, half of which he spent in a coma. During that time he had eight major surgeries, and his family was told there was no hope for him. If he lived he would be a vegetable. He finally came home to his dazed family three days before Christmas, totally blind, with a tracheotomy, having seizures and unable to move anything except one hand. He couldn't even suck well enough to drink his formula from a bottle, so he was fed through a stomach tube.

I met Red for the first time when he entered a preschool program for severely handicapped children in Covelo. He was a little over three years old. He was just beginning to bear his weight on his hands and knees with the help of a physical therapist, and seemed to be enjoying the attention he was getting. Most little children whine and protest during physical therapy, but Red produced drooly little giggles every time the therapist touched him. Encouraged by my new student's enthusiasm, I kneeled down to join the party on the floor and rattled a noisy toy in front of Red to see if he would look for it or try to move towards it. He had no ability to do either, but turned his face my way and gave me a huge lopsided grin.

In the sixteen years since that day I met Red, I spent countless hours trying to teach him how to see—or rather to teach him how to make sense of the vision he has. Absolutely nothing went wrong with Red's eyes during his ordeal with meningitis, but the brain damage that resulted from the fever, the cardiac arrests and the seizures severely compromised his ability to effectively interpret the information coming from his eyes to his visual cortex. There's a name for that: Cortical Visual Impairment or "CVI". When Red came home from the hospital with no ability to process visual images, he was functionally totally blind. Now, all these years later, he can read many words in large print and play video games, but frequently cannot identify a simple picture of a familiar object or find a large building that is looming right across the street from him. Repeated practice at these challenges led to microscopic amounts of progress, which all added up over time to result in slow, steady improvement. It was an incredibly long haul, but the project never ceased to be rewarding. It also never ceased to make me laugh.

If Red had not gotten sick he undoubtedly would have been the class clown. Hiding just beneath all the disabilities and slow reactions, there is an intact kid. He did not lose his quick and silly sense of humor or his uncanny ability to time his wisecracks to get the best results. On a walk practicing his white cane technique with me, he stumbled, as he did frequently, but made an uncharacteristically quick two-footed jump to regain his balance. I couldn't resist a dig at him, "What was that little dance all about?" Red looked me straight in the eye and deadpanned back, without missing a beat, "Cha cha cha."

Another day ages ago Red's special education teacher started venting his frustration on me at his inability to get Red's family tuned into the importance of helping Red regularly on assigned reading and writing homework. "Red's homework doesn't come back on time, and sometimes Scarlett doesn't even bother to send it back at all," the teacher practically whined to me. "Since you are going to be taking Red home this afternoon, you could help me by talking to his mother about it. She just doesn't pay any attention to me."

I dutifully passed this concern on to Scarlett an hour later when I delivered her son home after our mobility lesson. Scarlett rolled her eyes and I knew I was in for it. "I'll tell you how I deal with this homework nonsense," she fired at me. "We have a big blackboard set up in the kitchen. Red and I use it to write large-print words—we take turns, and he gets plenty of practice with both reading and spelling." Her eyes gleamed with a good memory and she continued. "He hadn't written anything for days, so I just wrote, 'Red is a brat.' Then I waited to see what would happen. Red didn't do a thing for about a week, and then I looked at the board one morning when I came in to fix breakfast. Sometime the night before he had erased my message and replaced it with 'Mom is a cow,' in huge letters. You just go tell that teacher what he can do with Red's homework assignments." I decided not to bother taking the teacher's side in any more homework disputes.

Red had so many problems when I started working with him that I needed to spend weeks just figuring out where to start. He couldn't crawl or even sit unaided, he couldn't talk, and he couldn't use his hands to reach for or manipulate toys that I hoped might be interesting to him. This wasn't a kid who could benefit from anything I had ever been trained to do in the realm of orientation and mobility, but I was being paid to provide two hours per week with him since he was functionally blind and clearly qualified for the services.

I figured out fairly quickly that Red was aware of the comings and goings of people and that he was happily responsive to any kind of human interaction. His hearing was intact, and it was clear that he could see light and movement, both of which he looked towards. He affirmed with his lopsided grin that he was enjoying whatever it was that he saw.

With that information and nothing else to go on, I decided to start taking Red outside for little adventures in a stroller. I had spent countless happy hours pushing or carrying my own offspring around outside when they were tiny, stopping to explore every interesting object or event we happened upon, and I figured this would be a way to help Red begin to connect his vision, hearing and touch. Maybe, with my help, he could begin to make some sense of the disconnected jumble of visual input that was flooding his brain.

So I flopped Red's wobbly five-year-old body into an undersized umbrella stroller and out we went. Twice a week, rain or shine, we trailed down hallways at his school, poked into offices and classrooms, watched flowers bloom and fade in front of neighborhood houses, counted trucks rumbling by on the main drag and looked for apples in the grocery store. I talked my head off, trying to help Red make the connection between the things he was looking at and their word labels. Through all of this Red was unmoving and silent, but always alert.

It dawned on me one day that Red could possibly understand more about his world, and have a pile more fun, if he could participate actively to make things happen to objects we encountered. I gave him his first little white cane and helped him hold it. With the cane we could make noise—*loud* noise. I remembered the racket I had made running into garbage cans during my mobility training at SF State, and I aimed Red's stroller for the nearest metal trash receptacle in the school hallway. I helped him smack it, softly the first time and then harder. Annoyed teachers stomped out of their classrooms to glare at me disparagingly and bang their doors shut with unspoken disdain, but the only thing that mattered to me was that Red was moving the hand that gripped the cane and trying to bang the garbage can again. Out of respect for elementary school protocol we moved out of the hallway to find a garbage can on the far side of the playground, and there we practiced. Red soon was able to see his unusual target as we approached and smack it all by himself. I couldn't help wondering what my college professors would think if they knew I was putting those difficult and expensive years of training to use teaching my students to whack garbage cans with their red-tipped, regulation, for-the-blind-only white canes.

Red quickly learned that he could make all sorts of commotion with other objects that we passed on our forays into the community. He could drag his cane along fences and achieve a huge variety of sounds depending on how fast we were going with the stroller and what kind of fence it was. Chain link fences were his favorite, and the faster we went, the better. I had to explain what we were doing to practically every senior citizen in the community as we startled them in the midst of doing their yard chores. The poor souls would hear us banging their fences and look up angrily, sucking in air preparing to yell at a juvenile delinquent up to no good, and then splutter disconcertedly when they discovered that it was a respectable looking adult with a handicapped child in tow creating the unseemly racket.

Another eye opener, literally, for Red was his discovery that he could reach up with his cane and clobber low hanging branches. The result was not only noise, but motion—a lovely frenzy of action, which motivated him to try harder to look for things and use his cane independently to touch them. In the summer he could create a show of light and shadow as the leafy branches he hit swayed back and forth in front of the sun, and in the fall he could knock down a shower of colorful leaves to take back to his classroom for a fall bouquet. On rainy days Red could shake all the water droplets off the leaves onto both of us—his favorite activity but not necessarily mine.

Even as Red learned to see more and more, he never seemed to notice anything below eye level. I decided to try to fix that one winter day after a good rainstorm. There were puddles everywhere and I parked the stroller next to a big, deep one. I took Red's cane and splashed it in the puddle, making as much noise as I could. Red grinned ear to ear like the naughty little boy he should have been, and actually looked down while I guided his hand on the cane to help him stir up the muddy water. Then he did it himself. And he did it again. We both ended up soaked. To this day Red knows that he can get a rise out of me by threatening to splash a puddle with his cane, laughing like it's a brand new joke as I take the bait and jump aside.

It was always easier for Red to notice and identify moving objects than stationary ones. While still in his stroller, he could watch a flock of crows fly overhead and see them land on a wire. One day he stared intently at a group of them squawking twenty feet off the ground and announced, "I see three crows." That same boy, walking with me six years later, still could not stand still, look directly across the street, and find the huge barn-red grocery store that he had seen and shopped in dozens of times. He just stared blankly, with the message "does not compute" written all over his face. Then I asked him to turn his head. The minute he did the light of recognition came on and he was able to point at the elusive edifice and tell me "There it is." The apparent motion created by moving his head was all he needed for what he was looking at to register in his brain as a building.

Red's stroller mobility lessons lasted for a long time, even after he was far too big for the stroller and beginning to walk with a walker. Red had to use his full cognitive powers to see. Vision for him happened only as the result of a supreme conscious effort—it was never the incidental, uncomplicated sense that the rest of us grow up taking for granted. When Red was focusing on the difficult new task of keeping his balance and taking alternating steps in the walker, he had no ability left to see, and consequently ran into things. Finding the peanut butter on Aisle 6 was out of the question, even though he knew perfectly well what a jar of peanut butter looked like. The solution we dreamed up was to alternate walking and looking. In a grocery store, where the dangers were minimal and the predictability at its maximum, Red learned to walk five or six steps and stop. Then, without having to worry about what he was doing physically, he could move his head back and forth, checking for obstacles and trying to recognize the item he was searching for. He'd finally spy the peanut butter display, light up like a Christmas tree, and point at it in triumph.

Years later, in a familiar place, Red finally learned to walk and stay oriented at the same time, navigating the hallways and sidewalks of his high school independently. He progressed beyond both the walker and a short-lived pair of forearm crutches, preferring to use a white cane in constant contact with the ground in front of him as an early warning system for unrecognized steps and drop-offs. He was still hopelessly slow, but his many friends accommodated willingly and altered their own pace to walk with him. Red knew practiced routes to a few favorite bakeries and snack shops within three or four blocks of his high school, which he reviewed weekly with me. He was never able to travel alone in the community, because one small error would cause him to lose his bearings and end up right back at the bottom of Alice's rabbit hole. What he saw there was vaguely familiar to him, but the details were nameless and distorted. He couldn't cope if one piece of his learned mental map got jostled out of place.

Working all of those years in the shops and on the streets of Red's small town, I became quite visible to his family's friends and neighbors. Everybody knows everybody else, and everybody knows the story of Red's terrible fever. The well-meaning citizens of the town seem to have agreed that Red will never have to do a thing for himself as long as one of them is within running distance to speak for him, open doors for him and anticipate his every need. My philosophy, to the contrary, is that the more my student can do for himself, the better. So I made myself stand and pretend not to watch as Red struggled with a heavy door or fumbled with his fanny pack to get his money out to make a purchase at the general store. Reports of my meanness and lack of basic human kindness reached home to his parents with regularity. People everywhere considered it their moral duty to telephone Red's mother to inform her of my shortcomings, in case she was unaware of the bad treatment Red was getting at my hands. Scarlett gleefully passed every complaint on to me and shared her own irreverent take on her life with her handicapped son.

Bad reports about me weren't all that came Scarlett's way. Her face was lit up with mischief one day when I delivered Red to her after a lesson, and she didn't even wait for me to get out of the car before launching into her story. "You'll never believe this, Laura, but I got a call this morning from this logger who works with Red's dad. It seems that this nutcase thinks he's in the market for a wife, and he goes and tells me that he's spent the last few weeks eyeing you while you and Red are walking around downtown!" Scarlett sucked air and continued, "So now he's got this cockamamie notion that he could get away with asking *me* what *I* thought *he* should do to get *you* to the altar." By then, Scarlett was laughing so hard she could barely talk, but she finished, "I told him he's been in the woods too long!" I'll bet Scarlett told him a few more things than that, and in no uncertain terms. And she reminds me periodically that I owe her—big time.

Red's family members may not have been eager to help me with my love life, but I drew no such lines when it came to helping their son learn to date. In his junior year in high school Red met a cute, nutty, constantly chattering freshman girl who knocked him off his feet. I lost no time in letting Red know that the Junior/Senior Ball was coming up, and described the whole thing to him. We walked the hallways, stopping while I pointed out all the details of the posters announcing the event. Downtown, in addition to having our usual bakery treat, we went into the store that rented tuxedos so Red could see what they were like. We visited the flower shop so he could learn about corsages and the ritual of giving one to a date to wear to the prom. We even explored some restaurants so Red would understand my descriptions of going out for a special candlelight dinner that was different from the fast food he was used to.

Red seemed thoroughly interested in this prom concept, so I took it a step further. I suggested to him that, since he was now a junior, he could attend. I also dropped the hint that he might invite Tania to be his date, since they enjoyed each other's company. This my eager student did the next day, without running the idea by his parents first. Red told his special education teacher about his plans, the teacher immediately told Scarlett, and what I heard next was Scarlett's frantic voice on the phone.

"What's all this about Red wanting to take some girl to the prom?" was the first thing out of Scarlett's mouth. "He's out of his mind! There's no way he can do that! The answer is no, and I'd thank you for not putting any more of those cockeyed notions into his head!" Scarlett sounded more panicked than angry, so I decided I was going to win this one. I had enough sense to let her vent as much as she needed to. When she ran out of steam I gently asked her what was really going on. Dating, and everything associated with it, it turned out, was a door Scarlett had unconsciously shut for her baby when he first came home from the hospital irreparably damaged and disabled. There were so many things he wouldn't be able to do, and the safest approach for Scarlett emotionally was to remove all of those activities from her projections and expectations for the future. Scratch football. Scratch boy scouts. Scratch dating. That way there wouldn't be so many disappointments as each was proven to be impossible. Don't dare to dream.

With that door to the erased possibilities unexpectedly re-opened in Scarlett's face, the old pain came pouring out—all the guilt and fear and grief about what had happened to Red so long ago. To allow Red this date with his friend Tania was to set him up for the rejection, disappointment and insecurity that goes with the territory of teenage dating, all of which would undoubtedly be exaggerated in Red's case on account of his immature social skills. Could Scarlett face that risk for her son, and for herself?

True to form, Scarlett ranted and raved some more, and then took the plunge that she and I both knew she would eventually come around to. "Yes, he can go, but if it's a disaster it will be all your fault, Laura." And also true to form, Red's whole family got together to make sure that the evening would be a monumental success. They rented a tuxedo for Red and bought a corsage for Tania. Red's older brother and his girlfriend dressed up and drove Red to pick Tania up for a restaurant dinner, and set them up at their own private table with candlelight. At the prom Red and Tania had their pictures taken as they walked in, just like all the other couples, and they danced until the party shut down. Scarlett spent the next week handing out the stunningly handsome prom pictures to everybody she knew.

After the flurry of the prom and the other end-of-school festivities, Red was bored by the second day of summer vacation. He told his mom that he missed seeing Tania, and Scarlett phoned to ask if I might have any bright ideas for summer entertainment for her son. I dreamed up some half-day mobility lessons that would involve Red inviting Tania to "go out." Red had no way of knowing what kinds of activities existed in town that he could enjoy with Tania, nor did he know how to plan a date with her. Other people had always done the social organizing and facilitating for him.

Our first "dating" lesson was simply to walk around town by ourselves and preview the possibilities for an eventual date. It was necessary to actually poke our heads into a number of places and watch people while I described what they were doing to Red, since he couldn't rely on his imagination to visualize the activities. We scanned the posters on the wall outside the movie theater and walked in to check out the snack bar. Down the street was a convenience store with pool tables and video games in a back room, so we went in to see what people were doing. We walked through an alcove full of tables and chairs, and I read the list of foods that were served, so Red would have some idea what he could order if he and Tania came there. Our last stop was the health club, which we toured with an employee to check out the pool, lockers and snack bar. With a fairly concrete understanding of what the three places had to offer, Red chose to invite Tania to go swimming with him at the health club.

With support from me, Red phoned Tania and invited her to our planned outing the next week. It wasn't until we arrived at the health club that I realized I was going to have to deal with an almost adult male student who needed to change his clothes in a locker room that he was unable to find his way around in. I hastily worked out a plan. I had Red stand out in the hallway and remove all the clothing that he could decently take off, and sent him in with just his pants left on, carrying his swim trunks. I could see a bench through the door as he opened it, so I told him to go straight ahead, sit on the bench to change, and wait there for me to call him before getting up to come out. After what seemed like an appropriate interval, I opened the door a crack, yelled Red's name, and told him to get up and walk towards my voice. It worked perfectly.

I had never had much success in swimming pools with Red. With little ability to see where he was going and without the motor control to stabilize himself in the buoyant water, he had always been fearful of swimming, even with a float or tube to hang onto. Tania proved to be the perfect antidote to Red's reluctance to get in the pool. With her in the water it all of a sudden seemed attractive to Red, and he was more than willing to allow me to guide him in and assist him in a splashy game of catch with a bright beach ball. Once soaked, Red got into the spirit of the fun with his chatty little friend, and we devised an arrangement of "noodles" that would keep him floating with his head safely out of the water. With Tania noisily egging him on, Red kicked and flailed around enough to propel himself all the way across the pool. Thanks to Tania, Red had a good enough time in the water that he chose to return to the health club several more times over the summer. He achieved an extraordinary level of independence, once it occurred to me to outfit him in a snug life jacket that he could float in without having to hold onto it. With his arms free and his confidence at an all-time high, Red discovered that he could control himself in the water and happily pursue Tania from one side of the pool to the other.

Red didn't exactly turn into a social butterfly as the result of his summer dating experiences with me, but he began talking with a few of his school friends on the phone and inviting Tania and another girl over to his house every so often for backyard swimming. The biggest barrier to Red's social life with peers was the location of his family's home in a small, remote town; most of his potential friends lived more than an hour away in Ukiah. In spite of the long bus ride, Red's family allowed him to make the jump in September to a well-run, community-oriented adult transition program in Ukiah, which he attended until he reached the mandatory graduation age of 22.

Red did not go on to accomplish big things. Staying home was the choice his family made for him. Their biggest concern was always for his safety—they had completely reasonable fears that some predator could take advantage of Red's inherent friendliness and willingness to comply with anything that was asked of him. My own hopes, which I didn't keep secret from Scarlett, were that Red would eventually move into a group home in Ukiah and go on a daily basis to some form of sheltered employment. I thought he would be happiest in a setting where he and other people with disabilities would be coming and going and talking and managing their activities of daily living in the kind of structured, supported, interactive way that is fostered by an educational or residential program. I was worried that Red would get bored and lonely at home and lose the skills he had worked so hard to achieve. I was wrong. I've seen Red many times since he became an adult, and he is as alert and sociable and happy to see me as he ever was. He always has a story to tell me about something he has done with his family, or a picture to show me of his new twin nephews, whom he utterly adores. I'm still not thrilled that he is home, but I've got to hand it to Scarlett. Life with her is *not* boring.

THE MUNCHIES

When frustrations occur that I can't solve, which is frequently, I succumb to the munchies. The munchies strike the minute I settle into the county car—with no regard for what I'm doing, where I am going, or what the weather is like. No matter how long it's been since my most recent feeding, my stomach begins to rumble the instant I turn the key in the ignition. Even if I have just downed a huge breakfast of French toast covered with fruit and yogurt, or an entire nourishing lunch, something about the feel of my hands on the steering wheel makes my fingers itch for delectable goodies to grasp and ferry repeatedly to my mouth. The longer I hold out, the longer I obsess on my desire to eat, and the longer I obsess, the more pressing my appetite becomes. I have learned to get the inevitable over with and just give in to my cravings.

Most of my lunches get eaten behind the wheel, for the simple reason that it makes more sense to eat while driving the great distances I have to cover than to take a relaxed lunch hour and arrive at the next school on my schedule after it has let out for the day. I know where every faculty room microwave in Mendocino County is located, and I make use of them to heat up my tried and true (and rather dry, but dripless) bean and cheese burritos before dashing out to the car for my meal on wheels. I was on a cream cheese and bagel kick for a while, but couldn't fill them with enough additional goodies to make them interesting without leaking—plus it's nice to have something hot to hold and eat on rainy winter days. Peanut butter and jelly is a last resort, but there's no way to make it warm and edible in the car, and it reminds me too much of being in grade school myself. Any other kind of sandwiches are a lost cause, since a bite on one end invariably results in half the ingredients being squished out the other end unless I have two hands available to contain the mess, which I don't while driving.

I am by now an expert at selecting good road food. The single most important criterion is safety, with neatness coming in a close second. The two go hand-in-hand. Morsels that can be eaten whole win out over larger delicacies that have to be bitten into, as the biting frequently causes disastrous leakage or uncontrolled dripping, which in turn causes the diversion of an undue amount of my attention from the critical job of looking where I am going on our winding roads. I peel and quarter my apples ahead of time, and go to the bother of sectioning my oranges into a lidded plastic container before I leave home. Anything that can be eaten in one neat, vision-free bite prevents me from arriving at my next school with slopped juice, sauce or oil staining my front or my lap.

When I'm feeling particularly conscientious about my health, I select carrots, snow peas, green beans, jicama fingers, and spears of lightly steamed broccoli for my on-the-road snacking. All of these can be eaten without looking. Better yet, they can be crunched in large quantities while basking in imagined approval from Dr. Dean Edell, or whichever health guru I have just heard on the public radio station expostulating about healthy eating and prolonging one's life. Cherry tomatoes are also fine. Regular-sized tomatoes aren't, for the simple reason that they frequently shoot their red juice and sticky little seeds all over the car when I break their skin in the process of taking that first bite.

Trail mix also works well in the car, as long as it doesn't have chocolate chips lurking in it. I learned the hard way that chocolate, in any shape or form, *always* melts in a parked car—even in our chilly wintertime—resulting in a gooey little time bomb that is more likely than not to plop into my lap as I concentrate on rounding a turn. That's a pity, but it's the one reason my waistline hasn't ballooned over all these years of snacking in the car.

Cookies are my current downfall. I know where to get the best ones, as I have visited every bakery in the county. The Point Arena Bakery makes unbelievably wonderful chocolate ginger cookies—large and chewy, with bittersweet chocolate chunks and an exciting amount of grated fresh ginger neatly incorporated into the cookie, as opposed to being sprinkled loosely on top of it. They are also outrageously expensive, so I rarely buy more than one at a time. That single, huge cookie should be big enough to keep me happy for at least a couple of days, but it usually doesn't last more than a couple of miles. I have tried forcing myself to break the cookie in half and stow the part I don't intend to eat in some part of the car that I can't access while driving, but that just makes it necessary to pull off the road somewhere and retrieve the thing after trying not to think about it for twenty miles. My current philosophy is "Why bother with the denial nonsense when it clearly isn't going to work anyway?" Luckily for my waistline, I only work in Point Arena once a week. And luckily for my emotional well-being, the munchies do actually offer me some solace on those frequent days when things don't work out.

CHAOS AND CONTROL

Shaynna. She was the best and the worst, the funniest and the sad-dest, the one child of all the children I will never forget. She grew with me and I grew with her through hours and years of intense time together. During my offbeat, improvised and frequently messy lessons with Shaynna, I re-discovered the best of my childhood, and through her I also began learning to accept the adult pain of letting go.

Shaynna was born a survivor. Nineteen-year-old Samantha waited in a motel room with her husband Raymond while the first of their ter-ribly premature twins died, and they refused to grant the doctors' request to take her remaining infant off life support. Samantha knew on some wordless level deep in her heart that this tiny, unformed being meant to live. Live Shaynna did, in spite of a birth weight of less than two pounds, a Grade IV brain bleed, hydrocephalus, and Cerebral Palsy which left her seriously restricted in her ability to use both her arms and legs. Total blindness was the least of Shaynna's problems when she was finally sent home from her long hospitalization to begin her life with her shocked and completely unprepared parents.

No child comes with directions, but most new mothers and fathers are lucky enough to have the support of their own parents, siblings or friends who have managed to raise offspring somehow or other, without too many things going irreparably wrong in the struggle. Raymond and Samantha were not so fortunate. Even without the birth of a severely handicapped child they would have been challenged beyond their abili-ties to nurture a helpless, constantly needy infant. Samantha herself had a major learning disability and was the product of an abusive childhood. She suffered from chronic depression and hadn't learned any effective means of dealing with stress. She didn't drive. Desperate to find some of what was missing in her life, she had married Raymond, a hearing im-paired Vietnam veteran with Post-Traumatic Stress Syndrome who was more than twice her age. Intensely intelligent and well-meaning, and committed to moving himself and his family out of their state of poverty, Raymond was unable to cope with the constant noisy disruptions caused by his new family. He spent most of his time out of the house. He worked in the driveway tinkering on the third-hand car that was his lifeline to his community. He immersed himself in earning a college diploma the slow hard way, by correspondence, escaping to the library to do required reading for hours at a time. He was also busy writing a book. Raymond rarely lifted a finger to help with whatever household crisis was raising the decibel level to intolerable, but he was responsible about getting his daughter to school and medical appointments. I got to like Raymond quite well as the years rolled by.

I felt a gnawing need for a good omen as I drove up north to meet Shaynna for the first time. I had already heard quite a bit about this family, and I was overwhelmed with waves of self-doubt and trepidation as I tried to imagine how I could possibly find some useful ways to support them. I had been teaching for ten years, long enough to know that home visits require an intuitive combination of tact and directness, but I wasn't confident that I would find the right amount of either. I took my eyes off the road, scanned the slope to my left, and breathed a sigh of relief. I saw what I was looking for—the white deer.

The white deer are my personal omen for good luck. I see them just often enough to be thoroughly convinced that they do, in fact, exist, though other people who live here have driven the Ridgewood grade a hundred times and never noticed them. The deer make an eerie impression, standing unaware of their startling beauty, grazing as though they had ordinary deer bodies to nourish. To me they are spirits from some distant enchanted world, visible only to those mortals who truly believe.

I've driven the grade often enough in all these years of commuting to Laytonville and the coast that I know exactly where to look for my phantom deer. They move around, as wild things do, in rhythm with the cycles of the changing seasons. Sometimes the deer stand within twenty feet of the highway—so close that I can see the steam of their breath hovering in the winter air, lending them an even more ghost-like quality. When I see them I am reminded that magic is possible on an ordinary day if I just take a minute to let it happen.

Feeling more hopeful about my first meeting with Shaynna and her parents, I drove on to find them. Shaynna was then almost three years old, and her family had just moved to Mendocino County in search of more affordable housing. I switchbacked through the convoluted roads of an ill-planned subdivision in the hills to the west of Laytonville, and eventually located their shabby, low-income apartment building. It loomed at the end of a partially paved cul-de-sac, separated by a low hill from the finer homes surrounding the golf course. I parked among a litter of dilapidated cars and weather-beaten children's toys. There was no shade in this ragged clearing that had been hacked out of the beautiful inland forest of fir, madrone and oak. In this island of ugliness Samantha waited for me outside, chain-smoking next to the laundry drying on the balcony railing. She did not greet me.

Feeling intensely awkward, I introduced myself in a weak voice. I guessed by looking at Samantha's dark hair and unwrinkled skin that she was considerably younger than I, but she was still the person of authority in this place where I was a visitor. My habitual good manners required that she make the first move to welcome me to her home. Samantha didn't do anything. She barely looked at me. She did not offer to accompany me inside, nor did she appear to be in the mood to talk. I squirmed in the silence. Finally I asked, "Can I go in and see Shaynna?"

"She's in there," Samantha indicated with a jerk of her head as she exhaled smoke. She lit another cigarette, a clear signal that she intended to stay out on the balcony. Lacking alternatives, I pushed open the battered sliding glass door and walked inside alone.

The lights were off and the blinds were drawn tight. The air conditioning blasted at full speed, making me wish for a sweater on this intensely hot summer day. I stood in the doorway to adjust to the climate and figure out what to do, and after a silent minute or two was able to make out a high chair standing in the middle of the gloomy kitchen. Hunkered down in the chair was a small, feral-looking child, bare except for her diaper. The tray of the high chair was piled with slobbery Cheerios, which Shaynna was chucking down without benefit of a bowl, a spoon, or even her one useable hand. The German verb "fressen" came to mind—it's the word for how animals eat. Samantha banged in, interrupting my train of thought, and upended the Cheerios box over the high chair tray before pitching it into the overflowing garbage can. She retreated to her post on the balcony, lighting another cigarette, without saying a word to either Shaynna or me. Shaynna hunched over, face-to-tray, greedily attacking the new pile of Cheerios.

My awareness shifted to an unexpected sound coming from the dim recesses of the living room. A human baby sound, from a younger sister who had been lying on the floor all this time without moving or vocalizing. It was Shaynna's baby sister, six months old, who could not yet roll over. She lay without light or toys, awake, silent and still, for the entire time I was in the apartment on this unnerving day. A forgotten child, left to her own non-existent resources in a family too full of tragedy to cope with one more demand.

Recollections of my college-acquired skills in the stimulation of blind babies ricocheted in my brain as I desperately tried to think of something to do with Shaynna. Just one thing to start with. I needed to define a point of entry into this sensory black hole where everything imaginable needed to be done all at once. Everything that should have been done today and yesterday and last year, and everything that would have to be done in all the years ahead that I could see marching their resolute way towards me, whether I figured out what to do or not. There weren't any answers on the textbook pages floating around in my mind. The skills and techniques I could recollect from my practicum class on multi-handicapped infants seemed utterly irrelevant in the face of Shaynna.

I moved quietly across the kitchen and turned on the light in a somewhat desperate attempt to affirm my own presence. I couldn't tolerate the spookiness of standing in the dark, even though the light, or lack of light, couldn't possibly make any difference to this totally blind little girl. Shaynna startled a bit at the click of the light switch, but continued shoveling in her Cheerios.

I needed to let Shaynna know there was somebody new in the room with her. I started talking to her, softly, saying her name and telling her mine. She quieted immediately, quitting her chewing with her mouth still full, so she could hear every sound made by my unfamiliar presence. She kept her head down. Staring whitely back at me, cutting an unnatural jagged part in her un-brushed, food-caked hair, was the surgery scar from her shunt operation.

Walking closer, not wanting to scare or intimidate Shaynna on this first encounter, I reverted to the universal adult-child connection. A nursery song. I don't remember any longer which silly little ditty popped into my head, but the result was what I'd been praying for. Shaynna listened, slumped on the tray, as I sang verse after verse and then repeated them all in my most animated singing-to-children voice. Shaynna remained motionless and I kept going, feeling less sure of myself with every repeated verse. Finally Shaynna raised her head. Just a little at first, and then all the way up with a tremendous effort. She wriggled her crooked little body from head to toe with unconstrained delight, and suddenly grinned from ear to ear.

There was the connection, the place for me to start. I saw directly through the white, cataract-clouded pupils of Sahynna's misshapen and useless eyes. Looking back at me was that enormous soul her mother had recognized and fought to save three years before. This child wanted to be alive and she was ready to be a part of her world. Bringing that world to her was what I knew how to do, or so I thought.

Working with Shaynna was never easy. Having lived her entire life of three years in an environment where almost nothing made any sense to her, she had no reference point upon which to build. She did not have a context in which to put new information. Shaynna existed in a world where people and things came at her without warning or words, and where she would be handled or abandoned just as abruptly. Sounds were not connected to the objects that made them, and activities did not have a predictable beginning, middle and end. Food appeared from nowhere, her clothes vanished when they were taken off her, and voices were disembodied sounds which came and went without connection. Shaynna might be picked up and deposited in another space at any moment, with no idea whether she had been moved half a foot or to the other end of the house. Without the physical ability to sit or crawl, a room could not be explored, and a toy that had been pushed an inch out of her reach simply ceased to exist.

Shaynna had no awareness of the cause and effect principle, no notion of object permanence, and no internal map of any part of the space in which she lived. And, without vision, she had no motivation to move. She couldn't see other people getting around. Nor could she see interesting objects that would entice a sighted child to roll or crawl, or, at the least, reach, to explore them. Shaynna's world consisted of what she could feel in the moment with her contracted limbs. She would only tolerate being in her bed and her high chair, both familiar places where at least some predictable events occurred.

How could I teach Shaynna that socks go on feet and mittens go on hands? She didn't know her hands from her feet or even that her hands and feet were different from mine. What about learning that her Cheerios came from a box in the cupboard and her scrambled eggs (the only other food she would eat) came from a carton of eggs in the refrigerator and got cooked on the stove in a pan that came from the shelf under the counter? When I tried to lift Shaynna to find the cupboard or the refrigerator, she was so fearful of being off the floor or out of her familiar chair that she hung onto me like a panicked little monkey and refused to let me pry her one good hand loose from its stranglehold on my shirt. How could I teach Shaynna to explore with her hands, when one was tightly contracted from her Cerebral Palsy and the other recoiled at every unfamiliar touch? Everything that is fun and interesting to a sighted child was unfamiliar and terrifying to Shaynna.

Preschool, luckily, was a godsend for Shaynna. Raymond took on the challenge of riding the bus with his daughter until she got used to it. Shaynna quickly responded to the structure of her daily trips to and from school and the schedule of indoor and outdoor activities. She liked sounds and caught on quickly to the rhythms and tunes sung at circle time. In her safe little wooden school chair with armrests, a solid foot-rest, and a snug seat belt, she dared to let go and lift her hands to reach for noisy toys that she had learned to like. As she became comfortable enough to trust, Shaynna's nutty little personality began to emerge, as did her unexpected intelligence. She let her therapists entice her to start moving around the room, using a modified commando crawl. She learned to use her hearing to follow people and toys across the rug and out the door, and eventually crawled down the steps and across the lawn to the tire swing, which she tried and adored.

Shaynna started talking. Her early speech was echolalic, full of meaningless repetitions of words she didn't comprehend. She repeated entire radio commercials, complete with accurate intonation, without a clue what they were about. She also had a mania for spelling. For some reason Shaynna could hear any word and make a reasonably accurate effort to sound it out, letter by letter. The first time I told her how to spell "bed" and then asked her to spell "red," she got it. However, even by the age of five she couldn't express a simple thought such as "I am hungry" or "My ear hurts." I realized that oral language might be too nebulous for Shaynna, too lacking in solidity for her to literally get a handle on. My mind wandered crazily to the possibility of teaching her braille as a tangible, concrete vehicle for the introduction and organization of new language.

My time with Shaynna was shared with the other teacher of the visually impaired, Suzanne, who somewhat dubiously agreed to take on the challenge of this outrageous braille idea. Suzanne put her heart and a tremendous amount of energy and creativity into the project. As the years went by, Shaynna learned all of the letters of the alphabet, followed by most of the complicated braille contractions, and was able to read and write an increasingly long list of words. She eventually used her braille to read simple books, learn words to songs, and write shopping lists which she could read back to me in the grocery store, to her endless delight.

More importantly, braille gave Shaynna the ability to process new concepts far better than she was able to just by hearing people talk to her. With braille, she could read sentences over and over to herself or to her aide, until the meaning of the words sank in. We used braille to help explain something new that was going to happen on a certain day, such as "Mommy is going to come to school for a visit and she will go on a mobility lesson with us." Forewarned in writing, and given plenty of time to go over the words, Shaynna could handle the alteration to her routine without falling apart. If we simply told her that her mother would be coming for a visit, Shaynna would start yowling the minute she heard Samantha's voice in the classroom, unable to assimilate the fact that this person who "belonged" at home had somehow shown up at school, which, in Shaynna's rigid little mind, was *not* a place for family members. Trying to talk Shaynna out of such a fit never worked, but allowing her to read herself to calmness was successful more often than not.

Shaynna's disabilities frequently allowed her to get away with behavior that would absolutely not have been tolerated in a more able student. That usually drove me nuts, because it made it difficult to teach Shaynna that rules existed at all, let alone that they might apply to her. However, on rare occasions, this inequity delighted me. During Shaynna's fourth grade winter of too many rained-out lunch recesses, the din of cooped-up children in the school cafeteria rose to such a pitch that the teacher in charge resorted to using the microphone to try to shout the kids into silence. Unsuccessful in her effort, she summoned the school principal, Mr. Gunderson, to her assistance. He strode with glowering and purposeful demeanor into the clamor, seized the microphone, and commenced at full roar to harangue the offending student body with all of his blustering principal power. "This racket has GOT to stop. There will be NO outside recess for the rest of the WEEK. Notes will be sent home to the PARENTS of ANY student caught making a PEEP from now until the BELL rings, and you will spend the REST of the day in my OFFICE! Do I make myself absolutely CLEAR?" Mr. Gunderson stood menacingly tall and red-faced from his efforts, glaring—daring just one child to disobey his ultimatum.

In the utter, stunned stillness Shaynna piped up, unusually loudly and with perfect diction, "Good speech, Mr. Gunderson!"

With Suzanne working tirelessly on the academic front, I was free to spirit Shaynna away from the confines of the classroom for hours at a time. I always characterized our lessons as adventures, in an attempt to imbue them with a sense of excitement and fun. One day when I announced my arrival to Shaynna at the end of her classroom circle time, she piped up with her first complete sentence, "Here comes the adventure lady!" Shaynna loved mobility lessons, and with such a responsive student I was able to devise endless means to put her into contact with the world she could neither see nor reach.

White canes were designed for people who walk. They are supposed to be used in a proper arc, in the regulation "touch technique." Shaynna couldn't walk. She was pushed everywhere in a wheelchair, and she didn't have the strength or coordination in her deformed hands to hold a cane correctly and move it back and forth in front of her. I didn't see any reason why she shouldn't have a cane, though, to explore her immediate environment and get some information about all the fascinating things that she was getting wheeled past without touching. I figured that my college mentor, Pete Wurzburger, would forgive me for being creative instead of correct, and I found a lightweight cane with a fat grip to put in Shaynna's stronger hand. I sawed the bottom two feet off the cane to make it the right length for my tiny student. It was an instant hit.

Shaynna had developed an eager and effective sense of touch, and she quickly learned to use her cane like an extension of her fingers. With her zany amusement at the details of how people go around living their everyday lives, she learned to detect with a swipe of her cane whether a lawn in front of a house was freshly mowed or in need of cutting. If she felt tall grass swatting her cane as she poked it around, she would gleefully holler out, "Somebody tell these people to mow their lawn." Likewise, she was adept at finding out if the fall leaves had been raked out of a front yard we passed.

I wasn't sure Shaynna knew exactly what "raked" meant, and the opportunity to learn leapt out at us with no planning on my part. On the way downtown one fall day, we approached the house of an elderly widow, Mabel, who always waved as we walked by. Mabel was home, busy in her front yard with a rake and a litter of fallen sycamore leaves. I hailed Mabel and stopped pushing Shaynna so she could hear the scratching of Mabel's rake on the lawn. Listening was interesting, but certainly not enough for Shaynna to grasp the entire concept of raking. I abandoned my plans for our downtown lesson and hollered across the lawn at Mabel, "Have you got another rake?"

"Whatever for?" Mabel asked.

"Shaynna and I want to help you. She's never raked leaves before."

"Well, if you insist, I guess that would be all right." Mabel sounded a bit dubious, but she pointed out the location of the extra rake. I parked Shaynna and dashed behind the house to fetch it. I returned to Shaynna, helped her out of her wheelchair, and balanced her from behind while assisting her to hold her rake and swipe it around in a loose approximation of the activity of raking. Shaynna squealed at the crunching of the dinner plate-sized leaves. We laboriously made a messy little pile, which I plopped Shaynna on top of while I seized the rake and swept up more leaves. I dumped them over Shaynna's head, and soon had her buried up to her neck. She was delighted and thrashed around to make as much noise as possible, spreading the leaves all over our poor friend Mabel's lawn again.

"It doesn't look like you're getting much accomplished." Mabel commented, surveying the mess and moving to defend the leaf pile she had just finished. I grabbed my rake once more and helped Mabel create one tremendous heap of leaves. Mabel thought her yard work was finished for the day, but I picked Shaynna up and tossed her wiggling little body right into the middle of the neat pile, which resulted in most of the lawn looking like no yard work had been done at all.

Mabel laughed this time. "Don't worry about cleaning it all up again," she told me. "My son is coming by tomorrow and he can do it. I had so much fun watching Shaynna that it was worth the mess. Stop and visit again any time you want."

Rain was another concept that eluded Shaynna. Being severely handicapped, she was automatically protected from getting wet. All she had ever experienced about rain was a few drops on her head as she was hustled from house to school bus to classroom under the protection of a huge umbrella. Unless she had to go to school, she was kept in on rainy days. I decided it was time for Shaynna to learn something new about her world, given the reality that the town of Laytonville gets soaked under about four feet of rain annually.

I waited for a good stormy afternoon with dumping clouds and overflowing gutters. Armed with permission from Samantha to give her daughter a good soaking, I loaded Shaynna into her wheelchair. Instead of dashing for the county car all safely umbrella-ed and driving to a nice dry store, we set out into the weather. Not wanting to terrify Shaynna with too sudden a transition from dry to wet, I paused her wheelchair under the overhanging roof to let her listen to the water pounding on the shingles overhead. I pushed her a couple of feet forward to where she could reach her hand out to catch some raindrops in her palm, and then retreated to our dry shelter to explore the droplets on her hand. Shaynna rubbed her hands together and sampled the wetness with her tongue. She wriggled and giggled in delight. I started to sing her favorite song, "It's raining, it's pouring," waiting for Shaynna to finish the verse.

"Shaynna is snoring," she chimed in right on cue.

We made another foray out from under the protective roof and stayed in the rain long enough for Shaynna's head to get wet. She was ecstatic. "Uh oh, don't let the rain come down," she started to chant. "My roof's got a hole in it and I might drown." Thus dampened, we were ready to plunge in, but not with the wheelchair keeping Shaynna's feet a dry six inches above the soggy ground. I unbuckled my student's seatbelt, pulled her up to standing and marched her on foot into the deluge.

The concept of "puddle" was first on my agenda. So many children's storybooks are full of references to puddles, and Shaynna was familiar with the word. She could even spell it. However, the word puddle was hollow language for her, with no visual image or actual experience to give it meaning. That's the hardest thing about growing up blind. It's impossible to pick up on casually presented information. Sighted students can understand a concept at first glance when they are presented with a picture.

They can grasp the complicated meaning of tornado, dinosaur, shooting star or castle without leaving the room. Even everyday concepts such as puppy, birthday card, mailman, or train, the images that fill the colorful pages of preschool books, are meaningless word sounds unless they are accompanied by hands-on experience for a blind child. Where a sighted child could accurately grasp twenty new concepts from a book in a single sitting in the classroom, a child like Shaynna has to have multiple field trips to physically touch the object and interact with it from as many perspectives as possible. And, with all that, they still might not get it.

I was determined that Shaynna would have a thorough first-hand comprehension of the concept of puddle by the end of our lesson. As we headed towards the street, we came to a lovely little body of rainwater in the middle of the sidewalk—the sort of thing we would usually circumnavigate fastidiously with the wheelchair to avoid getting Shaynna splashed or muddy. I stopped her by the puddle's edge and stomped my foot in the water so she could hear the satisfying splash. Shaynna stomped her foot, once tentatively, and again with more conviction. Then she went at it with both wobbly little feet, gleefully yelling, "My shoes are getting all squishy and my toes are all wet!"

The two of us slopped and splashed our way along the sidewalk until we came to the gutter alongside the street. It was swollen to overflowing with runoff—the perfect place for Shaynna to find out where all the falling rain goes. I sat her down on the sidewalk and let her explore the fast-flowing water with her hands. We picked a spot right next to a drain, so we could hear the water cascading into the culvert deep below the street and feel the power of the waterfall created by the sudden drop. Shaynna plopped her already soaked feet over the curb and into the gutter, letting the cold water swirl up over her ankles. Before I knew it she had maneuvered to lower her entire body into the miniature river in the gutter. People passing by in cars stared at us dumfounded while Shaynna thrashed her uncoordinated legs to splash as much water as she could. I grinned and waved back at the people. When Shaynna began to shiver I packed her into her wheelchair and ran her through the deluge to her home, luckily just two blocks away from the school, and helped her amused mother peel her for a hot bath.

Many of my countless lessons with Shaynna, like our rain experience, were at least somewhat planned ahead of time. I was always willing to modify my mental script at the last minute to take advantage of the weather or some unexpected activity going on, but I did try to maintain some relationship between each lesson and the previous one. Continuity is a big issue in the teaching of students without sight. Every now and then, however, some magnificent possibility that had nothing to do with anything would present itself squarely in our faces.

One of these "have-to-drop-everything-and-go-with-it" opportunities fell out of the sky in the form of a complete stranger, who introduced himself as Bob. Shaynna and I were poking along on a lesson looking for spring flowers in downtown planter boxes, when this somewhat scruffy character walked up and asked me if Shaynna was blind. I wasn't too excited about getting into a conversation with this guy for many reasons; nothing about Shaynna was any of his business, Shaynna and I were busy with our lesson, and I try to model "don't talk to strangers" behavior to my students. Bob, however, dodged the "get-out-of-our-space" glare I aimed at him. He held out a business card and politely informed me that he could see I was busy, but he had invented a bicycle that he thought my student might be able to enjoy riding.

The word "bicycle" cut right through my negativity towards this unknown man. I love bicycles. I have always used one for transportation when it's not absolutely necessary to drive a car, and my idea of a perfect weekend get-away is pedaling a hundred-mile round trip on the back roads between our inland valley and the coast. Bicycles are fun. They are great exercise. They travel at the perfect speed for me to see the hills and valleys and flowers and animals, but fast enough that I can actually get somewhere in a day. Bicycles are the perfect way to have a great time with kids, and I had worked with a number of legally blind students on tandem bikes. I hadn't ever thought of a way to get Shaynna on a bike though; with her cerebral palsy she wouldn't be able to hang onto her perch on the seat behind me, and pedaling would be totally impossible for her.

I realized the man I had meant to get rid of was still talking to me and still holding his card out for me to take. "This isn't an ordinary tandem bike," he was saying. "You can see from this picture how the bike is set up for two people to ride it, but the passenger rides in front, and the pilot rides behind. See how these long handlebars completely wrap around the passenger? I call it the 'Love Bike' since you ride it with your arms around your passenger. It not only accommodates general riders of all ages, but allows people with disabilities to ride safely."

"Give me a break!" I thought. "This is a bit too 'Mendocino County' to take seriously." However, I couldn't manage to completely dismiss Bob and his invention, and began asking questions about how the bike could be adapted for Shaynna. She would never be able to keep her feet on the pedals, but with the pilot's arms close to her for security and her hands firmly gripping the handlebars, she could probably enjoy the chance to go bike riding for the first time in her life. Bob thought about it and came up with the idea of installing motorcycle foot pegs on the frame for her feet, so she would have the stability she would need to keep balanced. Bob and I agreed that he would make the necessary addition to his bike and meet us in town with it for our next lesson.

Two days later Bob was waiting for Shaynna and me near the park, as planned, the "Love Bike" leaning in shiny pink splendor against his battered pick-up. I had prepared Shaynna for what she was going to get to do by pushing her around school on a child-sized bike, and she was excited. I let her touch all of the parts of the "Love Bike" and showed her where she was going to sit before helping her out of her wheelchair. Bob braced the bike while I guided one of Shaynna's braced legs over the center frame and boosted her up onto the seat. It took both Bob and me to help her bend her knees enough to get her feet on the foot pegs, but the position was comfortable for her once she realized where she was supposed to be. I secured her feet to the pegs with Velcro strips I had brought for the occasion. With my already delighted student clamoring to go, I squeezed a helmet over her pigtails and rehearsed the plan with her one final time. "You are going to ride with Bob to the bakery and I am going to drive the car behind you. When you get to the bakery you will have to wait a few minutes for me, and then you can have a treat. Got it?"

"Got it, got it, got it," Shaynna yelled back at me, "I'm going to ride with Bob!"

Bob climbed on behind Shaynna, grabbed the foam-covered handlebars, and pedaled off on a short loop around the small park, as we had agreed. I wanted to make sure Shaynna was enjoying this new form of locomotion, in a place where I could watch her, before letting her go all the way downtown with a man she did not yet know very well. As Shaynna and Bob rounded the last turn and approached me, I was greeted with the delightful sight of Shaynna with her head up, hair blowing out of her borrowed helmet, grinning ear-to-ear. I motioned to Bob to keep going and I dashed for my car.

I followed my student and our new friend closely, but it took me a couple of minutes to find a place to park the car once I got mixed up in the downtown congestion. I sprinted to the bakery, a bit concerned that Shaynna might be distressed by not finding me there immediately. I shouldn't have worried. There, on the crowded sidewalk in front of the bakery, sat Shaynna in contented splendor, still perched on the bike since she was unable to get off. She had a pastry in one hand and Bob was holding her cup of hot chocolate. Around the two of them were gathered half a dozen well-dressed lawyers and business people, out on their morning coffee break, all helping to support the bike, fetch napkins, or call for an ice cube to cool Shaynna's drink. All of them were laughing. Shaynna, between sticky bites, was hollering to herself over and over, as though she needed to repeat it to believe it, "I rode a bike, I rode a bike!"

These adventures with Shaynna were always so much fun for me, and so easy to organize, that I frequently wondered why her parents didn't manage to take her out for much besides doctor appointments. It wouldn't be that huge an effort for them to just go on a little walk around the block on a nice day, or bring Shaynna when they went grocery shopping. I had taught Shaynna to love going to the market—she could ride in the shopping cart, take specific items off the shelves and later hand them to the cashier when our turn came in the checkout line. She enjoyed identifying various fruits and vegetables by touching and smelling them, and she found handing cans or boxes one by one to the cashier to be uproariously funny. However, when Shaynna was not in school she stayed home, mostly indoors, lost in a world of her own amid the noise and confusion of her disorganized family.

Shaynna's mother was solidly supportive of all my efforts to teach her firstborn anything I wanted, but it just had to be on my time, not hers. I spent many frustrating hours in Samantha's home trying to demonstrate certain skills that I wanted her to learn in order to help with Shaynna's development, but finally realized that my efforts were in vain. Samantha said it directly after she knew me for a while, and I was both surprised and moved by her clarity. "I can only manage to keep a couple of things under control on account of my own disabilities," she told me. "I'm really sorry about that, but I have to be realistic and not drive myself over the edge trying to accomplish more than I can handle. Too much stress makes me crazy, and if I get too crazy I can't function at all. I want Shaynna to get all that sensory stuff you keep trying to teach me to do, but you just have to realize that you and the other teachers at school are going to have to do that part yourselves."

I could see Samantha's point. With Shaynna plus a new baby, and a diagnosis of mental retardation on her middle daughter, she already had more issues to deal with than most people could comprehend. Samantha had a plan, though. She explained to me, "My choice is to enroll in the parenting classes offered by the county, because I feel that I can do my best for all three of my daughters that way."

The harshness of my mother's lessons echoed in my head as I faced Samantha in her dilapidated trailer. As a child, I was thoroughly in-doctrinated to look down upon or avoid those less educated or of lower economic status than my own family. My mother had been brought up dirt-poor on a rural farm, the first child of immigrants from Ireland and Wales. In spite of serious abuse at the hands of her parents and lack of support from any outside agency, she had "pulled herself up by the boot-straps" as she frequently reminded me. She had made a success of herself. In a dogged counter-reaction to being kicked out of her poor excuse for a home during the Depression, to make it on her own as a servant in a succession of more fortunate households, my mother became the first member of her family to graduate from high school. She continued to work her way through college, and earned a BA degree after a long and laborious eight years. She was fiercely, vocally and justifiably proud of that accomplishment.

My mother was also terrified that association with those of lesser accomplishment would pull her right back down to the hell of her be-ginnings. Worse yet, she believed that exposure to "low class" habits or "Oakie" English would drag her children down too. She moved us to a home she could barely afford in the suburbs, knowing that well-to-do folk paid high taxes for their schools and would consequently have the best teachers. She stated disapproval of any friends my brother and I made who had "foreign" surnames or divorced parents. She hinted her disdain of Catholics, Jews, Italians and everything they ate or celebrated. She didn't have to say anything negative about blacks or Mexicans, because the suburb she had chosen for us was almost one hundred percent white.

The only people of color we ever saw came on the Greyhound bus from Oakland to do house and yard work for the wealthier residents of our town. In my mother's eyes they didn't even rate a put-down.

Most confusing to me at the time was my mother's essential excommunication of both her and my father's relatives from our little nuclear family. In her crusade to protect her children from bad influences, even blood relations had no free ticket to acceptance. They had to earn approval from my mother, and it was far easier to lose points with her than to win them. These relatives had "trashy" children, "cheap" homes and talked like "hillbillies." My mother was afraid that their habits might wear off on her offspring. Consequently I spent my entire childhood not knowing two aunts, four uncles and twenty first cousins, most of whom lived within a couple of hours of our home.

My mother's final and most profound statement of disapproval of a "low class" lifestyle came when I was divorced, several years before I met Shaynna. My three children and I moved temporarily into a newish two-bedroom mobile home owned by the parents of an acquaintance. I was depressed and struggling to make ends meet, and fearful about being alone and single for the first time in my life. My mother offered her sympathy over the telephone, but she refused my plea to come and stay with me for a couple of weeks. Her stated reason was, "I will not come to see you as long as you're in a mobile home. Let me know when you quit living like an 'Oakie'."

Samantha certainly fit in this unfortunate category so disdained by my mother, and I initially made stereotypical assumptions about her. Samantha tolerated me with an amazing amount of grace, considering that I was a regular intruder into her chaotic home, and that I came with an undisguised mission to change her. She made no attempt to apologize, clean up her house, or otherwise alter her lifestyle for my benefit. Her unspoken statement was that she was good enough as she was. She waited for me to figure it out; to finally get it that I, a stranger in her land, was the one who needed to make some changes.

Samantha knew about grief and she knew about loss. She could sense both in another person, and immediately tuned in to what they couldn't say. Over-reactive and unsure of herself in most of her dealings with the world around her, Samantha became the steady one when somebody near her was hurting. Of all the people who tried to comfort me and say the right things when my mother died, it was Samantha who was the most effectively empathetic. She was immensely compassionate, though she used few words. Her touch went straight to my heart, though she did nothing extravagant. What I felt from Samantha was unconditional caring, something I had never experienced before.

I wish I could have been there for Samantha when things got really bad with Shaynna. When Shaynna was about twelve, her family moved to a neighboring county, and it was decided by Shaynna's entire educational team, including me, that she would benefit from going to the California School for the Blind in Fremont. Initially, it seemed like an exciting possibility for Shaynna to have access to blind classmates and relevant schoolwork in braille, especially since there wasn't a teacher of the visually impaired or a mobility instructor in her new county of residence. We all expected that this would be the opportunity of her lifetime for Shaynna to grow. The School for the Blind had always been the ultimate goal of the entire team of educational professionals who worked with Shaynna, and we were delighted that our dream was about to be realized.

Shaynna's first months in her new school setting seemed promising. Suzanne and I went to observe her on a couple of occasions and we were pleased that she was indeed responding to new academic challenges. Shaynna's highly skilled, legally blind teacher was adept at presenting materials that were meaningful and accessible to Shaynna and her five blind classmates, and we were thrilled to see Shaynna raising her hand in class, waiting until she was called on, and giving correct answers to math problems. We had never been able to achieve anything like this in Shaynna's seven years of education in her home school district. The ever-present problem in public school was that Shaynna was "mainstreamed" with sighted, same age "peers," who were years ahead of her in general knowledge and academic achievement. Shaynna consequently spent hours of every day marooned in the back of the classroom, doing unrelated independent tasks with an aide, or talking to herself and doing nothing at all. We all congratulated ourselves on finally achieving this new placement that had been our long-term dream for Shaynna.

Neither Shaynna's family nor the professionals who worked with her predicted that things would get worse instead of better for Shaynna. Always affected negatively by disorganization in her environment or unexpected changes in her schedule, Shaynna did not adapt well to the necessity of getting bused back and forth between her new, unfamiliar, home and the distant School for the Blind. Every Sunday she would be driven by her father over an hour to meet the bus that would transport her another four hours south. When the school week was over at midday on Friday she would have to do the entire trip in reverse. Every week.

The tantrums that had been a serious problem at home and at her school in Mendocino County became unmanageable on the bus. Shaynna howled, soiled herself and tore her clothes off. Soon it wasn't just the bus ride that set Shaynna off—the mere mention of a family member's name or one of her old friends or teachers would precipitate spasms of persistent screaming. Shaynna mixed events in her mind, combining remembered details from upsetting experiences in her past with emotions, current and past, that she had no words to express. She could not say she was worried, but she could recall a negative memory associated with worry and reenact all of the emotions of that scene. Every stress-filled memory Shaynna dredged up seemed to trigger another one, until she became utterly hysterical. Her fits could last for hours.

Concerned phone consultations were taking place among all of the professionals who were working, or who ever had worked, with Shaynna. Nobody could figure out what to do to help her. Then, out of the blue, we got the shocking news that Shaynna and her sisters had been removed from their home over the weekend and placed in emergency foster care. Over the course of the next six months, the three sisters became wards of the court and were split up to go to separate foster homes. Shaynna was terminated at the School for the Blind, returned to Mendocino county and became my student again in a home schooling program at her foster home.

Though Shaynna no longer traveled back and forth to the School for the Blind, her emotional situation continued to deteriorate. By the end of the year Shaynna was transferred to a residential program in southern California for severely emotionally disturbed children with multiple handicaps. None of us in Mendocino County were allowed any contact with her or her new therapist. It had been decided by the psychiatrists on her case that Shaynna needed to sever all connections with her past in order to defuse her tantrums and avoid her downward-spiraling negative reactions to her traumatic memories.

Cutting Shaynna loose was not easy for me. In that wracked and confused adolescent body was still the goofy spirit of the child who loved the Adventure Lady. And I still loved her. I was convinced that I, more than any other person in the world, had the skills and intimate knowledge of Shaynna's quirks and abilities to be able to communicate successfully with her. How could strangers, even the most well-trained and advanced-degreed of strangers, know enough of Shaynna's experiences to choose the words that would have meaning for her, or to use an ironic turn of phrase at the right moment to sidetrack her with humor as she was boiling towards a tantrum? Shaynna wasn't just any blind child—she was *Shaynna*. Did anybody in her new setting even know that she could read and write braille? Would they care how much the changing seasons meant to her? Was her white cane—the white cane I spent seven years teaching her to use—even packed with her belongings?

I called the new institution repeatedly over the next several weeks, hoping that somebody would want to hear from me—to learn from me. I left messages. Nobody ever called me back.

WHERE DO I FIT IN?

Selena was beautiful and intelligent. She attended middle school in her hometown of Willits. She was blessed with a family who loved her and expected her to participate as much as she was able in chores around the house. Her parents and siblings included her in all of their outings and activities. What wasn't apparent at first glance was the reality that Selena was functionally deaf-blind.

Deaf-blind is a world unto itself. It is not just blind with a hearing impairment or deaf with compromised vision. Even if they have some vision and some hearing, as Selena had, a person with this dual disability does not have an intact "distant" sense to compensate for the other impaired sense. A blind person with good hearing can use it to detect walls, localize traffic, and get a reasonably accurate idea of what is going on around them. They can converse easily with most of the people they have to interact with, understand verbal explanations, and keep up with the fads in popular music. A deaf person with vision can communicate effectively in real time with the use of sign language, and walk or drive around independently by paying extra attention to visual cues in their environment. These adaptations don't work for a person who has neither vision nor hearing. A deaf-blind person experiences an exponential increase in the barriers to achieving an independent and fulfilling life. Deaf-blindness leaves a person walled off from natural communication, intellectually stranded, and socially isolated.

I first met Selena when she was in the seventh grade. She was stylishly and expensively dressed, with every detail perfect, right down to the bangle bracelets and large gold hoop earrings worn by all of her classmates. Selena's glasses, though rather thick, were framed in the latest fashion. Her hearing aids, on the days when she could be coerced into wearing them, were completely hidden behind a hairdo carefully combed and sprayed in place to cover her ears. Even her footwear was a fashion statement—she sported strappy plastic sandals with heels high enough to throw her off balance. I cringed at the shoes, thinking of all the unseen ugly things Selena could unexpectedly encounter with her unprotected toes.

Selena was "mainstreamed" into regular education classes for most of her school day, where she managed a certain amount of seventh grade math, science, English and social studies assignments with the assistance of her one-on-one aide, Mary. The pair was inseparable—Mary never left Selena's side, unless one of them had to use the bathroom. They were never more than three feet apart from the moment Selena was deposited on the sidewalk in front of the school by the yellow Special Education school bus in the morning, to the time at the end of the day when Selena re-boarded the bus to go home. Mary stationed herself a foot in front of Selena's face during classroom lectures and busily signed everything the teacher was saying, whether Selena was paying attention or not. Mary enlarged all reading assignments to print big enough for Selena to see. She patiently read paragraphs out loud into her charge's auditory amplification system, laboriously trying to explain all the words and concepts Selena didn't understand. She led Selena to her next class or to PE, and made sure Selena had the correct books and equipment with her at all times.

Selena, for her part, waited for a cue from Mary before lifting a pencil or making a move, and seemed to have no desire or ability to take even the smallest foray into the world of independent expression. Even though Selena was as bright as most of the students in her classes, she had missed out on so much of the visual and auditory concepts that her classmates had absorbed without even thinking about them, that she had a tremendous deficit in general knowledge. Her class was studying Christopher Columbus' arrival in the New World, but Selena had no idea where (or even what) Europe was, how the Atlantic Ocean connected Europe to North America, or how the Native Americans in the 1400's could have been surprised by the sight of white people with ships and weapons. She did not understand the difference between 1492 and 1992. The words "ship," "ocean," "Indian," and "year" all made some sense to her, but "voyage," "discovery," "foreign," and "century" were not concepts she could grasp. Consequently, the task of reading a chapter in a book, picking out the main points, and putting the information back together in a meaningful paragraph was impossible for Selena to accomplish on her own. Mary had to explain every third word as she read to Selena and basically draft sentences for her, asking "yes" and "no" questions in an attempt to elicit at least some participation from Selena.

I looked for a way to fit into this tight unit of Selena and Mary in some useful manner, and realized with dismay that there was no room for me. Mary was already doing it all, and, to her credit, she was clearly not inclined to sit around doing nothing while I took over assisting in some aspect of Selena's education that she already had covered. I followed Selena and Mary through a school day and scouted out a few areas where I thought some improvements might be possible. Why, I asked Mary, was Selena sitting on the far side of the classroom separated from her classmates by a wall of equipment, instead of being stationed front and center where she could see the teacher and have a better chance of participating spontaneously in at least some of what was going on around her? Mary didn't want to distract the other students with her signing or loud talking to Selena, and the large print books and enlarging machine took up too much room for a normal sized desk. I tried another tack—how about having Selena take on at least some of the responsibility of getting herself and her equipment from class to class? Selena's expensive Closed Circuit TV Magnifier (CCTV) was top-heavy on its rolling cart, and might topple to the ground if Selena failed to see a bump in the sidewalk or didn't manage to push it squarely over the threshold on the way into a classroom. Plus, there were too many students charging around during the passing time between classes for Selena to avoid running into them. One last question—how about encouraging Selena to have her lunch in the cafeteria with peers instead of eating in isolation with Mary in the Special Education classroom? Selena was overwhelmed by the noise and confusion in the cafeteria, and didn't have any friends anyway, so it was easier to continue eating separately. Reading between the lines, I guessed that it was really Mary who wasn't wild about spending thirty minutes each day trying to eat in the pandemonium of the middle school lunchroom, but I couldn't think of a subtle or polite way to challenge her established way of doing things.

I came up with one more suggestion for Selena—to start Orientation and Mobility lessons with me. She lived within easy walking distance of her school, and with some route training and street-crossing skills she would be able to walk there and back with a sibling or classmate. Selena's parents weren't the least bit interested in the idea of their deaf-blind daughter getting out of their sight without the support of school personnel, and Selena already got everyplace she wanted to go with Mary at school and with family members at home. She was terrified at the concept of any level of independence.

I sadly realized that Selena and Mary were perfectly happy in the symbiotic system they had spent years working out, and that they didn't perceive any need to fix any part of it. My tentative interventions were interpreted as interference, and were clearly unwelcome. I thought about it long and hard, and finally took the only option that made sense. I backed off and left my deaf-blind student and her aide to their own resources. Sometimes the best thing I can do as a teacher is simply to wait for somebody to decide that they need what I have to offer.

My ineffectiveness didn't last long. Selena entered high school a little over a year after I met her, and by then Mary was beginning to grow weary of being taken for granted by an increasingly uppity teen-ager. I enlisted the help of my colleague Kim, the teacher of the Deaf, to do a full day of observation of Selena and Mary in their new ninth grade routine. As Selena was walking from her English class to PE, followed by the three of us, she realized that she had forgotten to bring her gym shoes with her. She turned and ordered Mary to go back and fetch them for her. Kim and I exchanged a quick look, stepped as a unit between Selena and Mary, and took over. Kim faced Selena and signed to her that it was her responsibility to get a hall pass from the PE teacher to go back to her locker for the missing shoes, just like any other student would have to do. I stood with a newly receptive Mary and fast-talked her out of her habit-formed inclination to help Selena retrieve the forgotten sneakers. Kim and I then joined forces to show Selena how to get to her locker. I quickly chose a route I thought would be possible for Selena to comprehend and walk independently, while Kim translated my directions in American Sign Language for our charge to follow. A somewhat perplexed Selena accomplished her errand for herself, and returned to the gym, appropriately shod, to finish the period with her class.

Sensing a slight advantage for the first time in my ineffective history with Selena, I pressed her to start Orientation and Mobility lessons with a white cane. Selena had complained periodically that she was helpless in the dark, and mentioned that she would like to be able to go out at night with members of her family without having to hold hands with her sister or mother. She was embarrassed, though, at the idea of practicing at the high school or downtown, where she imagined people she knew would watch her and think she was weird. I suggested, with Kim's help interpreting, that we practice at the elementary school late in the afternoon after all of the students and most of the staff had gone home. During the winter it was dark already by 4:30, so Selena would have some meaning-ful practice at using her cane when she was night-blind. My suggestion was well-received by this young lady who was beginning to like the idea of increasing her level of independence in her almost adult life. For the first time in her school career, Selena made a decision for herself without waiting for Mary to answer for her.

Another great stride forward for Selena in high school was her new interest in having friends and interacting with them without Mary's assistance. Friends were hard to come by, though. Kids who knew Selena from being in class with her would greet her in the hallways, but get dis-couraged when she failed to respond. They thought she was stuck-up and rude. They didn't understand that Selena couldn't see well enough to rec-ognize them as they approached or see them waving to her, and that she couldn't hear well enough to know when they were talking to her. And Selena had no way to approach potential friends and start a conversation that would be mutually interesting.

Kim and I did some brainstorming with Selena, figuring that if she were part of the solution she would be more inclined to participate in whatever program we dreamed up instead of resisting it. The group of us came up with the idea of starting an American Sign Language club at lunchtime. We knew Selena would have an easier time interacting with a small number of students who were sitting still in a quiet room than she would have trying to pick out people to talk with in the noisy cafeteria. We also figured that she could gain some status by doing much of the sign language teaching, since she was fairly proficient at ASL by now. We helped Selena write up flyers and post them around the campus. Half a dozen girls showed up for the first class, and most of them stuck it out for the rest of the school year.

Selena did more with her signing class than just develop some friend-ships with a few girls interested in learning ASL. She started getting ideas. She wanted to learn more about other people who were deaf, and find out where they went to school and what they did for jobs. With Kim's guid-ance on the research, Selena learned about deaf communities, where ev-erybody in a neighborhood, including the shopkeepers and bus drivers, is deaf. She learned about deaf theater groups. She was slowly exposed to the concept of self-advocacy as she took charge of more of the decisions relating to her own life. In her last year of high school Selena informed her parents that she wanted to leave home and go to college.

Santiago and Ana had always expected that Selena would finish high school and live at home with them. Forever. Maybe she could work a few hours a day for some business in downtown Willits, where they would deliver her in the morning and pick her up at the end of her shift, or she might do some light housekeeping for family friends. They had no expectation that Selena would go to college, and the idea of their deaf-blind daughter leaving home to live in another town was out of the question. I, on the other hand, thought the experience of college would be wonderful for Selena. I wanted her to find out who she was away from the limited expectations, lifelong habits and careful supervision of her small community. I wanted her to learn to get around on her own and meet people like her who saw their handicaps as inconveniences rather than disabilities. I wanted Selena to step out and see if she could fly.

I developed a plan that I hoped would provide enough of a safe transition for Selena's family to eventually allow their daughter to realize her new dream. The California School for the Blind in Fremont ran a summer transition program for visually impaired high school students who wanted to go on to lives of employment and independence. I invited Santiago, Ana, and Selena to come with Kim and me to Fremont to check it out. I promised Selena's parents that I would not push my agenda. This would just be a trip to observe and get a more specific idea what the program was all about.

Our day in Fremont was perfect. We watched blind students moving confidently around the campus with their white canes. We observed others getting onto public buses to take classes at the local high school or junior college. We visited the transition program housing, a complex of attractive apartment units where the students managed their own shopping, cooking, cleaning and decorating with the support of trained staff. We ran into a group of students in the community, enjoying a lunch outing they had planned together, and we walked through the technology center where students were trained to use the latest computers and software for their academic and vocational needs. The last piece of the puzzle for Selena was the existence of the California School for the Deaf right next door. She was promised that, should she choose to attend the Transition Program, she would receive all the support she needed in her sign language skills.

Selena was convinced in her first half hour at the School for the Blind that she wanted to start the transition program within minutes of finishing high school. Her parents weren't so sure, but they weren't saying anything negative about what they had spent the day observing. Santiago mentioned to me that he had a cousin in Fremont who he would trust to look out for Selena if she went down there. I knew then that he was going to say "yes" to his daughter's request to leave her rural Mendocino County home.

Selena spent two years at the California School for the Blind. She wanted to pass enough courses at the community college and perfect her ASL skills to be accepted as a transfer student at Gallaudet University, the renowned college for the deaf on the east coast. She achieved her goal, while taking charge of organizing the social activities at the dorm in her spare time. Selena's parents, who never imagined that their daughter would ever be able to exist without them, saw her off on an airplane to her new life three thousand miles away.

I ran into Selena in downtown Ukiah a couple of months ago, walking down the street by herself, using perfect technique with the white cane that she held to its full, proud length in front of her. When I caught up with Selena and greeted her, she hugged me and invited me to join her for coffee. She knew the way to the favorite local bakery, and offered to treat me. She is back from her two-year stint at Gallaudet, and lives independently in a beautifully decorated apartment. She takes the bus to Willits to finish up her coursework at the community college there and visit her parents on weekends when she hasn't other activities planned. She has connected with the small deaf community in Ukiah and recently decided that "deaf pizza night" needs to be organized better. She's taken it on as her project.

THE ELUSIVE DEFINITION OF SUCCESS

All of my colleagues were talking about Karen within days of her birth. Afflicted with Fraser's Syndrome, she was the unwanted daughter of a scared fourteen-year-old immigrant girl who had been raped. Karen entered the world with none of the joy that is supposed to accompany the advent of a new life. The tragedy of her unfortunate beginning was compounded by her horrible facial dysmorphia. Where Karen should have had an upper lip, a palate, a nose and eyes, there was a gaping hole. What, in less extreme cases, would have been a cleft lip or palate, was essentially, in Karen's case, a cleft face. The halves of the embryonic beginnings that should have grown together in the first weeks of gestation didn't. The result was the unformed face, and along with that, no eyes or even eye slits. Compounding the obvious disabilities were major malformations of the pituitary gland, sinuses and GI tract—and certain severe mental retardation. The prognosis was that Karen would die within days, like the vast majority of infants born with her syndrome.

Both Karen and her child mother were placed in foster care before they were even released from the hospital. I screwed up my courage and went immediately to do a home visit, dreading the sight I knew I would encounter. My squeamish nature makes me uncomfortable looking at people who have disfiguring disabilities until I get to know them a bit, and I was afraid I would recoil when I saw Karen's face for the first time. To my relief, I was greeted by the sight of a beautiful young mother in her bed, cradling a tiny bundle completely wrapped in a pink blanket. My heart immediately went out to them both, and by the time the blanket was lifted from Karen's face I had lost enough of my sense of horror to override the gasp that I feared would be audible. What I saw hurt every bone in my body, but I was able to stay calm.

I tried to start a conversation, figuring that any help on my part would be useful, and hoping that my Spanish would be adequate for the situation. I was dead wrong on both counts. Karen's mother had her hands full just trying to manage the complicated tube feeding of her infant, whose blindness was a minor problem compared to the rest of the disaster she was dealing with. My Spanish was good enough for "Hello, how are you?" but I already knew the sad answer to that question, and it seemed mean and foolish to even ask it. I stammered around for a while about good ways to deal with a blind infant, and realized that nothing I had to say was going to be heard or understood, because it didn't matter right now. I left, wishing I hadn't come.

Somehow Karen managed not to die, and she was taken into surgery within a few weeks of her birth. The doctors closed her upper lip with skin borrowed from some other part of her body, and did the first of several operations to create a hard palate for her. They opened her vestigial eye slits to begin forming eye sockets that would eventually be large enough to accommodate artificial eyes. Her nose would have to wait for later. Even with the angry red scars left over from the surgery and her misshapen little flap of a nose confronting me with its central oversized nostril, Karen's face had already undergone a dramatic transformation. It no longer hurt me to look at her, and I could see the beginnings of a child who might one day be kind of cute.

In the present, however, things continued to go wrong. Karen, because of her mal-formed head and undersized Eustachian tubes, was plagued with massive sinus and ear infections. Her poorly educated, overwhelmed, non-English-speaking mother couldn't comprehend the need to regularly administer correct doses of the prescribed antibiotics until the bottle was empty. Constantly sick and feeding poorly, Karen was losing weight and clearly not thriving. The non-stop ear infections were causing her to lose her hearing. None of the visiting agency representatives could control the situation well enough to counteract what they could only define as parental neglect.

The court got involved again, removing Karen from her mother before she was three months old and placing her in another foster home. There, Karen got excellent care from a capable woman with a big heart, who was cheerfully enmeshed in the project of raising a large family of her own. I continued working with Karen in this first year of her life, glad to be able to communicate with her caregiver in English, and excited about the positive and energetic response I was getting to my suggestions about great ways to deal with the raising of a blind, hearing-impaired baby. As her first birthday approached, Karen was in good health more often than not. She was beginning to hold things in her hands, pull herself to sitting, and interact with me and her foster mother in small reciprocal ways. When Karen liked what was happening to her, a huge toothless grin would spread across her misshapen little face. Her favorite place was an adult lap, where she would nuzzle close to be held as tightly as possible.

Just as I was beginning to get excited about the progress I was making with Karen and her foster mother, I was informed that Karen was about to be adopted by a family from out of the county. The transition was handled beautifully by a thoughtful and experienced social worker. I was even allowed an opportunity to meet Karen's new family to demonstrate to them what I had been doing with her, and to discuss the special issues faced by a totally blind, hearing-impaired child. Karen's soon-to-be parents nodded their heads affirmatively at all the correct times, with vacant, non-comprehending expressions on their faces. Without pausing to talk to Karen and touch her gently to let her know something new was about to happen, as I had just explained to them as carefully and thoroughly as I could, they proceeded to snatch her out of my arms and glare at me when the terrified baby began to scream. My heart sank.

Karen stayed gone for ten years, and I didn't think about her much, assuming I'd never see her again. It works better for me that way; to let go as completely as I can when a child moves away, so I don't have to worry about them or grieve over their absence. I accept the reality that somebody else is managing their program and that other people are as capable as I of doing it well. There is no point in hanging on when there is nothing left to hang onto. New students came into my life to fill up the hole left by Karen.

After a decade of hearing nothing about Karen, the rumors started flying again—this time that an eleven-year-old girl with no eyes, from a different county, was going to be placed in foster care in Hopland. I knew instantly that Karen was about to re-appear in my life. Re-appear she did, now almost four feet tall and sporting an attitude. Still with the same flat, messy little face and still with the same delight in a good cuddle, Karen was used to doing exactly as she pleased. Unfortunately, that meant not doing much at all. For some unexplained reason she had never learned to walk or even crawl, and she was still in diapers. Karen's expressive communication was limited to a twisted open-mouthed frown, an ear-to-ear smile, and an incomprehensible gesture with her hand pushing into her neck. When those expressions failed to get the desired response, she resorted to exhibits of behavior, such as banging her head or throwing herself on the ground. There was no formal system of receptive language that Karen understood. There were also few useful documents or records from her past placements that could help our special education team in Mendocino County figure out what had been tried with Karen, what had worked and what had not worked. We had to figure it out for ourselves.

Though officially deaf-blind, it was clear that Karen had at least some hearing, but she made no visible response to people speaking to her. She didn't make noises or babble, let alone utter any words. Karen had no informal gestures or sign language skills either. She steadfastly refused to use her hands to explore objects or anything in her school environment, and all attempts to touch her hands were met with her stiffening up and clenching her hands into her armpits, out of our reach. Teachers' efforts to initiate any interactions with Karen, besides holding her in their laps, were frequently met with huge, open-mouth grimaces, and if that didn't discourage the intervention, Karen would throw herself on the floor and howl.

On top of all this, Karen didn't eat. No solid food ever passed her lips. She lived on a liquid diet of Ensure, which was unceremoniously poured down her throat three times a day. Between feedings Karen was most content to sit alone and unbothered for hours at a time, in one place, with her arms clenched around her knees, rocking quietly to some private rhythm inside her head. Her unstated but unmistakably clear declaration was that she preferred interacting with no things, ever.

There was nothing that *didn't* need to be done with Karen when she hit the Hopland school system. The problem was where to start with a child who had no vision or functional hearing, who had just been uprooted out of the only home she could possibly remember. With no explanation that she could understand, Karen had suddenly landed in a new home full of complete strangers. She was loaded daily onto an unfamiliar bus and trundled through unseen territory to a strange new school. That would have been far too many changes for a child with sight, hearing and language. For Karen, the total and complete lack of communication put an insurmountable wall solidly in front of any attempt on our part to help her with her transition to her new and different life.

All the special education teachers could do was try to help Karen get comfortable in her unfamiliar school setting and give her time to adjust to her new routines before we attempted to intervene directly with our own specialized programs. We established one corner of Karen's classroom as her "home base" space, where she would start and end all activities. We distinguished Karen's corner and made it identifiable to her by putting a loopy throw rug on the floor of her space, with a texture significantly different from the tightly woven wall-to-wall carpet that covered the rest of the room. We put the same toys in the same place every day, attempting to make at least some of the new environment predictable. We cuddled Karen quite a bit, hoping to at least establish some point of pleasant contact with her.

One decision that was made, before any of the multitude of service providers laid a hand on Karen, was to try to consolidate our services so she would have the smallest possible number of new people to get used to. With an orientation and mobility instructor, a teacher of the visually impaired, a teacher of the deaf and hard of hearing, a speech therapist, an occupational therapist, a Regional Center case worker, a Social Services case worker, a consultant from California Deaf-Blind Services, a special education teacher, a regular classroom teacher, a classroom aide or two, the bus driver and her foster mother all involved, Karen was faced with a cast of dozens coming and going on their complex and overlapping schedules. The professionals could barely keep each other straight; in fact, we had to make a "cheat sheet" with all of our names and responsibilities spelled out just so the classroom teacher and Karen's foster mother could keep track of us.

We picked a handful from among our ranks who would do the majority of the "hands-on" services for Karen, and decided that the other players would function as "hands-off" consultants. A smaller number of people working directly with Karen also increased the chances of our managing to provide her with as consistent a program as possible. We would do nothing but confuse her if some people communicated an action to her in one manner while other people did it differently. We were all aware that the planning of Karen's education was going to take as much, if not more, time than we would be spending working directly with her.

It all boiled down to the need to establish some (as yet undefined) simple, consistent, tangible form of communication for this child who had no idea that a word or sign can represent an object or action. The most critical need was to find a way to let Karen know what was about to happen to her; to tell her that she was going to be put on the bus, or that it was time for her lunch drink, or that she was going to be taken outside for recess. Her vehement resistance to going places and doing things was probably a direct result of her fear or dislike of the unknown, so we needed to do everything we possibly could to try to make at least some of her world predictable.

At the suggestion of the consultant from California Deaf-Blind Services, we began using a system known as "object communication" with Karen. Small tangible objects are chosen to represent different activities in a student's daily routine. The student is handed the appropriate object to feel and hold as a symbolic means of communicating that something specific is about to happen. For Karen, who had never seen anything in her life, we couldn't use something as seemingly obvious as a little toy school bus to represent her impending bus ride home. To her, the toy would just feel like a strange little piece of cold hard plastic with some sharp edges and little bits that moved if she fingered them. It would have no relation whatsoever to her experiences on a real school bus. We decided that it would be more relevant to hand Karen a small piece of vinyl that was similar to the upholstery on the bus seat, because she would touch that seat every time she sat on it. The vinyl would also be different from her wooden chair in the classroom or her hard plastic seat on the toilet. Similarly, we found a short length of chain to represent swinging (one of Karen's preferred activities), a plastic cup identical to her drinking cup at home to represent lunchtime, and a small "koosh" toy to indicate playtime in her box of sensory toys. The hope with all of this object communication was that Karen would eventually learn to reach for a familiar object as an expressive means of making a choice or indicating something she wanted to do.

Another means we employed to make Karen's school life as predictable as possible was to try to establish a regular routine for her daily activities. In this way, even if Karen couldn't make sense of the object cue that had just been handed to her, or the words that had been spoken to her, she would have a good idea, on a non-language level, what was going to happen next. She would be used to going to the bathroom as soon as she had finished her lunch drink, or going outside to the bus after rolling on the gym mat. Having her one-on-one sensory time with me right after coming in from swinging at lunch recess would be what she expected if it happened that way every day.

I was always careful to greet Karen verbally and physically every time I approached her, saying hello to her clearly. I always bumped her hand gently with the big watch I wear at work, so she could reach out to touch it to differentiate me from the last person who had been working with her. All of us teachers chose our own specific "name cues," and reminded each other to use them in the agreed-upon ceremony of greeting Karen and saying good-bye to her. Otherwise our comings and goings and changings-off would be utterly mysterious and meaningless to this child who could neither see nor hear people moving towards or away from her.

Karen's first years in the Hopland school system were frustrating and difficult for everybody involved with her. She continued to be plagued with recurring sinus and ear infections. And, even on days that she was sent to school healthy, she would suddenly start gushing unstoppable streams of mucous from her nose. She also suffered frequent attacks of acute gastric distress, of unknown cause, which would leave her doubled up and howling all of a sudden in the middle of a day that had heretofore been going pretty well. Grand mal seizures came and went, hugely and unpredictably, leaving both Karen and her teachers panic-stricken and exhausted. On top of all that, Karen underwent a number of necessary surgeries to continue the repair of her palate, nose and eye sockets. She missed days and weeks of school, and was so uncomfortable on many of the days she did show up, that she was unable to tolerate the activities we had planned for her. The itinerant professionals and classroom teacher struggled to work out an educational program that consistently dealt with all of Karen's needs, but the unfortunate result was that we mostly got nowhere.

The hardest aspect of my profession is occasionally encountering a student with whom I can make only negligible progress, or no progress at all. I'm used to the reality that many of the children on my caseload are so impaired that they take weeks and months to achieve only the slightest gains, but I am trained to tune into the tiniest of steps forward. I observe and document the details that would be unnoticeable in a typically developing child. I make video tapes of some of my students at six-month intervals, just so I can give myself, and their parents, visual proof that they are indeed doing something now that they couldn't do half a year ago (if that is actually the case). The validation that all of our program planning and hard work are worthwhile is critical for all of us. We need to believe that we are making progress so we can find the energy to do our teaching sequences again, and yet again.

Karen was doing worse than making no progress; she appeared to be backsliding. Her initial tentative curiosity about her environment and apparent interest in presenting her hands to the teacher for "co-active" signing diminished as she became more distressed with her physical symptoms. The child who had been willing to learn to walk howled every time she was prompted to stand up. She refused to drink her meals. Even swinging, Karen's favorite activity, ceased to amuse or console her.

Week after week I would show up at my appointed times to work with Karen, only to find her so unwilling/unable to respond to my prompts that she literally had to be dragged out of her chair and pushed into my planned activity. However, physically manhandling a student just proves that I am bigger or stronger than they are, and it certainly doesn't result in any learning on the student's part, unless it teaches them to dislike transitions to new activities even more than they do already. I hated being the cause of a meltdown on Karen's part, when she had previously been content in her chair.

Trying a different tack of engaging Karen where she was instead of trying to get her to move to a new location, I discovered one thing she not only tolerated, but appeared to like; staying seated in her familiar chair and interacting very slowly and gently with a variety of sensory objects. I chose a pleasant object or experience such as a soft brush, a warmed terrycloth towel, or my lotion-laden hands, and gradually worked up to firmly stroking Karen's outer arms, then her inner arms. My goal was to eventually move to her hypersensitive hands. It was necessary to keep all of this movement slow-paced and responsive to Karen's facial expression and posture, remembering that an "interaction" must, by definition, be a reciprocal event. I had to stay acutely conscious of Karen's subtle body language: was she reaching slightly towards me or pulling away, moving her fingers a tiny bit to explore, or closing her hands to protect them from my touch? If I got carried away and moved too fast, Karen would retreat, and I would not be able to coax her out of her defensive shell again. If I was careful, I could sometimes work up to some fairly active and enjoyable play with Karen. But only as long as I allowed her to stay seated and in control of the pace.

Karen's foster mother had managed to teach Karen to walk, but I had to retreat from all of my plans to teach her to carry a white cane to "shoreline" along the school hallways, or even to trail a section of the wall with her hand as she walked with a sighted guide. Karen just wasn't ready for that kind of stimulation, as she was not yet willing or able to use her hands for much exploration, let alone to hold a cane that she would have to "visualize" as an extension of her hand. I had wanted Karen to learn to identify certain meaningful destinations such as her classroom or the cafeteria by feeling for the room number or finding a certain pole in front of the door, but she was too resistant to the hand-over-hand prompting that was necessary to help her locate, explore, and identify the specified landmarks. I realized that her world was far more internal than I had initially understood. Our well-meaning educational program was apparently causing greater instead of lesser fragmentation in Karen's understanding of her strange and isolated world, and inadvertently reducing her ability to like and understand what was going on around her. We were having no luck at all helping Karen connect the conceptual dots, and our efforts were pushing her farther away from us.

The consultant from California Deaf/Blind Services paid another visit, and suggested that the best solution for Karen would be the employment of an "intervener." An intervener is a paraprofessional aide specifically trained in the complex issues of deaf/blindness, who works one-on-one with a student to essentially interpret their life to them, moment by moment, as events occur. The intervener uses whatever combination of sign language, gestures and object cues the student can learn to understand. The wonderful thing about an intervener is that there is a single person providing direct contact with the student throughout the school day. The result is that the deaf/blind child's entire educational program can be modified and presented in a constant and consistent manner—supported, but not interrupted by, all the teachers and specialists. Every aspect of the student's curriculum can be slowed down and made meaningful instead of being passed through without appropriate communication. The down side of using an intervener is that a full-time person has to be hired and trained, which is something most cash-strapped school districts are loath to do unless it is absolutely necessary.

An intervener was officially recommended for Karen by her educational planning team, including myself, and pushed relentlessly by her foster mother, who was just completing the process of adopting Karen. The hiring of the intervener was completed after a year of endless meetings, mediations, threatened lawsuits and large expenditures of district and state funds on lawyers to represent both the school district and Karen's adoptive mother. I sat wearily through some of the long meetings and wondered how much money was being spent on this one little child who would probably never be able to do anything completely independently in her entire life, with or without the services of this yet-to-be-hired intervener.

I firmly believe that everybody is entitled to the best possible education, and that extra effort must be made to support students who cannot achieve success on their own. I define success in special education as a child's learning to participate as independently as possible in all aspects of life: from planning for the future, to making choices about what to do in the present, to assisting on some level with the activities of daily living and recreation that make life meaningful and fun.

Many people with severe mental retardation and other disabilities can live semi-independently with the appropriate support, and that, to me, is success. My sister-in-law, who has Down Syndrome, went through an independent living training program in the mid '70s, where she was taught myriad daily living skills. In that program setting the only curriculum was learning at least some of the skills that were necessary for her to get through her day—from shampooing her hair and fixing her breakfast in the morning, to taking the bus to work, to making a list and shopping for her dinner. She has been out on her own, living sometimes alone and sometimes with a developmentally disabled roommate in a downtown apartment, for the last twenty-five years. She travels to her supported work setting, chooses her friends, plans her dates, manages her own shopping and cooking, and gets where she wants to go in her small town by bus and on foot. She enjoys visits and phone calls from her mother and participates in family celebrations and activities. She receives regular help with the balancing of her checkbook, an elusive skill which makes no sense to her, no matter how often people try to teach her basic math concepts. She gets other help as needed, and is seen several times per week by friendly staff from the local agency that supports adults with disabilities. The level of independence my sister-in-law can maintain is making her far less expensive for the State of California to support than if she were living in a more restrictive group home or a state hospital. And, far more importantly, she is proud of herself and she is happy. That seems to me like a terrific level of success.

For less able people, success might look quite different than it does for my sister-in-law. They might never be able to leave home independently, but at least have some way to make a choice about where they are taken or what they are going to wear on the outing. They might need physical assistance with every bite that goes into their mouth, but they will participate in choosing what will be cooked for dinner or whether the next thing in their mouth will be a piece of salmon or a sip of lemonade. The element of volition, which implies understanding of at least some of the concepts of what happens in one's daily life, is basic to my understanding of success.

I sometimes wonder how much effort should be put into a person who seems to lack volition, this most elemental building block for the achievement of success. When should we professionals decide to do the best we can to love and care for that person, and cut our losses in our efforts to try to teach her the skills of independence? Is there a line between being able to learn and not having the capacity to learn? If so, where is that line and when does it manifest? How much educational effort and funding should be poured into a person who looks like she is never going to be able to make the simplest choices for herself?

As the parent of three children who were identified early in their school careers as being gifted, I have experienced a huge amount of frustration at the system that could only support half a day per week of "enriched" education for them. Why does the school administration, or the State of California, or the government of the United States not understand that it is good for our society to keep these exceptionally bright kids engaged with a surplus of excellent material that is interesting and challenging to them, no matter the cost? So many of these smart students, tomorrow's potential scientists and leaders, get bored and turned off by school. They become troublemakers or dropouts or underachievers, all for the want of enough budgeted dollars to pay for the extra teacher or the great new mentor program or the cutting edge equipment in the science lab. Those dollars (yes, I do know those dollars come from different budget categories) get spent on Karen and children like her. They do not get spent in great enough quantity on my children. More importantly, not enough of those dollars get spent on the scores of intelligent but troubled kids who balance precariously on the fence between staying in school and succumbing to drug addiction, gangs or crime. Not enough of those dollars get spent on prevention of teen pregnancy or on conflict management strategies for kids. The money doesn't get spent on smaller class sizes for middle and high school students.

I often worry about those dollars while I sit in the frequent and lengthy meetings about Karen's program planning. I look around the room at the number of highly paid administrators and lawyers and specialists and find myself wondering what the district is spending that could otherwise be put to use on direct services to students who have the potential to be more productive members of our society. My specialist colleagues and I are taking time away from our other students to attend these meetings. The special education teachers are leaving their entire classes in the hands of substitutes or aides while they are dealing with the complex issues of one student who is not going to make a tremendous amount of progress no matter how much energy is focused on her. Karen is getting it all. I do not want to think she doesn't deserve the best, but, in my mind, the balance is skewed. I cannot look at the issue of what Karen is getting without thinking sadly about what other students are not getting.

I continue to work with Karen. I spent dozens of hours training and supervising her intervener during the half year before our efforts fell apart. I did the best I could, in spite of my reservations, because I could not make the decision that Karen didn't deserve what her new mother won for her. With the steady support of her intervener, Karen made slow progress learning some parts of the routines of daily living in her home, where her educational program was temporarily based. When handed articles of clothing in a prescribed order and oriented correctly, a process initiated by her mother, she learned to put them on with minimal assistance. Karen had regular schedules and routes that she followed every day, a few parts of which she learned to manage with minimal or no physical prompting. She used a basket to carry the ingredients for her blended breakfast from the kitchen counter to the dining room table in the morning, and took everything out of the basket when she got to the table. Sometimes she would drop the basket on the floor or throw the items on the table in a statement of resistance to being required to help with the process, and sometimes she did most of the job without complaining. Every step was prompted, or at least supervised, by the intervener. I doubt that Karen had any real understanding that the items she loaded onto the table had a relationship to what came out of the blender, but I hoped that might be something she could learn one day. In the meantime, Karen was verbally and physically prompted to hold down a switch that activated the blender, and in that way managed to participate as fully as she could in her breakfast preparation.

After half a year of working daily with her intervener, Karen was clearly comfortable with her now-familiar home routine. She was beginning to tentatively reach out to explore in a few of her favorite settings, where she felt most secure. She loved being in the family hot tub, where she stretched out her habitually clenched arms and voluntarily searched with her hands to find the seat she preferred. She was beginning to offer her hands to play interactive tactile games with a familiar adult, sometimes initiating movements or actions and controlling the rhythm of the reciprocal play. She would trail sections of established routes around her home, and she worked up to about a quarter of a mile of sighted guide walking with her intervener along the country road where she lives. Most exciting, Karen was occasionally able to respond to verbal prompts alone without needing an additional physical prompt.

Karen's program was just beginning to expand, to once again include her on a limited, part time basis in a mainstream school setting. I worked to help pave the way for her, which involved hours of "in-servicing" both staff and students in her new fifth grade class about everything that is special, and not so special, about Karen. Karen's non-handicapped peers needed to know ahead of time about her deaf-blindness and her unique communication system of objects and signs, so some of them would have enough skill and understanding to at least try to interact with her. More importantly, Karen's future friends needed to be guided past the obvious differences and made aware of how many ways Karen is just like them. They needed to realize that Karen has likes and dislikes, good moods and bad moods, a house, a family, chores, and lots of other activities in her life. They needed to learn to respect Karen as an autonomous person, rather than view her as an oversized doll; as someone who must be asked, rather than pulled, to play with them. The excitement for me was that twenty-five children in a regular education classroom couldn't wait for Karen's first visit to their school.

Karen did make a few appearances at school, none of which were especially successful. It was a time of tremendous stress for everybody, since disagreements between Karen's mother and school personnel were raging, and the intervener had been let go in the process. Karen's daily routine had been suddenly and radically changed, the cold winter weather was not conducive to her enjoying herself outside at recess with her new schoolmates, and she made it abundantly clear that she didn't like doing sensory activities in the classroom. Karen seemed to have a total negative reaction to being at school, and our hopeful plans to pave the way for her return to public education quietly died.

At the present time Karen is receiving minimal services in a home-based program that really isn't much of a program, because there is so little intervention. By agreement of her educational planning team, she only receives an hour a week of direct service from Suzanne, a speech therapist, and myself, in addition to some consultation from a teacher of the deaf/hard of hearing and an occupational therapist to augment her daily activities with her mother. I am not thrilled with this situation, but I am immensely relieved that Karen is staying far healthier and happier than she was over the past couple of years. And, as her mother puts it, "Karen has a wide circle of friends on account of all the shopping we do in the community. We know everybody."

Those of us who still work with Karen are endeavoring to stay in communication with each other and her mother over her progress and areas of need. I am resigned to this outcome, but still struggling to accept the reality that there are a whole lot of reasons why my ideas for a good program for Karen will never be realized.

RUNNING AROUND AND ACCOMPLISHING NOTHING

It was Tuesday, and I was doing my usual trip to Fort Bragg for a day of coastal students. I jerked to confused consciousness in the middle of Willits …

Oh dang—I just passed the left turn to Justin's school—but wait a minute—where am I going anyway? I can't believe this. I'm driving through downtown Willits, but I don't remember a thing about getting here. This is scary. I must have come all the way up the grade in a stupor, totally absorbed in some fantasy or other. Whoa—I hope I was paying enough attention to be safe. I guess if anything major had happened I would have snapped out of it and focused on my driving, but this whole thing is a bit unnerving—I must have driven at least fifteen miles without noticing any of it. I'd better pay a little more attention to where I'm going.

Come to think of it—where *am* I going? Oh my God—I really can't remember—my mind is utterly blank. I'm not even sure what day it is. Let's see … yesterday must have been Monday, so today is Tuesday, and it's 8:30, so that means it's not a Justin day, and I must have known subconsciously not to take that left turn back there. Tuesday, 8:30—got it. I'm supposed to be going to Fort Bragg, and there is the Hwy 20 turnoff. Quick—turn on the blinker—step on the brakes—light's still red. It would have been embarrassing to find myself halfway to Laytonville before I got this figured out. I'd better pay a little more attention. I sure don't want to drift over a cliff on this road—it could be an awfully long time before I got found and rescued. Maybe turning on the radio will help.

<click>

"…*eighteen bodies were discovered in a shallow…*"

No way—I can't take Amy Goodman at this hour of the morning. I wish they'd move her program back to 4:00 …

<click>

"…*reminding all of you that it's Pledge Week. Volunteers are waiting by the phones to…*"

Yeah yeah yeah—I paid up my membership last week, and if everybody else would just do the same we wouldn't have to listen to all this drivel over and over—what other station can I get on this road?

"... my baby left me standin'
all alone at the blue... "

No way—NOT Country Western. This is really the down side of living in the boondocks—if the public radio station is having its stupid pledge drive, there is NOTHING to listen to ...

<click>

Ah—silence. That's not so bad. Wasn't I going to try to be more present in the moment anyway? Breathe in, breathe out, open my eyes and mind to what is happening NOW. Pay attention, since NOW is the only reality that I'll ever have. I really believe that, but it's so hard to keep that focus, there is so much other stuff going on. Youch, my neck sure hurts. Maybe if I sit like the physical therapist suggested—yeah, that makes me about three inches taller, and I'm supposed to remember to relax my shoulder muscles. Now—that's a bit better—bring my head all the way back to the headrest. Got it. Since I'm paying the therapist all that money, I might as well try to follow some of the suggestions he's made. It's so hard to remember though.

Oh for heaven's sake—with the sun shining on my face I can see a monster chin hair in the rearview mirror. Why don't those stupid things ever show up when I'm in front of the bathroom mirror with the tweezers? It's white too—what an insult. OK, grab it, pinch really hard and pull. Can't go to the next school with this thing sprouting like a tree on my face. Got it. What was I thinking a minute ago? Bother—it didn't take me long to forget that I was practicing being here in the moment—some Buddhist I'd make.

It's really awfully pretty out there, with the maples just beginning to go yellow. Mmmmm ... the air smells good—kind of leafy and still a little damp from that rain yesterday. I love this time of year—there is such a vibrancy about the changing of the seasons. Oooooh ... lovely—watch those bright leaves kicking up in the breeze and dancing and catching the light—they just swirl like they have no weight—and there they all go upwards again. I guess it's going to be windy on the coast. I hope I remembered my Polarfleece—yep, there it is.

Rats—it's going to be too cold to take Amanda to the beach. She really wanted to collect rocks, and I promised her we'd do that today, but maybe she'll be happy searching for acorns instead. That'll work—I'll take her out behind the school where that big oak tree is—she can stomp around and find them with her feet, and we can more or less stay out of the wind. I've got to get her assessment written. Gads—her IEP is in two weeks, so I'd better take a look at how she is doing on her route to the cafeteria. We can do that first. I should have paid better attention to the assessment deadline, but I didn't—I've got to do better next time. I had no idea it was going to get this windy …

Wind … wasn't I trying to pay attention to what's happening out here in this beautiful world as I'm driving through it instead of getting all lost in stewing about what hasn't even happened yet? I can't remember even noticing the view from the top of Seven Mile Hill—I must have driven right past it ten minutes ago. Paul says he always stops up there on his way to Ukiah from the coast—at the turnout where you can see all the way to the ocean—and he actually gets out of his car for five minutes, rain or shine, just to take it all in. He does that every day of the week, and I've just driven right past the turnout without even realizing where I was—how can Paul be that much more aware than I am? He said something pretty profound about how all of us who spend so much time *getting* there can so easily forget all about *being* there. Half my day is spent in this car—getting there, because I have to get there. If I didn't, I'd never manage to do my job. But that's true for Paul too—he drives even more than I do. I should practice *being* there.

Here comes that little day use area by the river. Nobody's behind me—I can turn in. It'll only make me five minutes late for Amanda—It's so beautiful. I'm stopping …

After taking a minute to walk around the car a few times and stretch my body back to consciousness, I miraculously managed to finish the drive to Fort Bragg without getting lost or driving off the road and killing myself. I cruised to a halt in front of the elementary school and dashed in to grab Amanda for the somewhat re-designed lesson I had spent the last part of my drive planning. I walked in to find her, and saw only her clean desk with an empty chair in front of it. No Amanda. Her teacher looked up from his reading group and reminded me that Amanda was at a doctor's appointment—he had told me about that the week before, but I had forgotten to write it down. "Oh well." I thought, "I'll just go to the office and use the time to see how much of her report I can get done."

The little building the county staff used for an office was locked tight when I walked up, with a note on the door to the effect that the secretary was out sick for the day. That wasn't a problem because I was lucky enough to have a key. I dug it out of the bottom of my purse, feeling smug that I actually knew where to find it, and let myself in. A couple of seconds later an unfamiliar alarm started beeping, and I wasn't lucky enough to have any idea how to stop it. The last time I had been in the office by myself the alarm wasn't there, and now a siren was going off, and I had no idea what to do about it. A police car cruised up. It took the remainder of the hour I didn't have with Amanda to get that mess sorted out, so I gave up on doing my paperwork and headed over to the middle school to find Dylan.

The door to Dylan's classroom was locked. I looked in the window and saw a dark, empty space. Not finding my student or any of his classmates on the playground or in the cafeteria, I headed to the office to see if anybody knew what was going on. The whole class was on a field trip that nobody had remembered to tell me about, and they wouldn't be back until the end of the day. So much for my lesson with Dylan.

I decided to kill the hour eating my lunch at the Seal Point overlook while making another attempt to get some writing on Amanda's report done by hand. I wasn't about to make a second effort to get into the booby-trapped office to use the computer. The time went quickly and I started the car to make the hour-long drive down the coast to Point Arena for Rachael. I was looking forward to seeing her, because we had just started integrating her into a preschool class, and I had made a whole pile of suggestions about activities they might try. I wanted to see if any of my ideas had been successful.

I rounded the last curve before the Point Arena elementary school and noticed that there weren't as many cars parked out front as usual. The school also seemed uncharacteristically silent, with no sign of kids on the playground. The main door was open though, so I walked on in to do my usual signing of the visitor log in the office. The secretary was surprised to see me. "Didn't anybody tell you it's an in-service day?" she asked me. "No students today—just teachers."

"No," I squawked. "There is nothing about this on the calendar you gave me at the beginning of the year."

"Oh, it was just added," the nice lady informed me. "Somebody should have told you."

So much for my entire day. I had driven well over a hundred miles and spent a good three hours doing it. Plus wasting the time in Fort Bragg dealing with the stupid alarm and looking for two kids who weren't there. Now I had another fifty miles to endure over one of the worst roads in the county, and it would take me at least an hour and a half to get back to Ukiah. I set out feeling more than a little bit crabby, but my mood began to improve as the road turned away from the ocean and started its steep climb through the coastal mountains. Soon I was surrounded by maple trees glowing brightly yellow in the waning afternoon sunlight. Of all the seasons, fall is my favorite. Maybe that's because fall is the closest to my own stage of life. I feel it as a time of deep excitement—a sustained celebration of all that is beautiful before the Earth hunkers down to survive the discomforts of winter.

I finally crunched into the gravel of my driveway. Bad mood long forgotten, I realized that I had thoroughly enjoyed most of this long and useless day. I showed up where I was supposed to be, when I was supposed to be there, and most of the glitches were not my doing. My final thought, as I prepared to light a cozy fire and start my dinner, was that I'm endlessly grateful to get to spend futile days driving around Mendocino County instead of having to negotiate the madness of the congested Bay Area. Whatever I end up doing on any particular day in this beautiful place, it feels like a gift. I made the right move to come up here.

IT'S ALL ABOUT FRIENDS

Cari is smart. She's cute. She is really Carridwyn, a fairy queen from Celtic mythology, but her name got unofficially shortened long before I met her at the age of two. This now-budding adolescent considers herself to be quite grounded in *this* world, and, in spite of her pixie demeanor, disparages any mention of her fairy origins. She is currently thrilled to be reunited with her old fourth grade friends, plus another girl she remembers from her third grade class, as she launches into the first week of fifth grade. The news that really warms my heart is the fact that this gaggle of bright, able-bodied girls is equally delighted to welcome Cari back into their circle. They are her friends.

Cari is challenged with more physical impairments than most of the kids I work with. She is legally blind and ought to be a braille user, but her arms and hands tremble so uncontrollably from some undiagnosed neurological palsy that she can't keep her fingers on the page with enough steadiness to track a line of braille, let alone recognize a word with the delicate touch that is required to decipher the tiny raised dots. Other vision-related problems are a complete absence of depth perception, extreme light sensitivity, lack of ability to see much of anything farther than five feet away, and vertigo if she looks up. Cari wears molded plastic braces to support her ankles and can independently careen a few unsteady yards through space without physical assistance, but she ordinarily relies on her walker or her wheelchair to get around. One hopeful mobility instructor tried a white cane with her years ago, but Cari lacks the strength and balance to grip it and hold it out in front of her while she walks, and it is impossible for her hold anything when both of her hands are engaged with pushing her walker. On top of all of this, Cari has a moderate hearing impairment, which requires her to wear hearing aids in both ears. Even with the hearing aids she misses much of the conversation going on around her. Cari's combination of disabilities not only prevents her from using the tools and adaptations that would ordinarily be available to a visually impaired student, but it creates a tremendous obstacle to her participation in activities that other people can enjoy as an expected part of their daily routine.

Cari didn't start her educational career with an easy ability to make friends. As a preschooler, she retreated in fright from the noise and commotion created by the other children as they ran and scrambled over each other in the classroom and on the playground. Cari had a couple of favorite familiar places at school that she could find and essentially hide in. She liked the playhouse indoors and the sandbox outside, both of which were small spaces defined by a solid boundary that walled out much of the action, and both of which contained the same toys day after day. Cari's play with the dolls and sandbox toys was solitary and ritualized, and she would become visibly upset if other children tried to interact with her or her toys in any way.

Of course I immediately made an effort to push Cari to expand her tiny world. I had no doubt that she was intelligent, and I knew from her conversation with me that she was aware of objects and processes that she couldn't see. I wanted to show her more of her world and I wanted to introduce her to the excitement of being curious. I was determined to pull her out of her shell.

"Hey, Princess Cari," I addressed her in my musical preschool voice after I had spent a couple of days getting to know her, "I see a swing. Let's go find it so we can go swing swing swing swing."

Cari tightened her grasp on her little shovel and stiffened. I continued to cajole her to get up out of her safe-haven sandbox. "It'll be fun! Let's go one, two, three and jump up like a bunny!" Cari wobbled to her feet with my support, but her eyes stayed focused downward. She clearly didn't want to budge from her spot or engage with me. I took her hand and gently pulled her past her resistance, slowly helping her walk with me over to the swing. I thought she might enjoy gently exploring a part of the playground she had never experienced, or even seen clearly from her sandbox corner. I imagined that sitting on my lap and swinging back and forth a little would be fun for Cari once she got over her apprehensions.

The minute I grasped Cari around her middle to hoist her up she stiffened in fear. As I lifted her to my lap she arched backwards and started whimpering. Fairly certain that I knew what I was doing, I continued my effort to prove to Cari that swinging is fun. Holding her closely didn't help, though—it made the situation worse. I wasn't a familiar person who had earned enough trust to calm her. Singing to her didn't help, and even stopping the swinging didn't solve the problem I had created. Cari was terrified by the swing, and the only solution was to abandon my plan and carry her back to the familiar boundaries of her sandbox. There I put her down in her accustomed corner and left her alone so she could slowly regain control without my interference.

Cari didn't have to tell me again that my do-it-now enthusiasm was completely misguided. For starters, the short walk out to the playground, followed by struggling to her feet and walking from the sandbox to the swing, had completely used up her small reserve of physical strength. Add to that the fact that being lifted up onto the swing, even if it was into what I thought was the comfort of my familiar lap, did not feel at all safe to this child who had no control over her exhausted body and no ability to visually gauge her distance from the ground. She couldn't hang onto the chains with her trembling hands, she couldn't balance herself securely on the moving surface of my lap, and she was lost in space. This activity that I thought would be fun did nothing but assault every one of Cari's impaired senses.

I felt bad that I hadn't been aware enough to predict Cari's reaction and think up a more sensitive approach for my introductory playground lesson with her. I wondered why, after all these years of teaching challenging students, I still felt the pressure to jump into getting the lesson done instead of sitting back for a while until I knew what my student needed. It's always uncomfortable for me to walk into a classroom and look like I'm doing nothing. I'm a specialist, after all, and specialists are supposed to come in and solve problems that none of the school staff have been able to figure out how to manage. We are supposed to know what to do. We are supposed to act. My failed lesson with Cari reminded me that I was going to have to throw away the book and create a program for this child that would look nothing like any orientation and mobility program I had ever imagined. I was going to have to forget about my fears of being scrutinized by others, risk looking useless, and trust my instincts.

The first thing I changed the following day was how we got Cari out to the playground. Realizing that walking, even for a short distance, used up all the strength she needed for playing outside, I suggested pulling her out in a wagon. That was an age-appropriate solution that also could include a peer; all of the preschoolers wanted to be pulled in the wagon. Of course the peers leapt out of the wagon the minute it stopped moving and abandoned Cari to her habitual isolation. So much for that bright idea.

I decided to give up on peer interaction for the present, and re-intro-duce Cari to the swing in slow stages that she could control and learn to enjoy. The first step was simply to pull her in the solitary comfort of the wagon as close as we could get to an unoccupied swing. I gave Cari plenty of time to look at the chains and the seat. She stared down at her crossed legs and clutched the sides of the wagon with hands that she had no inten-tion of using to explore anything unfamiliar. I pushed the swing gently so she could see it in her peripheral vision, rattling the chains slightly to catch her attention. I resisted my teacher impulse to guide Cari's hand to the swing, and resolutely reminded myself to let her decide for herself when she wanted to engage with me and imitate my action. Cari hun-kered in the wagon with her head down and moved her arms to clench them tightly across her chest. The preschool teacher watched us from the other side of the playground.

I absolutely know that learning happens for blind children when they are allowed to act out of their own volition and are permitted to directly experience the result of that action for themselves. They cannot learn if I jump in and physically motor them through an activity, essentially do-ing their playing for them. Nor can they learn if I overload them with too much sensory stimulation and make the experience overwhelming or, worse yet, frightening or aversive. I am also a teacher. I am paid to guide my students through the correct sequence of developmental milestones so they can achieve their maximum potential, and I am usually really good at determining what they need to do next on their own personal journey towards that end. These two realities can be completely incom-patible when a student refuses to follow my lead and reach out. It can be incredibly frustrating to me.

I glanced again at the staring preschool teacher and I looked at Cari sitting in the wagon trying her darndest to avoid any interaction with either me or the swing. She wasn't happy and neither was I, but I knew that giving up on this lesson was only going to please one of us. Quitting in defeat didn't feel like a satisfactory outcome to me. I realized that the bottom line here was the issue of trust—Cari's trust of me. Without be-ing absolutely sure that I wouldn't ever put her in real danger, Cari was never going to allow me to lead her out of her narrow zone of comfort. She needed to believe in me enough to let me talk her into trying new things that were scary to her. My "win/win" solution for the moment was to ask Cari to use her words to tell me "I don't want to touch the swing." Rather than simply getting her way by shutting down to avoid the activity, making her needs known verbally would teach Cari to be assertive about her limits. I hoped that my honoring her verbal request would set the stage for her eventual trust of me.

Instead of swinging our way through the first weeks of preschool and learning how to play with the other children as I had eagerly envisioned, Cari and I practiced our new "Tell me what you want" form of interaction. I repeatedly showed her the swing and asked her if she would like to touch it. She repeatedly said no. I spent a lot of time taking her back to her favorite corner in the sandbox and interacting with her there. In the safety of her preferred surroundings, Cari gradually warmed to me and allowed me to show her how to dig holes and fill buckets with sand. Sensing some progress, I started swinging Cari gently in my arms when I held her. She liked being held, and tolerated the swinging motion when I told her I was going to do it. She learned to tell me "More swinging" or "Stop swinging." We counted how many swings she wanted. I prayed that my back would hold out.

I finally told Cari I was going to carry her to the playground swing and hold her while we swung back and forth three times. Her body stiffened as I settled the two of us onto the seat with my arm tightly around her, but she didn't protest. I pushed off as gently as I could, we counted the promised three swings, and I paused for Cari to tell me what she wanted. "I would like to go back to the sandbox now," she stated in a voice that was emphatic in spite of its uncontrollable wavering. That was exactly what we did.

I was thrilled. Cari and I had just established the foundation that we would need for all of our future years of stepping out and trying new things. I knew she would let me take her back to the swing the next day, and I was reasonably confident that she would eventually understand the concept of swinging and possibly even enjoy it a little. Far more importantly, I had a new hope that Cari was now ready to allow me to introduce her to other new and unfamiliar experiences, some of which, with a little luck, she might learn to like.

In the weeks it took to establish my own trust with Cari we had not been able to address my pet issue of helping her make friends with her peers. Cari cowered when her classmates approached her, and with good reason—three and four-year-olds in a special education preschool are not especially well socialized. Most of them yelled, grabbed the toys Cari was playing with, ran into her and otherwise invaded her space. Even at the table, where the kids were seated and most of the energy was contained, kids grabbed food, had tantrums and made noise. Cari's whisper-quiet, halting speech was completely ignored by the children, leaving only the adults to socialize with her. We redirected Cari's conversation where we could, repeated her words so the other children could understand what she had just said, and prompted brief conversational exchanges, but we couldn't begin to phase ourselves out. The minute the adults backed off from social facilitation duties, Cari shut down and quit talking.

Once again I had to reassess what I was trying to accomplish with Cari. I was putting so much effort into facilitating her active participation in all aspects of her preschool life, while she desired nothing more than to be left in peace. As I sat back and observed her more carefully, I began to understand with greater clarity that absolutely every movement this child was required to make during the school day was hard work for her. Every simple activity demanded her total mental concentration as well as a tremendous amount of physical energy. Just getting out of a chair was a taxing combined effort of visual attention, motor planning, balance control and physical exertion, which left Cari drained of any ability to carry on a conversation or focus on what another child was trying to show her. I realized that Cari must be on total overload for most of her school day, and was probably exhausted much of the time. I was amazed that she performed as well as she did.

I started paying more attention to how Cari functioned. She had obviously learned a tremendous number of meaningful concepts from her family, judging by her high verbal skills and interest in the parent-related processes that made her mostly home-based, indoor world work. Cari knew more about appointments and phone messages and making shopping lists than most children her age, and she understood schedules, deadlines and the flow of time through past, present and future. She was keenly interested in the details of her family life, and quite competent at one-on-one interactions with people she perceived to be non-threatening. The rest of the world, especially the big, uncontrollable outside world, was alien and menacing to her. Animals, forests, big stores, city streets and amusement parks were all impossible to see, too big to understand and too challenging to get a handle on. Many of these things were also noisy and prone to unexpected movement.

As I thought about it, I began to understand Cari's terror of noise. People with good vision and adequate physical skills can hear a noise, look around to instantly identify its source, and choose to either ignore it or scurry out of the way if necessary. Cari, on the other hand, could not see or hear well enough to figure out what was making the noise or determine if it was coming closer, and she was consequently unable to prevent the natural shot of "fight or flight" adrenaline in her veins. She knew she didn't have the ability to run away, and her instinctive fear, exacerbated by the adrenaline, instantly transformed into panic. I realized that I would always have to be careful to work with Cari in settings that were calm enough not to push her into that panic.

Kindergarten started. As Cari lived in a neighboring county, I was unable to spend enough time with her to have much of an effect on either her or her program. My periodic observations confirmed that Cari was utterly lost in the mainstream kindergarten with all of her busy little classmates running circles around her. She couldn't see them, hear them or physically perform fast enough to be included fully in any of their activities. In a classroom of eighteen students, Cari was sadly and completely isolated. The aide hired to work with her essentially did all of Cari's assignments for her, with the misguided understanding that neatly completed products were more important than allowing Cari to go through the process of trying her own wobbly hand at worksheets and art projects. The aide also did most of Cari's interacting for her by speaking for her and prompting her through every response to the people around her. Children talked to the aide and ignored Cari.

Cari was equally lost during her subsequent couple of years in a pullout classroom for severely handicapped children. There, because of their physical disabilities, the students didn't move around as much as the kindergartners in the regular classroom, but their mental disabilities prevented them from talking fluently or sharing interests with Cari. The curriculum was far below Cari's intellectual ability, and the endless repetition bored her. She was as isolated as she had been in her mainstream kindergarten class, but for a completely different set of reasons.

I regretted that I was not able to be an effective consultant for Cari during her first three years of school. I was an alien and inconsistent voice from a different county, and apparently viewed by school staff with a certain amount of suspicion and resentment. I could not show up often enough to follow up thoroughly on the recommendations I made, and I didn't know the school well enough to be able to identify or build a relationship with the key people who could have had the most positive influence on Cari's program. I made the same recommendations over and over again with few if any noticeable results, and I got tired of trying. I was an outsider who was tolerated with civility, but unwelcome in reality, and I couldn't figure out how to change that. The news that Cari's family was going to move to Ukiah was an unexpected and welcome thrill.

I knew Cari and the Ukiah school system would be a good match. Ukiah Unified School District is committed to "full inclusion" for students in special education. I am the first to complain that many severely handicapped students do not thrive when they are required to spend their entire day doing modified assignments in a regular education classroom, but this concept seemed tailor-made for Cari. She didn't have any behavior problems that would distract other students from their work, and even though she was far behind her peers on the academic front, Cari still had enough interest and ability to make at least some progress in reading, writing, math, social studies and science. Plus, there were the PE classes, art and music activities, lunch and recess times and field trips that could all be designed to be accessible and fun for Cari. With my colleague Suzanne signed on to provide competent and creative classroom support for Cari's visual needs, I gave myself the green light to design whatever I wanted for a white cane-less mobility program.

Remembering back to my preschool days with Cari, with her significant issues of fear of the unknown and physical overload, I decided to concentrate first on a low-key program of exposure to interesting concepts and events in town and at school. I wasn't especially concerned about teaching Cari any true mobility skills, since it didn't look like independent travel in the community would ever be a possibility for her. I felt that her quality of life would be improved the most by achieving a better understanding of all those too-far-away-to-see phenomena that were going on around her on a daily basis. I also wanted to slowly introduce peers into all of my activities with Cari and teach them things they could do with her on days when I wasn't there to facilitate their interaction.

We started with weekly after-school walks downtown, just the two of us. I walked—and pushed. Cari rode in her wheelchair, which she related to as a portable sandbox-like comfort zone, harkening back to her pre-school years. I liked using the wheelchair. I wanted Cari to be as relaxed and unstressed as possible, with a maximum amount of precious energy available to allow her to use her vision and interact with people. We did my errands at the grocery store, farmer's market, post office, bank and bookstore. We did errands for Cari's mother, bought birthday cards for people Cari knew, and stopped for treats at various eateries. As Cari became familiar with major downtown landmarks, I asked her to pick our route or decide where she wanted to go to purchase whatever it was that we needed to buy that day. I gave her choices of errands and encouraged her to problem-solve when things weren't working out as planned.

Cari, always interested in processes, came up with a great solution on a day when we arrived at the bakery right after a huge gang of soccer-uniformed kids had lined up ahead of us. I was explaining to Cari that we might have to give up on the idea of buying a snack because it would be time to go home before we even got served. She looked up at me and carefully articulated in her halting speech, "I have a better idea. How about if we go to the Coffee Critic instead? My dad takes me there, and I think they probably won't have a line." That's just what we did. I didn't care that the walk to the somewhat distant Coffee Critic made us just as late as standing in line at the bakery would have.

We spent most of a year enjoying these after-school adventures. Every day was different, and every season had something new to offer, all of it fun. I loved it. I'm good at planning spontaneous lessons around whatever is happening in the moment, and Cari was a mostly cooperative partici-pant. We played like I remembered playing with my own children when they were tiny and wide-eyed and just beginning to make their first little mother-supported forays into the big world. Cari was making satisfying progress and not only tolerating, but enjoying an expanded world. I came up with another bright idea for a way to guide Cari, through the process of having a good time, into the bigger community of fun and friends.

For the previous four or five years I had organized an event for a whole group of high-functioning students with orthopedic and visual disabilities. We called it the "Walk 'N Roll" celebration, and it was held in the most visible part of Ukiah, the old downtown business district. The primary goal was for these kids to get together, team up with each other and able-bodied friends, and have the time of their lives while attracting a large amount of positive notice. That was important to me, because most children with visible handicaps are looked on with pity by ordinary citizens, if they are seen at all. I wanted the citizens of our town to be surprised in the middle of doing their errands and have a chance to unexpectedly see my students as a bunch of goofy, happy kids. I wanted the shoppers' first reactions to be humor, admiration or even annoyance—anything but pity. In the context of this party, I wanted to give all of my students the opportunity to meet people like themselves, including older students with similar disabilities who could be mentors, as most of them were the only blind or physically impaired pupil in their school. I wanted my students to be loud and silly and proud of themselves as they caroused around town. I wanted them to have something to talk about with each other after the race and a story to tell to their friends at their respective schools the next day. I wanted their families to see them cutting loose and taking some safe chances at exercising their budding social and mobility skills.

The official focus of the "Walk 'N Roll" event was for the teams to race each other to collect a list of specific items at about a dozen stores located along the 4-block route. It was like a glorified treasure hunt with built-in handicaps for all of the participants. All members of each team were required to stay together, and the entire group had to go into each store to use whatever skills they could pool to locate the item they were searching for. Kids who couldn't physically open the door might have enough vision to see the counter, and somebody else might have enough verbal skills to ask a clerk for help. The ambulatory blind kids could help their team move faster by pushing somebody's wheelchair. They all had to cooperate to decide which store to go to next and figure out how to get there. Adults who accompanied the teams were only permitted to act as safety monitors, not consultants.

In the interest of making the event as festive as possible, all of the wheelchairs, walkers and cycles were festooned with large and colorful balloons—four to five per vehicle, all tied to long garden stakes that held them aloft above each student's head. This served the secondary purpose of providing increased visibility as the kids wheeled around town and across streets in their not always safety-conscious packs. I collected as many oddball cycles and mobility contraptions as possible to make our "Walk 'N Roll" event colorful and memorable for participants and spectators alike. I borrowed a huge four-wheeled cycle with two side-by-side seats that an able-bodied person could share with a physically impaired friend. An agency lent us a three-wheeled cycle that could be ridden independently by a student with poor balance, with a basket on the back that could carry a couple of small blind or non-ambulatory children. Another agency lent us half a dozen manual wheelchairs for friends and family members of our students, city council members, and the like to try out for the occasion. I pilfered a variety of wagons from friends and coworkers with small children. Best of all, I brought the "Afterburner" out of storage for the occasion.

The "Afterburner" was a find from a catalogue full of orthopedic equipment. I was looking for something else entirely, when this amazing piece of equipment leapt off the page at me. It was basically a bicycle minus the front wheel and handlebars. In place of the front wheel it had an articulated mounting device designed to clamp onto the rear axle of a manual wheelchair. When the whole thing was assembled, the person in back, on the "Afterburner," could pedal and steer his friend in front, in the wheelchair, by holding the push handles on the back of the wheelchair and turning wherever he wanted to go. I immediately envisioned Cari in the wheelchair with a friend pedaling behind her on this ridiculous contraption. I'm not sure whether it was the name of the thing or the delightful mental picture of it being used by my student that tickled my fancy, but I put in a purchase order that afternoon and was lucky enough to have it approved.

The "Afterburner" arrived and I hastened to borrow Cari's wheelchair and bring it to the office so I could get the mounting hardware installed. That accomplished, it seemed necessary and appropriate to take my new toy out into the parking lot for a test run. Of course it was also critical to involve a few other teachers who happened to be in the office, and pretty soon our hoots and laughter had attracted half of the staff in our office complex to come out to enjoy the show. I knew I had a hit for the upcoming "Walk 'N Roll" party.

My next project was to introduce Cari to her new means of locomotion. I crammed the "Afterburner" into the back of the county car, hauled it to summer school, and dragged it across the campus to Cari's classroom. I mounted the thing to my student's wheelchair while she was busy doing a writing assignment at her seat, feeling clever for remembering exactly which pieces went where. Then I was ready to launch myself on a trial spin around the classroom, to the distraction of the entire class. I wanted Cari to get a look at how her fun new toy worked as I cruised past her. I stopped, started, turned and pedaled backwards, all up close where she could see the show. All of the students got up from their seats and gathered around me, clamoring for a turn—except for Cari. She clutched the wooden arms of her orthopedic chair, hunkered down in that "no way" posture that I recognized so well, and refused to watch.

I did manage to convince Cari to give the "Afterburner" a low-key try at the end of the school day, after taking great pains to show her that nothing had changed about her wheelchair itself. The only difference was that I would be pushing her from a bicycle instead of on foot. I promised that I would go really slowly. Cari cooperated reluctantly and allowed me to assist her into her wheelchair. We squeezed through the door and puttered around the hallways, at what I considered to be a snail's pace, amid a gaggle of fascinated summer school onlookers. After about five short minutes we met Cari's mom in the parking lot. Her face told me what I didn't want to hear. "She looks terrified," Rena said.

In spite of the fact that I should have predicted Cari's reaction, I was bitterly disappointed. I saw the "Afterburner" as the means to some fun new possibilities for this isolated little student of mine. I envisioned her and some schoolmates using it to cruise spectacularly out to PE on what would have otherwise been an uneventful day. I figured kids would be lined up to do the honors of pedaling, and I saw Cari basking in some unaccustomed popularity. Not to mention the fun I imagined she could have at the "Walk 'N Roll" party. Hoping for a miracle, I offered the "Afterburner" to Rena to take home and try to use for family walks around the block, figuring that Cari might learn to accept it attached to the back of her wheelchair in the more comfortable home environment. Rena agreed, but my glorious toy spent the summer sitting unused in their carport. The truth I reluctantly came to accept was that the "Afterburner" was my idea of fun, not Cari's. I needed to give up on this one. Cari came to the "Walk 'N Roll" event in her wheelchair with her parents and a couple of invited schoolmates, and she had a good time participating in all of the activities. The "Afterburner" went into the storage shed at the office to wait for somebody else who might like it.

School was about to start again, and it was time to try a different tack on this ongoing project of helping Cari gain some confidence in her ability to relate to peers in her world. That had to come first, before the goal of making real friends could become a reality. The change occurred naturally, when Cari switched schools for the new year to be in a program that had excellent support for its full-inclusion students.

At Cari's new school I was welcome to design activities both on and off-campus to include selected classmates who were not yet friends of Cari's. The special education resource teacher and Cari's fourth grade classroom teacher were happy to collaborate on the choosing of students who seemed interested in Cari without wanting to treat her like a baby doll. We started with a couple of PE "helpers" who would hang out with Cari and do adapted activities with her. I put quite a bit of energy into designing the activities to be both inclusive and silly enough to hold the interest of the energetic fourth graders. With either a chair to sit in or a helper for balance on each side, and a third student carefully demonstrating directly in front of her, Cari learned to do simplified versions of many of the calisthenics taught in regular PE. I relied heavily and purposefully on the students to come up with their own ideas for how to make the exercises do-able for Cari, and they rose to the occasion with all kinds of creative ideas. The kids and I modified this activity further to create a new version of the "Simon Says" game that Cari could enjoy at recess. We also experimented with slow motion relay races, strange permutations of basketball tossing, Nerf ball golf and balloon batting contests. The all-time favorite was a wheelchair obstacle course race where Cari wheeled herself against friends who were "handicapped" by being required to dribble soccer balls backwards around the cones I set up on the gym floor. Cari's schoolmates liked our raucous games far better than the mainstream PE activities, so we were never without eager volunteers.

On days that we stayed with the entire PE class, I decreed that Cari and her two selected friends would function as one person. With a pre-trained pal on each side for both guidance and support, Cari could more or less play baseball or kickball by trying to kick a large, partly-inflated ball that the pitcher slowly rolled towards her. No matter what happened when Cari's wildly aimed foot connected with the ball, she and her buddies got to "run" all the way around the bases without being tagged out, scoring a point for their team. The PE teacher never quite got used to this blatant disregard for the rules of the game, but players on both teams cheered wildly for this three-headed, six-legged "person" as it/they ran. Kids even started wanting Cari on their team since she was guaranteed to score a point for them. Cari never had a clear idea what she was doing, but she liked the attention and had a mile-wide smile as she staggered around the bases with her pair of sighted guides. Cari didn't realize it, but as a result of all that fun she was learning to trust her peers and tolerate a high level of noise and commotion.

What I liked best was seeing the helpers happily hanging out with Cari during the post-PE recess. The kids never managed to independently dream up their own games to play with Cari, but they remembered the activities I had taught them on pullout days and were untiringly interested in repeating them with her. When the lunch bell rang, Cari and her buddies walked towards the cafeteria in a pack, still chatting and laughing about the games they had just been playing. Cari's experienced and well-trained one-on-one aide smartly backed off to let this kid interaction continue without adult interference.

With Cari's "helper" connections at school beginning to develop into possible friendships, I figured it was time to start inviting some of these kids on after-school lessons with Cari and me. School staff facilitated this idea with permission slips and phone calls to the students' parents, and a small group of delightful boys and girls became part of our weekly afternoon activities that passed for mobility lessons. We started out doing the shopping for a school grant project to choose and buy healthy snacks for the entire classroom, which helped Cari achieve status among her other classroom peers. Being part of the lucky group chosen to go buy the food was quite an honor.

We later expanded to doing a few baking projects at my own house, the most memorable of which was making a large batch of cookies for the entire class. Cari and two friends were belted into the back seat of the county car as we drove to the grocery store, so I decided to make the trip educational by asking them what ingredients they would like to buy to make healthy cookies. Nobody offered an idea, so I asked, "What do you think about raisins?"

"Yuk … raisins are icky!" one of the girls protested loudly.

"Well then, how about sunflower seeds? " I suggested.

The giggly chorus in the back seat responded in unison, "Aaaaaagh … sunflower seeds are bird food! We hate them."

"OK, if you hate the things I come up with, what shall we get that you like?" I asked. "Remember, it's got to be healthy."

"How about broccoli?" Cari piped up without hesitation. The back seat dissolved into peals of crazed giggles. I looked in the rearview mirror and couldn't pick out which of the three silly fourth graders behind me was supposed to be handicapped.

In the years between third and fifth grades, Cari and her mother hosted some successful birthday parties with her school companions. An even greater barometer of social success is that a few of Cari's school friends invited her to their homes for parties and occasional after-school visits. And more wonderful yet, Cari gained a best friend. The teachers and administrators who are responsible for choosing which students will be placed with which teacher for the new school year made a point of keeping Cari and her closest fourth grade friends together for another year, because they liked what they were seeing in all of the girls. However, the adults did not facilitate anybody choosing Cari for their best friend. That happened because Veronica and Cari made their own decision to like each other better than anybody else.

I wanted to do everything I could to keep the friend-related momentum going over the summer between fourth and fifth grades. I was afraid that Cari and her friends would drift apart if they didn't see much of each other and share at least a few fun activities. With this in mind, I planned weekly adventures for a small group of bright visually impaired students from the inland part of Mendocino County. Each of the children was invited to bring friends and family members, and my plan was to give my students plenty of time to thoroughly enjoy activities that ordinarily would not be accessible to them. I also planned the outings to be as engaging as possible for their friends. We went to a farm where we picked raspberries, petted animals and squirted each other with water blasters in the creek. We went horseback riding and found another great creek to soak everybody in. We went bowling and had a build-your-own pizza party and a tour of the pizza parlor. We went to a local museum full of century-old Mendocino County artifacts, and followed that with an ice cream party and a visit to the restaurant kitchen.

Cari came to every outing with a friend or two and one of her parents. She wasn't wild about any of the activities, but with the support of her friends and parents she was able to engage in at least some of what we were doing. Even if she was frightened, she allowed a friend to guide her hand long enough to reach out and pick a couple of berries for herself and pat a horse on the nose. Her friends encouraged her calmly and stayed with her, chatting and picking flowers, when she had had enough. That was a huge change compared to the scared and isolated little girl I had met eight years before, but I was still disappointed that Cari was obviously having a hard time with activities that everybody else was thoroughly enjoying. Her favorite part of each trip was getting back into her parent's familiar car.

Cari baffles me more than I like to admit. I still can't figure out what is and what isn't going to work for her. Her continuing terrors of the outdoors, large interior spaces and noise don't always make sense to me, as they seem to wax and wane in intensity without relating to a rhythm or pattern I can identify. A reasonably calm and predictable activity like shopping in a big store that she has visited dozens of times can cause Cari to clamp down on the armrests of her wheelchair and focus all of her energy on not wanting to be there. The next day she can be positively gung-ho about a far wilder and more taxing activity, like an all-day field trip to the Exploratorium with her class. I predicted she'd hate that trip and shut down in the first half hour, and instead she had a ball for the entire day and yakked tirelessly with her seatmate during the three hour bus ride home.

I try hard to plan lessons and activities that will be fun and engaging for Cari, while at the same time adding to her understanding of how the world works. It's frustrating to get an entire lesson wrong—still. I wonder what it is about myself that makes me incapable of figuring this child out. Do I push her too hard, do I fail to explain what we are gong to do, or do I just plain bore her? I know Cari gets tired—maybe her kind of tired is incomprehensibly different from my kind of tired. I can be utterly exhausted after a long day, but spring to life in an instant if an attractive plan of action suddenly presents itself. Maybe Cari has no energy reserve at all. Maybe I am asking her to interact and process information when she is literally running on empty. But then, there are times when I push her a bit and she suddenly perks up, gets interested, and stays a hundred percent with me for an hour or more. It seems likely that I am never going to figure this girl out, but I am going to continue trying.

After three years of weekly lessons with me in Ukiah, Cari still has extremely limited mobility skills. I don't care. That was never the point. Cari will always be a person who will have a terrible time seeing and hearing and walking. I don't think she will ever be competent to cross a street independently. That's not important to me. What is important is Cari's increasing ability to connect socially and enjoy herself with other people. It probably doesn't matter much whether or not she likes all the activities I try to get her interested in doing, but it does matter that she continue to explore possibilities. We'll keep what works and eventually give up on what doesn't, and we'll do as much of it as we can with friends.

I think social skills are far more important than any amount of math or reading Cari can acquire in school. She will get along in her supported life whether or not she can add correctly, and even if she learns a few more sight words reading will still be an arduous task that will probably bring her little, if any, pleasure. Friends, however, can make a boring day fun or an ordinary activity exciting. Friends bring laughter and conversation and an escape from the repetitive routine of solitary play. Cari is developing a critical ability to like her peers, and that will help her like her life. I see myself continuing to offer my special brand of non-orientation and mobility lessons to Cari, because her inability to learn the skills of independent travel no longer feels like a defeat. I have found an unconventional niche that works for both Cari and me, as well as for her friends. I have promised her mother that I will continue until Cari finishes high school, even if I retire before then.

MY DREAMS COME TRUE

Michael was getting close to the end of kindergarten when I met him. He didn't live in Mendocino County. My co-worker Suzanne and I were somewhat desperately requested to drive east as consultants, to try to make any recommendations we could to piece together a plan for delivery of services to this academically able blind child in a county more rural than our own. That was the first of dozens of trips I have subsequently made along the tourist-infested three hours of Highway 20 between Ukiah and Mike's home.

With the summer influx of tourists comes the inevitable invading swarm of motor homes. Each year, at the end of May, I am suddenly reminded in longing retrospect how much I appreciate the icy wet winters of California's north coast. With the constant wind of incoming storms and so few hours of welcoming daylight, the winter roads are all but deserted. And each year, on the weekend of Memorial Day, the motor homes return en masse to clutter the roadways of our world-renowned vacationland.

The roads are mine during the winter. I may not enjoy driving them all that much in bad weather, but the inconveniences and occasional dangers are caused by nature, not by a huge piece of sheet metal with a gas-guzzling motor and a frightened driver from out of state. Nature in all of her tempers is spectacular, and if I am slowed down or stopped entirely by the weather conditions there is always something going on that is worth watching. I am awed by fog that is too dense to drive through or ice that prevents me from getting to my next student on time. I feel the presence of a power far greater than myself when a section of our precious man-made roadway is dashed into the ocean or covered by a landslide whose movement cannot be controlled by crews of men with bulldozers and dump trucks. I am thrilled when the occasional snow closes the roads and schools, allowing me an extra day to stay home and read by the fire or to go out and play with the happy kids trying to build snowmen in the street.

I am *not* thrilled when I suddenly realize that, for the third or fourth time in a single trip to work with Mike, my view of the mountains or my speed on the drive home is impeded by a sixty-foot-long house on wheels looming up on the road in front of me. There weren't any of these things in my way yesterday, and suddenly today they have shown up in fleets. It seems that these lumbering machines all come back to life when they reach a certain temperature, like hibernating reptiles after the long winter. But, unlike the reptiles whose environment rarely overlaps mine, these metal beasts are in *my* space, on *my* roads, in *my* piece of the world.

I reason with myself to accept the return of the motor homes, because there will not be a day between Memorial Day and sometime in late September when the roads and parking lots are not clogged with them. Then the first rains will come, and one day I will realize that I haven't seen a travel-trailer for weeks. I will then be able to enjoy quiet trips to see my distant student and allow myself time to marvel at the flood-famous Cache Creek as it winds through its majestic canyon, home to bald eagles. I have learned to love the drive, no matter what is happening, because only a quarter of my long day will be spent with Mike. The rest of it will be on the road. I take time to think about my lesson with Mike and decide what to teach him in our precious short hours together. I wonder if this will be the day when he finally finds the courage to use his cane with a blindfold instead of trying to rely on what little is left of his vision.

By the age of six, Mike was almost totally blind as the result of an inoperable brain tumor. His parents were faced with a difficult choice: to either irradiate the tumor, which would probably leave Mike with permanent mental and physical disabilities in addition to his irreversible blindness, or decide against radiation and try to manage the cancer with unpredictable chemotherapy. Given Mike's far above average intelligence, Anna and Patrick made the only choice they could—to go with chemotherapy for as long as possible. Through the years I have known Mike, he has been through five or six different courses of intense drug therapy. All take him out of school for days at a time. Most have nasty side effects—one left his skin hurting so much that he could not bear to be touched for a couple of years afterwards. And, sadly, all but the most recent have quit working after tantalizingly hopeful periods of success.

The medication Mike is currently taking is experimental, and is only licensed for distribution through a prominent university on the east coast. That has made it necessary for Mike to fly across the country with his parents and younger sister every three weeks, for most of the last two years, for treatment or monitoring. The good news is that Mike's tumor has shrunk, and he is currently completely off chemo. His family is looking forward to trying to remember what a normal life of staying home feels like.

What Mike is looking forward to more than anything is being able to walk to school for the first time in his life. He is now eleven years old, and is one of a handful of blind children in the world who use a guide dog. Mike is my success story. Actually, though, to be more accurate, he's truly his own success story. The rest of the credit belongs to his family for their unflagging and constantly creative support of their son's long-term goals and daily problem solving of the many challenges that face him. I've been along for much of the ride, supporting my highly specialized piece of Mike's life, and I wouldn't have missed it for the world. Mike is the kid who has made me work harder and stretch my limits farther than any other blind person I've ever taught, and he is also the student who has made me happiest in my unusual profession.

I was the one who unintentionally planted the seed for this guide dog idea in Mike's head. It began as a field trip six years ago. I always try my hardest to plan great field trips for my far-flung students, knowing that most of them are the only blind kid in their school, and that they are too isolated to be aware of how the rest of the blind world functions. The perfect idea dawned on me to get Mike together with a group of relatively local peers. I teamed him up with a boy close to his age from neighboring Lake County, whose vision was almost as bad as Mike's, plus three older legally blind students from Mendocino County. With the support of Mike's mother and my co-worker Suzanne, I drove them all to the guide dog school in San Rafael.

Guide Dogs for the Blind is incredibly generous with time when it comes to conducting tours for the general public, and they outdid themselves for our group of visually impaired students. We were put under the care of a young blind woman with her beautiful guide dog, the pair of whom shepherded us flawlessly throughout the entire extensive campus. This lovely woman made an extra effort to ensure that Mike was able to touch and explore every aspect of her guide dog and its harness before she gave the dog the "forward" command to commence the tour of the classrooms, dormitories and gardens. Six-year-old Mike asked questions nonstop, far more tuned into the experience than the three high school students in our group.

The highlight of the tour was the visit to the kennels. Litters of rubber-legged, fuzzy-coated puppies bumbled over each other to greet us through the chain link fencing, eagerly sticking out their little wet noses to be patted by my five delighted students. Through it all, Mike wanted to know everything—how long do the puppies stay in the kennels, how old are they when they get trained, who trains them, do all the puppies become guide dogs? Mike was the only student in our group who could see clearly past the immediacy of all the endearing puppy cuteness, and visualize the eventual miracle of a guide dog for himself.

A week after the trip to San Rafael I received a big envelope in the mail. It was a crayon picture drawn by Mike, with an unevenly written sentence under it thanking me for taking him on the trip. He had painstakingly outlined a boxy guide dog with stick legs in dark brown, with every detail of the harness rendered perfectly. Next to the dog, with a hand gripping the harness, Mike had drawn himself. I showed the picture to everybody in the office, happily tacked it on the wall next to my desk, and more or less forgot about it. Mike, I realize now, did not forget anything about that day.

Years rolled by with my driving the six-hour round trip east every four to six weeks to give Mike a white cane lesson. I also squeezed in a half-hour program or talk on some aspect of blindness for Mike's eagerly interested classmates. That isn't exactly the recommended approach to teaching a child the complicated skills of blind navigation, but, given the distance I had to travel to see Mike, it wasn't possible to do the job any other way. Mike, astonishingly, made rapid progress. He learned everything I showed him on the first, or at most, the second try, and spent the time between lessons practicing what I had taught him. His parents encouraged him to use his white cane in the many airports they traveled through on their endless trips to and from the east coast. I never had to teach Mike the same skill twice.

Though Mike's cane technique was almost flawless after a few years of my sporadic teaching and his dutiful practicing, he wasn't able to make the jump to using his cane for safe, independent travel. In familiar locations Mike still tried to use his remaining vision as his primary means of getting information. Even though he couldn't see reliably enough to be safe, he was inclined to ignore the more accurate information coming to him through his cane. He was constantly running into things and stumbling over curbs that he would have found with his cane if he had not been trying so hard to see. An additional, insurmountable problem was that Mike's family lived in a house near a busy arterial street with a 55 mph speed limit and no stop sign within half a mile in either direction. Mike's school and everything he would have enjoyed walking to after school were on the other side of this street. So, even though Mike lived an otherwise easy four blocks from his school, he could never walk there like the rest of the kids in his neighborhood.

Mike's lack of independence frustrated him. His family took him kayaking, bought a four-wheeler that he could ride around a track at their weekend cabin in the woods, put up a safety-fenced trampoline in their garage, installed a swimming pool, introduced him to a climbing wall, and tried dozens of other indoor and outdoor activities. Mike could never go as far or as fast as he wanted to.

Mike's parents were game to try just about anything that would help their son lead an active life full of fun and physical challenges, and when Anna and Patrick heard about the Blind Space Camp in Huntsville, Alabama, they gave Mike the chance to apply. He wrote his own application essay about why he wanted to go, and I happily produced a letter of recommendation for him when he phoned me himself to ask for my support. I knew Mike would have a great time meeting blind students from all over the country, and fervently hoped that he would be accepted.

Sooner than I expected, I got another call from Mike. He was so excited he could barely articulate his torrent of words. "Guess what?" he jumped in before I finished saying hello. Interrupting me as I started to ask if he had heard from Space Camp, he continued, "I got a letter today and I'm accepted and I'm leaving in five weeks and I've decided to do 'Aviation Challenge' instead of 'Outer Space' and they have a real fighter jet with all of the controls and I get to go in it." He paused to gasp air, "And my mom wants to talk with you."

"Hello?" I heard Anna's voice after waiting for Mike to shout for her. "I'll bet you can tell we're pretty excited around here."

"It sounds like it," I responded. "I didn't even get a chance to congratulate Mike, he was talking so fast."

"Thanks so much for the letter you wrote for him. I'm sure it helped a lot. Now there's one more thing I'd like to ask of you. Please say no if you don't want to do it, but Patrick and I just realized that Mike will have a much better time if you go as his chaperone instead of us. He's used to working with you, and I think you would give him the opportunity to be as independent as he can. I'm afraid if Patrick or I go we would hold him back."

All of the reasons to say yes and all of the reasons to say no spun around in my mind. Mike was far too young to make the trip alone, so it was clear that somebody would have to accompany him. But attending any kind of space camp, let alone Blind Space Camp, was about the farthest thing from any conscious desire of mine that I could imagine. My hobbies were mostly outdoor activities on terra firma, and all I knew about space was that stars and planets are different from each other and that the smartest people on Earth still can't completely comprehend black holes. I wondered if it would be possible to get the week off work and worried about whether Mike would really have all that much fun with me. Yet, his mother was right; who could do it better?

"Are you still there?" I heard Anna ask. "Please believe me when I say there is no pressure. I'm sure Mike will have a great time even if you don't go."

"No, I've just decided to go. It sounds like a great idea."

I had no way to prepare myself for an entire week of this unexpected adventure to the muggy August South with more than a hundred fifty unknown blind kids of all ages from half the states in the country. The chaperone information sheet that was sent to me about three days before our departure date stated in bold print that all adults would be on duty 24 hours a day for the entire week, and that we were expected to take our responsibilities seriously. We would eat, sleep and go to classes with our charges. They repeated several times on the page, *"Do not expect this to be a vacation!"* "Vacation" was about the farthest notion from my mind; I was thinking more in terms of "ordeal" or "trial by fire." It had been quite a number of years since I last participated in camping trips with my own offspring, and I was feeling a little too old to anticipate much fun on this one.

The adventure started with a long day of travel for Mike and me. After three hours of driving from Ukiah just to get to the airport, we flew out of San Francisco to change planes in Dallas. Mike and I were frisked and thoroughly searched for the second time in the day by airport security, who were not about to let Mike's white cane go past unexamined. We hurried past the food vendors with barely enough time to make our connection to Huntsville, and went lunchless. Looking morosely out the airplane window (the nice thing about flying with a blind companion was that I didn't have to give him the window seat), I saw cumulus clouds piling up, ever thicker, as we flew into the night darkening around Huntsville. By the time we were in our landing pattern, we were completely surrounded by massive black billows pressing right up to the plane's windows, out of which jumped ferocious zigzags of lightning. We eventually dropped out of the clouds and managed an uneventful landing on the soaking wet Huntsville runway. Through all of this Mike kept busy chattering about all of his fantasies about how wonderful Space Camp was going to be and how much he hoped he would win the "Top Gun" award for flying jet fighters on the simulators he had heard about.

In the terminal we connected with hordes of white cane-toting high school kids and a couple of flight-suited Space Camp representatives, who shepherded the entire noisy gang of us to a waiting bus. We were whisked past a few miles of wet woods and nondescript shopping malls that bordered the highway, and delivered promptly to the US Space and Aviation Center—our home for the coming week. I never saw any other part of Huntsville beyond this military-style fenced compound.

Rampant disorganization greeted us inside the "Habitat," a cavernous metal building that resembled a prison block more closely than anything I'd seen since my last visit to Alcatraz. In the echoing interior, hordes of blind and visually impaired kids and their tired chaperones milled and clattered loudly and aimlessly about, while scrambled dorm assignments were worked out by the hopelessly overwhelmed camp staff. Mike and I were eventually led through the continuing downpour to our dreary digs in an adjacent Quonset hut. Mike was assigned a room where about a dozen rambunctious boys were busily engaged in a pillow fight from the top bunks. He entered cautiously, ill at ease with the high decibel level of the unsupervised commotion. I was guided to an identical, but empty, room next door. My biggest thrill of that endless day was the realization that I was not going to be required to sleep with any of the hyped-up campers.

Every one of the thirty eight metal bunk beds in my room had a sprung, humid mattress sprawled across it, covered with a crackling plastic cover in a nauseating shade of yellowish brown. I chose the least offensive pillow from a pile of damp, plastic-covered lumps, and made the best nest I could in what I hoped would remain a forlorn corner of the hideous room. The chaperone instructions had one thing completely right—this *wasn't* going to be a vacation.

I woke up to my alarm with no clue in my windowless domicile whether it was pouring or sunny, light or dark out in the world. I was good and hungry, having turned my nose up at the previous night's 9:30 p.m. offering of squashed ham sandwiches on white bread, delivered to the tired campers from a garbage can dragged through the "Habitat" by a couple of staff. I picked up my groggy student from his dorm, aware that he was fighting a deepening disappointment that his dream camp was turning out to be a bit of a nightmare. He marched stoic and unspeaking towards breakfast, pushing away the arm I offered to guide him. Not that it was worth the effort it took us to get there—what awaited us was a choice of Fruit Loops or Cocoa Puffs, dry sausage patties, rubber eggs, or white bread French toast in sloppy fake syrup, each item lurking un-embellished in its own throw-away Styrofoam container. I found myself regretting my addiction to fresh, homemade, organic food. I went for the eggs and slipped a couple of extra bananas in my backpack for sustenance during the remainder of the day.

All of the Space Campers and Aviation Challenge participants had the morning free to explore the museum, the space simulation rides, and the outdoor exhibit of out-of-date missiles, shuttles and lunar landers. It was all pretty interesting, even for me, who had never been especially fascinated with the NASA space program or the war machines used by our armed services. Everything was set up for visitors to touch and view from all sides, so Mike was able to make some sense out of what we were looking at. He chickened out, however, on the "Space Shot" ride that he had been dying to do until he realized how high up it went, and wanted more than anything to go straight to the gift shop to plan how he was going to squander the money he had brought with him.

I stumped around for the remainder of the morning with my charge, bored to death after the first hour, until it was time for lunch and our first meeting with Mike's team for the official beginning of the "Aviation Challenge" week. We waited half an hour while incoming campers milled around, and were told to come back an hour later, which we did, only to be shuttled noisily to another location where we waited again for the rest of our young "Mach 1" sub-group to straggle in. I realized, with some regret, that much of this week was going to be spent waiting for blind kids to figure out where they were supposed to be going.

Once things finally got moving, our enthusiastic and reassuringly well-trained college-aged counselors led our group of the nine youngest kids in camp through our initial introduction. There were three students from the Missouri School for the Blind (two of whom were totally blind), three partially sighted kids from another school for the blind somewhere in the South, a couple of cute and goofy pre-adolescent boys (one the sighted brother of a blind camper in a different group) and nine-year-old Mike. They ranged in age from about eight to eleven. Everybody in our little gang was immediately assigned a silly or embarrassing call name to use for duration of camp. Mike hated his, and we agreed never to say it again after camp was over. The entire group chose to call itself the "Thunderbolts."

The first project our energetic Thunderbolts tackled after the naming ceremony was using flight simulators with video screens and controls that most of them could barely see, or not see at all, to practice take-off in virtual Eagle jets. My charges' blindness coupled with my complete incompetence at computer games added up to one sorry mess. Apparently the chaperones were supposed to have been trained on the "SIMs," as the video simulators were affectionately called, some time during the previous day's chaos, but that never happened. So Mike and I "crashed" an untold number of planes on our video screen, and inadvertently blew up a frightening number of hangers, fuel tanks, and other ground structures by driving our simulated plane right through them. Mike and I dogged on and eventually learned that his plane could survive that kind of carnage on the ground, so we just took off in any old direction without my trying to verbally guide him around obstacles he couldn't see on the screen. That was a fairly successful and far less stressful, if not officially sanctioned, technique—at least Mike was able to get his virtual fighter airborne without having to suffer through undue frustration on the runway.

Dinner was far more chaotic than lunch, with all one hundred-eighty space campers and more than sixty adult chaperones crashing around the dining room with white canes and trays. I found that I was far more useful dealing with logistics in the food line than in the SIM lab, and I helped a number of our group move along in line, select their meals, find our table, open their packets of throw-away utensils, administer Ketchup to hamburgers, and finally throw their huge piles of Styrofoam bowls and uneaten food into the garbage. Bedtime came blissfully early for the exhausted campers.

The next morning I got out early, an hour before the hordes of kids were released from their rooms for breakfast, to try to take a walk as an antidote for what I feared would be an entire week of completely sedentary days. I strolled out into a clean, rain-soaked world that was quite lovely except for the fact that I was trapped behind the six foot chain link fence that surrounded the Space Center. I finally found one guarded gate that was open, so I managed a quick circumnavigation of the parking lot before coming back in for breakfast duty. I discovered that I could walk from the dorms to the Aviation Challenge Center half a mile down the road, and beat the bus, since the kids took so long to get loaded up. That little airing became my multiple-times-per-day sanity saver.

We spent the entire morning doing more SIM time, allegedly learning how to land our virtual Eagle jets. That was a joke, with the airport and the details of the runway impossible for anybody in this gang (save the one sighted brother) to see on the little computer screens. The kids concentrated instead on enjoying their fiery crashes. Even those who were totally blind could relish the loudly and accurately simulated sound effects.

Our first scheduled afternoon water survival class ended up coinciding with an approaching thunderstorm, so the kids were blue and chattering with the cold by the time we cut the event short and fished them out of the lake for long, hot showers. After that fiasco it was back to the SIMs to learn how to shoot each other down. All the blamming and blow-ups got the kids revved up higher than kites, and they were impossible during dinner. They were loud. They were jumpy. They were in each other's faces and making food messes left and right. Mike, always incredibly good at following directions and behaving himself, looked miserable. I wondered if he was going to have any fun at all on this adventure he had been anticipating with so much enthusiasm. I started counting the days until we could go home.

I was relieved that the post-dinner activity was to begin Night Patrol. The kids were introduced to scouting maneuvers, which required the whole bunch of them to walk around quietly in the dark, in a line with each kid connected to the kid in front of him by a hand gripping his buddy's shoulder. Even the squirreliest boys were daunted by the imminent need to simmer down and pay attention as the fleeing daylight took most of their vision with it. Mike perked up and excelled, the tension lines gone from his face. The peaceful and cooperative mood prevailed until the campers were all deposited in their dorm.

Another day dawned with the entire camp going to a fascinating IMAX movie on the International Space Station, which I described to Mike who was on one side of me, and to a totally blind teammate on the other side. Amazingly, both boys seemed to enjoy the movie thoroughly in spite of the fact that they could see little or none of it, and they both asked me questions indicating that they had some well-developed concepts of rockets and outer space. I was pleased at the rare opportunity to talk to my blind students throughout a movie—that kind of behavior is impossible in a crowded theater full of sighted people. Here, where nobody could see, I noticed kids in the rows in front of and behind me straining to hear my narrative, rather than giving me dirty looks for disturbing them.

I didn't enjoy the afternoon in the SIM lab. The more sighted kids got greedy and wanted to practice the increasingly difficult "flying" maneuvers without giving up time at the controls to their blind partners. Some of them protested loudly and vehemently when they were told that they had to share the SIMs, and their complaints were rude and hurtful to the blind kids. Our new, young SIM instructor, a substitute for the day, had no idea how to handle the situation, so it fell on us three chaperones to reinforce the rules of the game. This was my first eye-opening to the social hierarchy in the blind school world that is based on the amount of vision a person has. At this Space Camp the more sighted kids found every opportunity to lord it over their blind compatriots, verbally bullying them and ostracizing them from their selective cliques. The "cool" kids with the most vision all sat together in the back of the bus, where the blind kids did not dare to venture. This unfortunate behavior reinforced my doubts about this entire project of trying to teach blind children to learn skills in the SIMs that were, by definition, impossible for them.

We had far more fun with our after-dinner "patrol" in the woods. The kids, partially sighted and blind alike, took it totally seriously once again.

They all got involved in doing up each others' faces in camouflage, using red clay that we dug up from a nearby stream and black charcoal that we helped them chip out of the fire pit. Once we finally helped everybody with their clothes changes and got bathroom stops orchestrated, we set off on a successful walk in the pitch-dark night. All nine of our adrenaline filled kids stayed quiet, worked as a team, and found some "clues" that they thought they could use for the next night's scheduled patrol.

I wished there could have been more of this kind of activity. Most of these blind and visually impaired students are so well-watched in their regular lives that they rarely get dirty, and probably most of them had never been in the woods. Each of them had magnified fears of bugs, snakes, getting wet or getting lost, but when they were all connected hand-to-shoulder and unified by their inability to see in the dark, they found the courage to work together. As a unit that could not exist in the daylight when most of them had some vision, they functioned as equals on their nighttime patrol and loved the experience. I loved the calm when they quit bickering, and enjoyed watching how each individual child dug deep and discovered his or her own strengths. Mike, always quiet and self-contained, worked past his tendency toward aloofness and interacted with his peers as a natural leader during these patrols. His extraordinary abilities to pay attention and remember facts served him well, and he was the guy who always knew what needed to be done. I saw Mike learning to believe in himself, and in the frightening dark I watched the other campers turn towards him.

With the experience of supporting each other as a unit beginning to make some sense to the Aviation Challenge campers, we finally managed an entire day of fun. For the first time in the week, the counselors had the SIM act together (as much as it is humanly possible to get any video act together for people who can't see the monitors), with pre-assigned partners and a stern lecture on the importance of teamwork. Anybody who whined about or put down their partner would be disqualified from the game. The "mission" was an exciting one; one side was to use all of the aviation and navigation skills they had learned so far to try to bomb the buildings and bridges of San Diego, while the other side was charged to defend the city by shooting the attackers down. Amid accidental destruction of team-mates' virtual fighter jets and unplanned kamikaze dives, enough noise and mayhem ensued to keep our group of pre-adolescents delighted. I was amazed that just the sound effects of the shooting and bombing were enough to get the adrenaline running in the veins of these kids. They had no need for the graphic visuals on the computer screens.

This high-energy morning was crowned with the much-awaited opportunity to climb into the cockpit of one of the rain-soaked fighter planes sitting out in the yard surrounding the classroom building. Every camper was allowed to become a fighter pilot for five exhilarating minutes, with real controls that they could touch in a real cockpit. The fact that the defunct old plane full of birds' nests was going nowhere was totally irrelevant to these happy flyers. Mike was in heaven; this was the activity that had made him choose the Aviation Challenge in the first place. I wished it could last longer for him.

Water sports were the focus of the afternoon. First the dunker, which simulated a helicopter crashing into the lake in slow motion, and then rolling over on its side. As the thing filled up with water, the life-jacketed kids all had to swim out the escape hatch and count off as they had been taught, to establish that all were present and accounted for. Everybody was scared to death on the way into the water, but within seconds they all popped up yelling in triumph, hollering over each other that they wanted to do it again.

With everybody soaked, it seemed logical to stay at the lake and commence raft training, since the prognosis for better weather later in the week was poor. Hurricane Isadora was looming, possibly heading towards Huntsville, and the balmy days of the earlier part of the week were not expected to re-appear. So, our fearless leader "FireStarter" proceeded to shepherd nine blind kids off the dock onto a big yellow pontoon raft. Jockeying the four blindest campers into position astride the pontoons took some major doing, since the concept of sitting on anything besides a chair was pretty foreign to most of them. Then paddles were added to the mix, with some of the kids needing hand-over-hand instruction on which end to hold and what to do with the other end. Somehow the whole motley crew started flailing with enough synchronization to achieve some distance from the dock, and they eventually floundered all the way across the small lake. As they were returning, I glanced down to look for something I had dropped, and when I looked up again the entire boat-load was flopping in the lake like a bunch of dying fish. FireStarter had knocked most of them off their precarious perches on the pontoons so they could savor the experience of getting dumped and rescued. The couple of kids who had managed to stay on the raft rose instantly to heroism, and enthusiastically began dragging their drowning companions into the boat. FireStarter's voice, choked with giggles, echoed across the lake as she attempted to admonish one overly enthusiastic young lifesaver, "Once you have rescued your companions you aren't supposed to throw them back into the lake!"

Finally it was time for showers, with a huge amount of time dedicated to re-uniting all of the campers with their respective towels, clothes and shoes. Most of the kids were obviously used to having other people keep track of their possessions and pick up after them. We straggled to the bus, dragging sodden towels and bathing suits, late for a dinner that consisted of leftovers from the previous three days of things that weren't all that appetizing the first time around. That was my own special cross to bear; nobody else seemed to mind what we ate.

We rushed through the meal and decamped immediately back to the Aviation Challenge site for some more Army-style drills. The kids loved to "sound off," yelling their respective numbers one through nine, followed by shouting more or less in unison, "Ma'am, all Thunderbolts present and accounted for, Ma'am!" The movements required for the drills were another story; every kid had a unique idea what "Attention" and "Right face" meant, and "About face" was beyond comprehension for about a third of the line. Our fearless leader announced tactfully that everybody had done great, and we patrolled off to the campground for the scheduled cookout. Not that any of us could figure out why were eating hot dogs, chips and sodas after our complete dinner two hours before—but we weren't running the show.

Midway through the charcoaly hotdogs, the announcement was made that our "E and E" (Escape and Evasion) mission had been changed from its scheduled time tomorrow night to *right now,* on account of the fact that Tropical Storm (downgraded from Hurricane) Isadora was on its way to Huntsville for sure. The weather forecast promised that it would be pouring over the entire area within a few hours. So it was now or never for this much-anticipated mission. For the highlight of the week, *never* was not an option.

We made haste with our excited charges through the bathroom, having figured out that it was wiser to enforce pit stops first. We had learned the hard way that getting everybody all suited up in full camo without an enforced usage of the bathroom beforehand inevitably resulted in making everybody stand around waiting while a couple of campers desperately tried to peel all their gear off to pee.

Amid the hubbub of the older "Mach II" and "Mach III" groups getting suited up, we retrieved our camouflage shirts from the airplane hanger where we had stored them for this occasion, and searched around for Army-style pants that were small enough to stay up around Puffer Fish's and Slippy's skinny little bottoms. Much adult help was required to re-locate and match shoes jettisoned in the disorganized pants try-on, and it was then that we discovered that our eleven-year-old Blusher had shown up for the evening turned out in her stylish, teen-age wanna-be high heeled sandals. There was no hope for her to belly crawl through the woods in that get-up, so a chaperone was dispatched to find a ride back to the dorm and fetch some more sensible footwear for the girl.

Meantime, the kids who had managed to get suited up were guided over to a bench where a couple of counselors were busy with green and brown camo paint—the real stuff as opposed to the mud and charcoal from the night before. Faces were smeared, glasses replaced, and too-large combat helmets buckled on top of the whole works. The campers, regardless of their age, strutted around looking ready to save the world from an imminent attack.

One task remained. We removed ourselves to a nearby grassy slope to conduct a hasty practice in combat crawling, an important detail that had originally been scheduled for the next morning. It was critical now, because none of our blind kids had a clue how to do it. We chaperones were kept busy doing tactile demonstrations of the technique, unsuccessfully trying to convey the concept of carrying the body's weight on forearms and knees with butts down. Most of our dirt-fearing little soldiers were inclined to spider walk on their hands and feet with their rear ends high in the air. We adults had to muffle laughter as we watched the ungainly and decidedly unmilitary show. The gathering clouds and first raindrops abruptly ended our practice, and order was established with a loud whistle and the barked command for the campers to sound off.

Teams of twos or threes were self-selected, and strategies for survival were discussed between partners. Every child was convinced that they were about to embark on a life-or-death mission, with success or failure dependent on their stealth and ability to remain undetected by whatever "enemy" was lurking out there unseen in the dark woods. As prepared as they were ever going to get, our pairs of blind soldiers joined the older kids for a final drill and briefing before marching off under the night-blackened trees in their best approximation of patrol formation. Once in the woods, the kids were helped down into a ravine by counselors stationed there for that purpose. I could read my charges' body English from the back, and what I saw was stark fear. None of them hesitated, though, as they were handed over a narrow, unstable bridge and launched into the ravine on their bellies, alone in the dark, to prevail over the imagined opposing forces for the length of the quarter mile trail to the finish line. Grasshopper bleated out in a wavering voice as he assumed his approximation of the commando-crawling position, "I'm praying for myself and everybody else!"

We three chaperones ran around to meet our little Thunderbolts at the finish line of the dark-shrouded course, all worried that somebody would get lost. We skirted the woods under low, inky clouds with occasional bolts of lightning flashing in the distance. Our group's counselor, Firestarter, suggested that we walk back into the woods from the finish line to find a place to sit and watch the action. We located a fallen tree about a hundred yards in, and perched silently in the darkness to see what would happen.

Sure enough, before long we heard some crashing in the distance. A pair of prostrate bodies bumped into view, passing inches in front of our toes with no awareness of our presence. One boy heard a noise, loudly shushed his teammate, and they both froze as they had been taught to do when threatened. A large male counselor with a flashlight strode over next to one of the still forms and boomed, "I need to see some ID—credit card, driver's license—what have you got?" The young soldiers froze in terror before finally being told that this was a friendly encounter and that they were to proceed to the finish line if they could find it.

It wasn't too long before a pair of short bodies appeared on the trail. I could just make out enough characteristics to identify Mike and his buddy Crusher, somehow far ahead of the dozens of older kids who had crossed the starting line a good quarter hour ahead of them. We could hear the boys whispering to each other in dead earnest, deciding when it would be safe to proceed and reminding each other to stay low. They scrambled, wary and determined, towards the hero's welcome that awaited them at the finish line looming ahead in its blaze of Tiki torches. Amid handshakes and cheers, they happily attributed their survival and unexpectedly early finish to their excellent teamwork. Crusher eloquently and repeatedly informed all who would listen, "I provided the brains and Mike provided the moral support."

"Aw, come on, I did plenty of thinking too!" Mike responded. "I think I deserve some of the credit!"

Our trio of students from the Missouri School for the Blind experienced a similar, if less organized, success, coming in a surprising third and way ahead of the rest of the older students. Skylover, Slippy, and Grasshopper had almost no useable vision among them and no clear concept of what it was that they were supposed to be doing out there in the damp night, but they knew they wanted to do it. They communicated the way all totally blind kids communicate, loudly and frequently. With no vision to inform them where their teammates were, they broadcast at high volume into the unknown. We could hear this unabashed trio halfway back to the starting point, alternately complaining and encouraging each other. They also did what most of the partially sighted soldiers forgot to do in their panic at not being able to see in the night. They used their hearing. They could hear the water in the creek and veer away from it before getting soaked, and they honed in on the commotion at the finish line as their goal. They weren't all that happy about getting cold and muddy on the ground, but they were used to navigating in the dark. When they crawled across the finish line their pride spilled out, still loudly. They were sure they had won the imagined war for their entire Thunderbolt team.

The kids from the other teams of junior high and high school students began straggling in, many of them dejected at having had to be rescued by counselors when they got scared in the dark or couldn't find their way out of the woods. They were honestly amazed to find most of our team of blind little Thunderbolts already safely returned to cheer them in. One of the oldest boys, a swaggering potential gang member who had been reprimanded and threatened with expulsion several times for bullying and putting down our students, came over to shake each of the Thunderbolt's hands. "You guys are awesome," he congratulated them like a proud older brother. "I can't believe you beat all of us. Hey, come on, give me five! How'd you all manage to get past that narrow place without falling in the creek? That's where I got stuck."

Rain began in earnest as we led our exhausted army back past the lake to the staging area. After all that independence, sighted guides were a welcome comfort to the four blindest kids, and for most of the others as well. The entire group accepted adult help peeling off their muddy camo pants and shirts. The piles they left were picked up by the chaperones without complaint this time. The kids were even told to skip showers—at the ridiculously late hour of 1 a.m. cursory face washings would do just fine.

Campers were up and milling around the hallways at the usual hour the next morning, waiting noisily for the walk to breakfast. None looked any the worse for wear after their late night "E and E" maneuvers, though on closer inspection traces of black and green paint were still visible on most of their necks and ears. The breakfast march was a soggy one—it had poured all night and was still raining buckets. Scheduled raft races and shelter-building demonstrations were quickly replaced by a second trip to the IMAX Theater, a free hour on the indoor climbing wall, and some energetic indoor drill practice. After six days of Aviation Camp I was still amazed that this unruly mob was, to a person, completely enamored of the "sound off" drill. Ten times a day they requested permission to do it, and when permission was granted they all came to immediate attention and did it perfectly. These same kids were prone to head off in completely different directions when the group was walking the familiar route to the cafeteria or Habitat. None of them could pay enough attention to stop when somebody yelled to one of them that he was about to run into a wall or fall off a step, but they could all hear and respond immediately to the command to "sound off," even if it was whispered.

I wasn't altogether sorry to awaken to the last day of Aviation Challenge Camp. It had been a long week of being on duty for everything from mediating personality clashes between my charges to locating misplaced swim trunks to helping campers through the cafeteria line three times a day. The food lines got particularly old. I quickly grew weary of being bumped repeatedly by whoever was behind me carrying a tray of syrupy pancakes or sloppy soft drinks. Several of our group needed to be guided to the bathroom after meals to wash their sticky hands—sticky hands that had to grasp my arm for the sighted guide technique. I decided I was suffering from a severe case of "SAS," otherwise known as Sticky Arm Syndrome.

Mike surprised me on the last morning of camp by requesting permission to walk to the bathroom by himself. I told him "Sure," trying to sound casually confident in his ability to accomplish this mission. As soon as he launched himself on his independent journey, however, I jumped up from the table and followed. I hovered in the hallway outside the boys' room until he re-appeared, and watched him hesitate with a worried expression on his face before he made a false start in the wrong direction, corrected, and headed the right way back to the table. I took a shortcut and scampered back to my seat so I'd be there, rock-solid and confident, when he returned.

Mike pulled off the same successful trip to the bathroom after lunch, with me brave enough this time to sit tight and let him go unwatched. Later, at dinner, he hopped up and confidently announced that he would guide Skylover through the tray return line. Next thing I knew Mike was off to the bathroom with Skylover's pizza-smeared hand locked onto his elbow. This successful mission of Mike's didn't have a lot to do with aviation, but to me it sure looked like flying.

In spite of continued light rain and the tornado warnings on the radio, it was decided that the previous day's put-off raft races should take place on this last afternoon. I was delighted to hear it, since the initial raft practice a couple of days before had been such a hit. Unfortunately, I missed the fun on account of being summoned to a chaperone meeting, but I got down to the lake in time to greet the victorious Thunderbolts as they emerged from the hanger where they had showered. There I witnessed a classic blind conundrum. In the doorway one sightless kid was trying to come out, pushing on the door that was jammed half shut by the foot of another camper who was in the way, but trying to move. This second camper, however, was pinned to the ground by the first camper's full weight on the end of his swim towel, which was dragging unnoticed on the ground. There the two boys stood, both unable to move, and both completely unaware of the presence of the other. The situation was spontaneously resolved when a third camper blundered towards the door unaware of the gridlock in front of him, bumping into the second boy on the way out and pushing him off the first boy's towel. Once loosened up, all three proceeded out the door.

The much-anticipated "Top Gun" war game was the last stage of the SIM training. Pairings of adults and campers were worked out ahead of time by the counselors to give the totally blind kids the greatest chance for fun and longevity in the air. We agreed that it was OK to tell the kids which way to move their joystick, but that we couldn't actually move it for anybody. Mike had confided to me after breakfast that he felt he had a good chance of winning the Top Gun award, since he and his partner Crusher had stayed in the air for quite a while the previous day. Mike wasn't fully taking into account the fact that Crusher was one of the more sighted kids of the bunch, and that today's game was going to be played individually rather than with a teammate. I wasn't about to burst Mike's bubble, but wished he could have somebody besides me for support on his SIM.

With my inexpert help, take-off went efficiently, if not exactly by the kosher route. Unable to see the runways and hangers on the screen, Mike kept to the un-veering straight line we had successfully practiced before, blasting colorfully through parked jet fighters and airport infrastructure. He achieved take-off after a spectacular cross-country dash through fields and houses surrounding the airport. I silently admired the exceptionally forgiving nature of this part of the computer program, but dreaded what would come next.

Once Mike became airborne, I placed my forearm along the wildly veering horizon on his computer screen to give him some visual feedback on where level was in his virtual sky, but he didn't find my help particularly useful. He became tense and angrily ignored my attempts to assist him. "Pay attention, Mike," I told him. "When I tell you you need to go up, pull back on your joystick a bit. No ... not that much ... now you're going straight up and you're going to stall. Push the joystick forward a little."

"I hate this. It's a stupid game. I don't see why they make us come in here anyway." I commiserated with Mike's disappointment as the reality sank in that he wouldn't win the coveted award. He thrust the control lever all the way forward and rapidly self-destructed in a loud, final crash. He banged his way out of the SIM and threw his cane on the floor when I tried to hand it to him. He stomped out of the room, trying to hide tears he didn't want me to see. As suddenly as his storm arrived, however, it passed. Mike stopped suddenly, mid-step in the hallway, and announced, to himself as much as to anybody else, "It's only a game. I tried my hardest and now it's over." He immediately perked up and joined the conversation some other kids were having about their previous day's dogfights in the pretend SIM sky. Mike was one of the first to jump up and congratulate the winner of the next round as the happy kid burst triumphantly into the hallway.

Ultimately, Bandit, a student with low vision and Grasshopper, with almost no vision at all, made the final round of competition. Grasshopper had to stand up in the SIM with his one partially functioning eye just a few inches from the screen, to see any of what was happening. It was a long, hard fight between foes of equal skill, despite the fact that one could see much better than the other. Bandit eventually won, but it was Grasshopper who commanded the most respect from the rest of the group. They surged to pound him on the back, shout their praise and exchange multiple high-fives.

After a week that had started with the more sighted campers pressing their advantage over the others, what I saw on the bus after the "Top Gun" competition looked like a bunch of old friends who had just enjoyed a fine adventure. Mike took his usual place next to me up front, thought about it for a second, then jumped up to join the pandemonium in the back of the bus. All of the kids bounced around together, sharing the elite seats that had previously been commandeered by the more sighted lords of the camp. Tales of triumph and disaster on the video screen were told and re-told by all as the bus made its last trip back to the Habitat.

On this final day of camp, the process of becoming friends and equals that had started on the "E and E" mission the night before became complete. Part of me wished there could be another week of camp so Mike could realize some of my hopes for him in both the areas of friendship and self-confidence. I liked seeing my quiet student's assertiveness bloom as he took on difficult, unplanned challenges and succeeded. I was happy to see him deciding for himself what he could realistically do and making a positive choice to let go of what was unachievable. I knew this Space Camp hadn't been as much fun as Mike had anticipated, but he had discovered some things about himself that he wouldn't have found during an easier week. I saw in myself a growing respect for Mike's intelligence, determination and autonomy, and I knew I would be one hundred percent behind him, whatever he wanted to tackle in his future.

The other part of me celebrated the end of the hectic week. I was relieved, upon returning home with Mike, when he announced, "I don't think I'm all that excited about going back to Blind Space Camp next summer. I think I'd like to give it a break for a while, and maybe do it again when I'm older—maybe in high school." Two summers later, what Mike wanted more than anything else in the world was to get a guide dog.

Children do not get guide dogs in the United States. Eighteen is the official minimum age, with an occasional exceptional sixteen-year-old getting accepted at a guide dog school. There is a reason for this. Actually, there are a lot of reasons. Guide dogs need to be constantly trained and disciplined through the careful managing of both corrections and rewards, which is something most guide dog trainers feel children are not capable of doing consistently. Working dogs cannot be played with, which is contrary to what most children want to do. Busy places like schools, where children spend much of their days, are too full of distractions and temptations for a dog. And children do not have the same need for independent mobility that adults have.

Mike didn't especially care about all of the reasons why he shouldn't have a dog. He was driven by a desire to walk to school by himself, and maybe to eventually go downtown or over to a friend's house without an adult by his side. At the age of eleven he felt that he was mature enough to go through any guide dog program in the country and be as responsible as the adults. He hounded his parents and they agreed with him. Anna searched the Internet and finally discovered a guide dog school that was open to working with children. Located in eastern Canada, it had recently begun holding one class a year for students between the ages of eleven and twenty-two. Only three times had they accepted a student younger than fourteen.

Mike's family decided that he could apply to the Canadian guide dog school. In a process identical to what he had gone through to be accepted at the Space Camp a couple of years earlier, he had to write an essay to explain why he wanted a guide dog. Anna and Patrick again requested that I write a letter of recommendation to be included in the package. The guide dog school immediately responded that they were interested in knowing more about Mike, so his family and I hurried to create a video that would accurately demonstrate all aspects of his orientation and mobility skills. The staff at the school wanted to see how straight Mike could walk, how he managed intersections, what kind of terrain he would be traversing at home, how much he used his residual vision, and how he used his hearing for orientation and traffic awareness. We did it all, mailed the tape off to Canada, and got the news back that Mike looked like a promising candidate *if* he could demonstrate competence in a whole list of completely new skills that he would need to work successfully with a dog guide.

There were six months to go before the summer class started, and some serious decisions needed to be made before Mike, his family and I could fully commit to embarking on the project of trying to get him prepared. First was the daunting list of required skills. I read every one of them to Mike over the phone, pausing after each to hear his affirmation that he could do it. "Check," he told me after I explained the first skill. "Check," again after the second. "Check," all the way through the list to the tenth and most difficult. I heard the quiet confidence in my student's voice and remembered how he had learned to believe in himself at Space Camp. Mike knew the guide dog school wouldn't be a game, and he thoroughly understood that it would be the greatest challenge he had ever taken on. He was convinced that he was ready.

"OK, Mike," I told him at the end of our conversation, "if you think you can do it, I know you can do it. We're on!"

Mike's parents already knew what lay ahead for them if I agreed that their son was ready to embark on the training. They made their typical decision to give Mike their unified and total support—changing their job schedules, putting their social lives on hold and finding alternate ways to make sure Mike's younger sister didn't get neglected. Patrick drove or flew Mike to Ukiah once a month in order to double the number of mobility lessons I could give him. Anna took time off work to accompany Mike and me on lessons in their hometown so she could learn a new set of skills each month. She took Mike out to practice those skills after school and on weekends, phoning me if she had questions. I continued to drive the six-hour round trip to work with Mike on a monthly basis.

I had never taught skills at this level of sophistication to an adult, let alone to an eleven-year-old. The bottom line for the guide dog school was that a potential student had to be able to walk straight, locate street corners and stay oriented by using hearing alone, *without a white cane.*

I understood their reasoning, since a person with a guide dog wouldn't have a cane in his hand for tactile feedback, and he would have to have some means of determining if his dog was straying from the intended course. However, I had taught Mike to depend almost entirely on his sense of touch to get around safely.

Mike, up to this point, had been reluctant to walk blindfolded when I suggested doing that as a means of teaching him to pay better attention to his hearing. Eliminating the vision he still depended on was a difficult task both physically and emotionally. Until he became obsessed with the idea of getting a guide dog, Mike didn't see any immediate need to wear an uncomfortable blindfold, struggle with the difficult new skill, and draw extra attention to himself on the streets of his small town. The most he would do was humor me by agreeing to shut his eyes for the last half of an occasional block. Now, with the incentive of a guide dog looming in his immediate future, Mike was all for the idea. He asked his parents to modify a sleepshade so it wouldn't press uncomfortably on his eyes for the long periods of time that he would be wearing it.

We started out using the sighted guide technique so Mike wouldn't be entirely lost in space while under the blindfold, and I set out to teach him to hear the echoes off buildings and the absence of those echoes when we got to intersections. Mike then learned to correlate the time it took him to walk a block with the amount of distance he had traveled, and he became successful at predicting almost exactly when he should be arriving at the next intersection. A more sophisticated extension of the skill of stopping at a corner without feeling it with his cane was learning to tune in to the sound of a car passing somewhere in the distance ahead and estimating exactly how far to keep walking before stopping at the point where that car had been. If his estimate was too short, Mike would stop before he reached the curb. If his estimate was too long, he'd stumble off the curb into the street. Mike learned, after a few lessons with me and some regular practice with his mother, to stop a consistent foot or two short of the curb.

Mike also had to learn to maintain a straight line of travel without using his cane to "shoreline" along the edge of a curb or a building, as he had previously been taught to do. I had to find a long stretch of sidewalk without landscape trees or driveway cuts for this one, so he wouldn't suffer needless crashes or stumbles, and turn him loose entirely on his own. His challenge was to walk forward and maintain an even distance between himself and the parallel traffic, accurately judging his distance from the cars going his way and the different distance from the cars going the opposite way on the other side of the street. Mike took to this challenge like a duck to water, and was walking arrow-straight and caneless by the second lesson.

To make the lessons more challenging for my entirely too capable student, I started guiding him with a piece of PVC pipe fashioned by Patrick to resemble a guide dog harness, as guide dog school staff had instructed us to do. Pretending I was his guide dog, I held one end of the pipe while Mike grasped the handle on the other end. Attracting stares that I was glad Mike couldn't see with his blindfold on, I would lead him straight down the sidewalk for a while, and then try to subtly veer towards or away from the traffic to see if he would notice. He did—every time. He corrected me the second he perceived me changing course by even a few degrees, and then threw in with a firm voice and a sharp tug on the fake harness, "Bad dog!" Every time he did this I looked back, and every time I saw Mike's slow smile spreading across his face.

I couldn't let this eleven-year-old be this good at his new skill without trying to lead him into at least a few mistakes. I started talking to Mike on our "guide dog" lessons, getting him going on any subject that I could think of that might interest him. I figured if he were good and distracted by our conversation, he would eventually forget to pay attention to what he was doing, and I would have at least one chance to say, "Ha … got you!" Mike would be yakking away with me and suddenly interrupt himself with "Bad dog, you're veering left." When the points were totaled between Mike and myself, Mike was the clear winner.

The last challenge for Mike, after learning to travel with a blindfold *on*, was taking his blindfold *off* to use his newly learned auditory skills in conjunction with his residual vision. What he mostly had to do was convince himself to ignore the vision, since the information he was getting auditorily was far more reliable. The guide dog school was adamant that Mike could not move his head around to try to see while he was walking, since that would sabotage his trust in his guide dog. It was difficult for Mike to ignore his vision at first, but he quickly decided for himself that the most effective tactic would be to keep his eyes shut in situations where he was inclined to try to see. As he practiced, it became more natural for him to walk with his eyes open and use his visual awareness of light and motion as secondary information to what he was hearing.

There was nothing left on the list that had seemed so daunting a few short months earlier. Mike was as prepared for getting a guide dog as I was able to help him be, and he departed for Canada with his whole family several weeks after school let out for the summer. We were still not completely sure if Mike would make the cut and be given a dog, but my telephone conversations with the school staff during my part of Mike's training had felt encouraging. There had been no questions about his progress that I couldn't answer successfully, and no doubts raised about any aspects of all the work we had done.

Mike had been gone for a couple of weeks when my telephone rang. It was Mike's voice on the line, contained and too quiet to hear easily, as was typical for him. He told me about the muggy weather in eastern Canada, the brailled card games he had played with a fellow student, the strangeness of hearing people speaking French all day, and the difficulty of fitting in with students who were in high school or older. Just as I was about to despair that something had gone wrong, Mike continued his sentence with sudden animation, "*and* there's a dog in my room—a black and brown Labernese named Sextant!"

Sextant, named after a part of a racing ship, was a cross between a Black Labrador and a Mountain Bernese, bred by the guide dog school for the qualities of health, size, physical appearance, intelligence, and personality. The dog's first step towards bonding with Mike as his new master was to be with him around the clock—working with Mike by day, sleeping in Mike's room by night, and receiving food from Mike alone. Mike's early lessons involved learning to take Sextant out on a regular schedule for elimination, preparing the correct amount of food at the mandated times, and simply learning to love his four-footed companion that he would soon depend on for his own independence.

Mike's remaining weeks in Canada were spent learning the skills he would need to follow Sextant correctly and to command his dog, in French, to go forward, left, right, or about face. They worked together six hours per day in the muggy summer heat, tackling ever more complicated challenges. Being a dog, Sextant did not always perform every task perfectly. It was necessary for Mike to learn to determine when a mistake was made, what that mistake had been, and to command Sextant through the sequence again, and again if necessary, to teach him how to do it right. For success at mastering his dog, Mike needed to develop a new level of assertiveness in both his voice and demeanor, so Sextant would get it that this new boy was indeed in charge now. If Mike were to let his dog get away with sloppy or unsafe work, Sextant could easily get lazy and careless in his maneuvers, which could end up being dangerous for Mike.

Of course Mike did exceptionally well, and he made it through the entire training with flying colors. The next challenge was to survive the long flight home with what was essentially a new member of the family and integrate the dog into their home routine. Anna phoned me shortly after they returned from Canada. She wasn't complaining, but I could hear some stress under the humor in her voice. "This dog has absolutely taken over our lives," she said. "We're all stumbling over him ten times a day, and there's dog hair everywhere. There's dog hair on the floor and dog hair on the furniture and there's even dog hair in our food." She paused. "And Sextant is absolutely gorgeous and we've all fallen in love with him!"

Now that Mike was home with the dog he had worked so hard to get, it was time for him to learn to use Sextant as a guide where it was really going to count—on the walk to school. Sylvia, an instructor from the guide dog school, made the trip to California to stay with Mike's family for the first week of critically important implementation of everything he had learned in Canada. I drove to Mike's hometown to watch the show for two days, and to learn what I would have to know to follow up on Mike's safety and orientation skills with his new guide dog.

Sextant was a beauty. His coat was jet black and shiny with good health, sporting some brown markings on the face and chest. Distinct brown spots hovered over his eyes, which gave him a perpetual interested expression. A tiny white tip on his constantly moving tail flicked around with excitement, or drooped when he was a bad boy. Resting on the rug while out of harness and off duty, Sextant watched every move that Mike made, waiting as he had been trained to do for the signal from his young master to get up and work. All Mike had to do was pick up the harness, rattle it, and hold it at Sextant's head level. The dog jumped up and walked neatly into the waiting harness, standing quietly while Mike fastened the Velcro bindings. When Sextant stood up, I realized how big he was. The trainers had selected one of their largest dogs for Mike, knowing that he would be growing at a rapid rate for the next eight or nine years. They didn't want Mike to get too tall for this dog that should work as a partner with him for at least twelve years.

When I arrived at his house, Mike and Sextant had already been working all morning with Sylvia to learn the route up the hill to the mailbox. I sat with a cup of tea that Anna offered, to decompress from the long drive. As we adults chatted, a neighbor child, a classmate of Mike's, knocked on the door to see if Mike could play. "Hey Mom," Mike yelled from the entryway, "can we take Sextant to get the mail?"

Anna looked at Sylvia and didn't voice the question I knew she wanted to ask. She made the difficult decision herself. "Sure!" she hollered back with confidence I knew she didn't feel. "Just come right back."

The kids, with Sextant leading the way, banged in the door ten minutes later. Mike's friend was big-eyed with excitement. "That was the most wonderful thing I have ever seen!" she told Anna.

With Mike's first solo voyage with his guide dog successfully completed, the next chore was to start on the walk to school. Never having worked in this particular area, Sextant didn't have a clue where he was supposed to be going, and he kept stopping at the top of the steep driveway when Mike gave him the "forward" command, instead of proceeding down the hill. Sylvia quietly coached Mike to shake the harness to indicate to the dog that it was time to buckle down and pay attention. When Sextant finally started moving hesitantly in the right direction, Sylvia instructed Mike to stop, remove the harness, and give the dog a food treat.

Sylvia explained to me that the harness was always removed for treats, since guide dogs are specifically trained to ignore all food while in harness. This would be a slow and cumbersome process the first few trips to school, but Sextant would eventually gain confidence and require fewer rewards, and the trip would get faster. Sylvia even corrected Mike when he brought out a handful of kibble from his pocket and allowed some of the pieces to fall on the ground for Sextant to lick up. She wanted Mike to only hold a few pieces in his hand and feed them to his dog without dropping any, so Sextant would not get the idea that it was okay to eat anything he wanted off the ground. That would be a necessary distinction to maintain in the school cafeteria and in restaurants.

The challenge for Mike and his dog was to walk about half a mile along a busy street with sporadic sections of sidewalk alternating with grass growing right up to the edge of the road. With the white cane, I had taught Mike to hug the edge of the road, "shorelining" along the grass or curb, ignoring the bits of sidewalk altogether since he couldn't tell where they were. Sextant could tell, so he was painstakingly trained and rewarded to step up on the sidewalk every time one began, and to go back into the street when the sidewalk ended. He also needed to be trained to walk closer to the edge of the road than he was naturally inclined to do, and Mike was required to correct him every time he could hear the traffic passing by too close. That first half-mile took almost two hours to put behind us.

Sextant began to work in earnest once we reached the part of the route that had sidewalks. He had been a city dog, and he knew what sidewalks were. He strode half a step ahead of Mike, veering carefully around garbage cans and power poles. He sailed in perfect form past the gas station that had posed some difficulties for Mike with his cane, since there was no line of demarcation between the sidewalk and the pavement surrounding the pumps. Sextant could see the sidewalk, and he stuck to it. He also made short work of a difficult street crossing that Mike had struggled with—a wide one where the painted crosswalk lines had a dogleg in the middle of the street that sent the pedestrians at an angle away from the parallel traffic. Sextant did what he knew how to do. He stopped at the curb with front paws down in the street to tell Mike there was a step down, started forward when Mike gave him the command, ignored the painted lines and made a beeline for the opposite curb, and stopped safely with front paws up on the sidewalk in exactly the right place.

The rest of this first walk to school went almost flawlessly. Mike knew the way, Sylvia confirmed that the route I had taught Mike was indeed the safest one, and Sextant was obviously confident. Anna and I noticed people up and down the street watching Mike, smiling to see him working his beautiful guide dog and calling out to greet him. "This reaction is so different from how people usually treat Mike when they see him coming with his white cane," Anna told me. "They always part like the Red Sea and either stare at or ignore him."

"Yeah, when we're on lessons nobody ever stops to talk with us," I agreed. "Humans seem to be programmed to admire good-looking animals," Anna observed. "When Mike uses the cane, it seems to present more of a barrier to strangers. Look how that lady just saw Sextant and came over to ask Mike about him. That's never happened before. I never thought a guide dog would be such an easy conversation opener. This is really going to change Mike's life."

Anna and I re-focused on Mike's walk to school. The only glitch on the route was a four-way stop sign at a corner with uneven traffic, where Mike had his usual difficulty deciding when to cross. It was up to him, not his dog, to decide when to step out into the traffic, and without cars coming at regular intervals it was hard for Mike to find the "holes" that he was looking for, the times when the cars on the perpendicular street in front of him were stopped. Drivers who noticed Mike waiting to cross would invariably be both polite and legal, and stay stopped to let him cross in front of them. Mike, not hearing any cars moving, could not judge when there was a safe hole in front of him, so he would stand on the corner without moving. Finally, hearing nothing, he would tentatively step out into the street, usually at the same time the driver got tired of waiting and accelerated into the intersection. Then they would both stop, and the whole waiting game would begin all over again. Sylvia solved the whole dilemma by instructing Mike to simply wave the cars on if he wanted to wait. That way he could hear one pass in front of him and step out safely with Sextant in its empty wake.

After an almost three-hour journey, we arrived at the middle school where Mike was about to begin the seventh grade. The principal and staff had been informed that Mike would be showing up with a guide dog, and were somewhat dubious, though mostly in support of the idea. Their biggest concerns had to do with where to seat Mike and his dog in the auditorium for assemblies, how to deal with the noisy chaos in the lunchroom, and what to do with the dog during recess and PE. Sylvia, Anna and I shared those concerns, and we set about trying to problem-solve as many of the potential disasters as possible. We introduced our-selves to a school secretary, who immediately gushed, "Oh, I'll have to get some special treats to keep in my desk for Sextant! Would that be all right?" Well, no, not exactly. Sylvia kindly explained to her that Sextant was to have only his special dog food, given to him by Mike, because anything else could make him sick or disrupt his elimination sched-ule. The secretary graciously said that would not be a problem, and we moved on to assess the auditorium.

Mike and Sextant would have to squeeze into the cramped old auditorium of his school with the other three hundred seventy-five students on the first day, and for all other school assemblies after that. His preference was to walk there with his class, guided by Sextant, as opposed to being led to his seat by an aide. The rows of fixed chairs were squeezed close together along the two narrow aisles without as much as a crack between them. Sylvia scouted out one possible seat on the far side of the back row, where there was an empty spot large enough for Sextant to curl up near the wall in front of a radiator, assuming that the radiator was not on. She had Mike and his dog practice walking to the chosen seat from the hallway, get in and out of it, and orient Sextant so he took up as little of peoples' foot room as possible. Plans would be made later to re-arrange the auditorium seating chart so Mike could sit with his classmates in the back instead of being stuck next unknown students from other grades.

The cafeteria was a bit more of a challenge. The quietest corner was on the far side of the room, but Sylvia was dubious about Sextant having to resist the temptation of food on the floor if he were required to walk across the entire room twice each day. Instead, she found a spot close to the main door, a bit too near the heavy traffic of kids entering and leaving the cafeteria, but more out of the way of the abundance of forbidden morsels of people food. With a small rug for Sextant laid on the floor as far out of the traffic as possible, she thought the dog could do just fine there.

It was decided, for the time being at least, that Mike would go to PE without his dog, to avoid exposing Sextant to kids running and playing with balls. The aide who helped Mike in class with his braille needs would be happy to keep Sextant with her in the classroom. Mike could still take Sextant out to relieve himself at the beginning of each recess, and then go on out to play while the aide kept the dog on his leash. Then Mike could walk back into class using his guide dog.

Hoping that we had most of the potential problems under control before they occurred, Sylvia finished her week of training with Mike and Sextant, and I headed home to enjoy the last weeks of my summer vacation. The day school started I was up before dawn to make the drive to Mike's hometown, eager for my own chance to see Mike and his dog in action. I planned to follow Mike and Sextant the entire mile-long route to school, but when I arrived Anna told me firmly that Mike was going to do it independently. The instructions from Sylvia at the guide dog school were that she could follow at a distance in the car if she absolutely had to, but that a person walking behind would distract Sextant and undermine everything he and Mike were doing. Of course I understood and supported the school's guidelines, but it was a blow to find myself dis-included from my favorite student's big moment. It didn't even occur to me to wonder, in the moment, what Anna must be going through. I was too full of my own disappointment. I had to be content to meet Mike at school, ask him how the walk had gone, and run my plans for the day past him.

Yes, they had had a successful walk to school. Yes, I was scheduled to give the entire student body a five-minute briefing on general behavior around a person who is using a guide dog, and that was fine. No, Mike didn't really want me doing the half hour guide dog in-service I had planned with the entire seventh grade after the main assembly. "I'd rather answer individual questions as they come up," Mike explained. "Up until now nobody has ever stopped to talk with me much, and everybody's really interested in Sextant. I really want to be a regular kid today, and if you go and talk to my whole class that's gonna make me stick out like I always used to."

"Is there anything at all that I can do for you today?"

"I just want to go to my homeroom and get to work—just like everybody else." Mike was polite but resolute.

I think Mike did the right thing on his first day at school with Sextant. He made his case that he wanted this big day to be his—note mine. I had told Mike many times that, since he was embarking into the adult world with this project of getting a guide dog for himself, I was going to treat him like an adult in all areas concerning the dog. This was my chance to make good on my promise. Granting my eleven-year-old student's request to move out of the limelight on his debut at school with his dog wasn't the easiest thing I've ever done in this ever-surprising job, but it was certainly the best. Now I will stand back, watch the show, and enjoy every minute of it.

GETTING OLDER

I was *really* young when I started this job. Young enough to have to prove to staff at the high school that I should be allowed in the teachers' room. Now the last of my own three offspring is five years older than I was when I launched myself on my initial tentative drive into Anderson Valley, seeking the home of my first little student in Mendocino County. This astonishes me—as long as I don't look into the mirror I maintain this happy image of myself as a youthful person.

The first blow came about twenty years ago, while I was working in a kindergarten class with my student Shaynna. As I sat doubled up in a seriously undersized chair next to Shaynna, a cute little classmate came over and regarded me with the un-self-conscious stare of an innocent. After a minute the darling child piped up, "Are you her grandmother?" My immediate reaction was to defensively splutter "Of course I'm not—I'm too young to be a grandmother!" but I managed to curb myself and tell the little girl calmly, "No sweetie, but I'd sure like to be."

Even in my state of shock, I was proud of my well-spoken rejoinder, but that kindergartners's question shook me. How could anybody take me for a *grandmother*? My own children were less than ten years older than Shaynna, and my long chestnut hair certainly didn't look like the white permed coifs sported by the old ladies of *my* grandparents' generation. Then it dawned on me. That lovely sun-highlighted hair of mine was indeed going gray. I now sported wide streaks of completely gray hair on both sides of my head, which I wore swept back behind my ears and held with clips. From a kindergartners's standing height next to my low perch on the tiny chair, those gray streaks would have been exactly at her eye level. What I could ignore with my preferred straight-on look into the bathroom mirror was literally in this child's face, and she instantly pegged me as old.

The gray didn't stop at my temples. It crept all over my head in a painless, deliberate march. I like it now—I can wear all those jewel colors that used to feel overpowering with brownish hair. I look classy now. The rest of me has managed to stay trim and healthy and energetic, so I still maintain the delusion that old age is somehow passing me by.

I'm caught off guard every so often by catching a glimpse of an unknown middle-aged woman reflected in a store window, only to realize that I am looking straight back at myself. I'm slowly getting used to that. As much as I am accepting the physical demeanor of middle age, however, I steadfastly refuse to respond to the bi-monthly application packets that come in the mail from AARP and Elderhostel. I'm not ready to go there.

I'm having a hard time getting used to the reality that my co-workers are beginning to retire. Juanita-Joy has *always* been around. Even though we have shared few students over thirty-five years of working out of the same office, we used to pass each other frequently while driving opposite ways on the Willits grade, and we have always managed to connect and enjoy each other at the office parties and meetings. Juanita-Joy is one of the people I count on to be there to listen when the going gets tough—she's a rock, she has an unimaginable amount of wisdom, and I really like her. The last I heard, she and her husband are off building a retirement cottage in Mexico. Her desk is now occupied by another person.

Juanita-Joy is the first of a knot of 50-somethings in our small group of itinerant teachers to actually retire, but the rest of us are not far behind. This truth hit me in the face on my last birthday. I was turning 58, and began musing about how fast the time was flying past. Only two more years until I would be 60—and then only twenty more years before I'd be 80! My hyperactive brain shouted a panic-stricken protest, "I don't want to be 80 already!!! If the years keep going by at this pace, I'll be 80 before I know it, and 80 means arthritic hands and artificial hips and macular degeneration. This *can't* be happening to *me*!!! "

I try to still my brain and wonder lucidly what retirement will bring. It is undeniably on the horizon, and I do enjoy the idea of having endless days of time to myself with a guaranteed income that I no longer have to work for. I can't wait to really sink myself into the art that I have never managed to find enough time to do the way I want to do it. Art, however, is by definition a sedentary and solitary occupation, and I am an active and social being. Maybe I'll travel, maybe there will be grandchildren in the near future, or maybe I'll contract with the county to do some of the fun parts of my job that I'm sure I'll miss. I'll probably do all of those things, and more. If I can keep that "turning 80" panic in check I'll be able to enjoy *all* of the intervening twenty-two years as they unfold.

And then who knows what?

In the meantime, the beat goes on. Students whom I have grown to love, enjoy, or maybe just put up with get older and graduate, or move out of the Mendocino County school system. Some go to better places. Some don't. A few I get to see occasionally in their adult lives, some I hear about periodically from mutual acquaintances, and others I lose track of completely. It's bitter-sweet; my students' successes don't always outnumber their hard falls.

I keep teaching. Every day is new, and every bend in the convoluted road, both literal and figurative, has the potential to lead me to a place yet undiscovered. I like what I do, and am constantly grateful for the lucky stroke that led me to this strange and specialized profession which allows me so much independence and creativity. I appreciate living in this beautiful county and getting paid to drive through the spectacular countryside that is a vacation destination for thousands of tourists in every season. Working here is a gift.

I wonder how the stories will unfold for a whole new group of visually impaired students who have replaced most of the children in this book. Will Jack learn to use his vision well enough to eventually communicate by pointing at pictures of what he wants? Will Kevin improve his cane skills to walk a block independently to get to a friend's house? Will I find a way to teach Jordan to look at and recognize a toy he wants to play with? And how about Sergio — is there a chance that he will become a Braille user? And what I wish for more than anything—will darling little Francesca focus her googly dark eyes on me one day as I am leaving, and wave good-bye to me?

And who are the children who haven't been born yet? Will anybody have Shaynna's zany sense of humor or match Michelle's unqualified joy in the moment? Will there ever be another child as eager and capable of learning as Mike? Will there be just one more student who can learn to cross a street with a white cane? And what about the families I haven't met yet? Who in the world will they be, and what will they teach me?

These questions intrigue me, but I don't mind not knowing the answers. As I have learned from the children who have been my students in the past, my unlikely teachers, the process is what is important. Each tiny little step I can teach them to take beyond the place where they are stuck is my focus for days, and sometimes months. I dream about the future of every student I teach, but I cannot control what will happen. I must dig deep, give it my best shot, and let go of the outcome. And hopefully get some more good laughs along the way.

And then, every so often, out of the blue, something wonderful happens that unexpectedly plunges me again into the life of a student or a family who has moved out of my sphere of influence. Maybe this happens to remind me that life goes on for these people, whether or not I am involved with them. Maybe it happens just to make me feel good, or maybe there is no reason at all.

One ordinary day a couple of weeks ago, I was walking out of a grocery store in Ukiah and came face-to-face with Shaynna's mother, Samantha, on her way in. I barely recognized her. This was a new Samantha, with a confident presence and a sure, direct gaze. A wonderful Samantha, who gave me the huge hug of a long-missed friend. She proudly introduced me to the people with her—her boyfriend, a good man whom she loves deeply, and her beautiful youngest daughter, who is about to leave home for art college. They just happened to be passing through Mendocino County, and made an impulse decision to take the freeway exit and grab a few things at the Co-op.

It had been ten years since I lost contact with Samantha, and during that time I never heard a word about either her or Shaynna. Samantha was eager to catch me up on all of her news. Her middle daughter is engaged and on her way to living independently. Samantha herself is employed in an elder care facility where her compassion and people skills are much appreciated. She drives now and owns a car. She is excited about her new life, but still practical. "I'm better now," she declared, "but it will be a long time before I'm all the way there. I've still got a lot to learn. I've got some regrets, and I wish I could go back and change the way I did some things, but all I can do is pay attention to the present. I'm trying to be the best person I can so I can be there for the people who are in my life now."

The rest of Samantha's news was about Shaynna, who is now twenty-four years old. She showed me a recent picture of her firstborn daughter, my favorite student from so long ago. In the photo Shaynna is slim, and she sits erect in her wheelchair with her head up. She looks good, and I am quick to imagine her able, once again, to pipe up with her madcap comments on life as she experiences it. "Shaynna," Samantha told me, "is stable. Not cured of her emotional disorders, but dealing with everyday issues a whole lot better than in the past. She's recently moved to a new facility. The people there are interested in learning about her past and helping her re-connect with her family and old friends. They asked if you would call. Is there any way you might be able to contact her?" Samantha phoned me the next day with the telephone number of Shaynna's new facility.

I'm hoping to go there in the near future, with Suzanne, to visit our newly found student. I wonder how much Shaynna will remember about the "Adventure Lady." I can't wait to find out, but I'm also scared. I feel like Red's mother must have when I talked her son into going to the prom, and unexpectedly opened a door that Scarlett thought was closed forever.

I thought I had closed and locked the door to Shaynna and her family, and, like Scarlett, I'm uneasy about allowing myself to step through. I was emotionally safe with Shaynna gone from my life, and now that the pain has worn off I'm not completely sure that I want to set myself up for another loss. What will happen to me if Shaynna freaks out when she hears my voice? How will I deal with my grief all over again if I re-connect with this young woman I loved as a child, and then have to cope with another institution-imposed separation? Is my heart resilient enough to handle another bout of Shaynna-induced turmoil? I look at myself and realize there are no guarantees in this life. My students and their families have taught me that a thousand times. Every day is a risk. Frustrations and disappointments and tragedies are inevitable. So are delightful surprises and joys of immeasurable proportion. One without the other is impossible. I cannot predict or control the outcome of a renewed connection with Shaynna, but the choice to take the chance is mine. I'm going to make that phone call and find out where it leads me.

Resource list

American Foundation for the Blind
    www.afb.org
    11 Penn Plaza, Suite 300
    New York, NY 10001
    (800) 232-5463

American Council of the Blind,
    www.acb.org
    1155 15th Street NW,
    Suite 1004,
    Washington, DC 20005
    (202) 467-5081
    (800) 424-8666

Blind Babies Foundation
    www.blindbabies.org
    1814 Franklin St, 11th Floor
    Oakland, CA 94612
    (510) 446-2229

California Association of Orientation and Mobility Specialists
    http://www.caoms.org or http://www.caoms.org/resources.htm
    1127 Broadway
    Alameda, CA 94501

CA Deaf/Blind Services
    http://www.sfsu.edu
    Maurice Belote
    1600 Holloway
    San Francisco CA 94132
    (415) 405-7560

California School for the Blind
    http://www.csb-cde.ca.gov
    500 Walnut Ave
    Fremont CA 94536
    (510) 794-3800

Guide Dogs for the Blind
    http://www.guidedogs.com
    California Campus:
    350 Los Ranchitos Road
    San Rafael, CA 94903
    (415) 499-4000

Journal of Visual Impairment and Blindness (JVIB)
    http://www.afb.org
    11 Pennn Plaza, Suite 300
    New York, NY 10001
    (212) 502-7619

Lighthouse for the Blind and Visually Impaired
    http://www.lighthouse-sf.org
    Produces The Lantern newsletter and has a store of products for VI
    214 VanNess Ave
    San Francisco CA 94102
    (415) 431-1481

Lighthouse International
    http://www.lighthouse.org
    The Sol and Lillian Goldman building
    111 East 59th St
    New York NY 10022-1202
    (212) 821-9760

Love Bike
   now known as the Buddy Bike
   www.buddybike.com
   2775 Sunny Isles Blvd, Suite 118
   North Miami Beach
   FL 33160
   707 456-0468

National Association for Parents of Children with Visual Impairments
   (NAPVI) produces "Awareness" magazine quarterly
   www.napvi.org
   PO Box 317
   Watertown MA 02471-0317
   (800) 562-6265

National Federation of the blind (NFB)
   http://www.nfb.org
   Produces the Braille Monitor monthly
   1800 Johnson St
   Baltimore Maryland 21230
   (410) 659-9314

National Library Service for the Blind and Physically Handicapped
   www.loc.gov/nls
   (202) 707-5100
   (888) NLS-READ
   local library 1-888-657-7323

Orientation and Mobility program at SF state
   http://online.sfsu.edu/~mobility/
   1600 Holloway
   San Francisco CA 94132
   (415) 338-1111